Myron Cope
Double Yoi!

———————————

A Revealing Memoir
by the Broadcaster/Writer

By
Myron Cope

Sports Publishing, L.L.C.
www.sportspublishingllc.com

Director of production: Susan M. Moyer
Developmental editor: Stephanie Fuqua
Dust jacket, photo insert design: Christine Mohrbacher

ISBN:1-58261-548-9

Printed in the United States of America

Sports Publishing, L.L.C.
www.sportspublishingllc.com

*To my daughter Elizabeth and son Danny,
in appreciation of their continuous love.*

Contents

Author's Note

There were times, now that I think about it, when I got extraordinarily lucky—when I "fell in," to use an expression from my youth. In the early 1960s, for example, I found myself on a writing assignment for *The Saturday Evening Post*, traveling with a Philadelphia freelance photographer for the better part of a week in dead winter. When we parted he said, "You ever feel like taking a vacation in Jamaica, call me. I'm related on my wife's side to a family that owns the finest hotel on the island, to say nothing of department stores and other things. I'll call ahead. You'll be treated well."

Indeed, when I arrived after nightfall at the hotel in Ocho Rios, the tuxedo-clad manager, himself a member of the entrepreneurial Issa family, showed me to a cottage near the swimming pool. The next day the family (including two attractive, Paris-educated women in their 20s) welcomed me into their company for the duration of my stay.

While we lazed in the pool at the cocktail hour, a clap of the hands by one or another of the Issas brought a white-jacketed waiter carrying a tray of martinis, to be accepted without our bothering to climb from the pool. Nights, after dinner and dancing at the hotel (I was single then), we traveled to cabarets where waiters fetched tables, chairs, and a calypso band to a flat rooftop for our private pleasure under the stars.

I could take being wealthy, I thought.

In 1968 Ray Cave, a *Sports Illustrated* editor, phoned me. "The U. S. Open will be coming up in June," he said. "Last year at the Open, a Mexican wearing dark glasses and constantly jabbering with the galleries came out of nowhere to finish fifth. He's the pro at a golf club near El Paso called Horizon Hills. Why don't you fly down there and see if he makes a story we can publish the week of the Open?"

The American Latino met me at the airport, chirping, "Let's go! Got a starting time to hustle some members. You can ride along in my cart."

The fivesome teed off, the Latino spotting the others anywhere from 40 to 100 yards at the tees and drilling one-irons low through the desert wind. Another handful of club members drove carts through the roughs, noisily wagering on almost every shot. The pro, Lee Trevino (all right, the reader already has guessed), informed me at the outset, "The rule is, first guy to his ball hits." In the cart I ducked for my life while golf balls whistled unannounced from every direction. Afterward, I phoned Ray Cave and said, "I believe I have a story."

At the Open at Oak Hill, Rochester, NY, Trevino took the lead. "Who the hell is this Trevino?" the golf writers asked, and were told, "Grab a copy of *SI*. He's in there." He was, and he won the Open, and *SI* took a full-page ad in the *New York Times* to reprint my article and trumpet:

"We're the selective that can write about memorable events ahead of time."

Again, as the saying went, I fell in. So I had great times —and a few less-than-great times. Allow me to share them, with an opinion or two thrown in.

Part One

Trying to Get There

Chapter One

Big Fish, Small Pond

"Just tell me when to start talking and when to shut up."

That's been my method throughout a broadcasting career that has spanned more than three decades, during which I have managed to remain spectacularly ignorant of ever-changing broadcast technology and of the right way to do things. I never studied to be a broadcaster or even aspired to be one, not for a minute. Nor had I ever so much as entertained the notion of becoming one. So in the television studios, for example, I simply waited for the camera's red light and for the floor director to point his finger, whereupon I began speaking. When he slashed that finger across his throat—the signal to wind down my sports commentary—I shut up, although sometimes not as quickly as the director wished.

One evening, in the midst of yapping through my gig in the six o'clock news, I spied from the corner of my eye a housefly circling lazily. It made a soft landing on the tip of my nose. It sat there. Turning cockeyed trying to see it, I cried out, "There's a fly on my nose!"

Never before had I seen a housefly invade a television studio, nor have I since. As I shooed it away, the entire studio—two anchorpersons, the weather man, the stagehands as well—burst into laughter, and I assume our viewers did the same. Why? Well, humor sometimes takes the form of the unexpected. Of course, other times, you can plan it; you can work at it, all right. As a magazine writer for the many years that preceded my broadcast career, a New York editor had dubbed me "our nut specialist"—he and other editors around Manhattan strove to direct me to unorthodox sports figures whose idiosyncrasies I could capture on paper. Among writers, you should know, humorists are almost as rare as stand-up comics at a Klan rally. I have known writers who at a party or at a bar could double up those around them with laughter as they told funny stories, yet could not write a humorous piece if the sale of one would stave off eviction. So kindly pardon my pride in mentioning that in 1968, Prentice-Hall, a major publishing house, found it worthwhile to publish a collection of my magazine articles, *Broken Cigars,* written in my role as roving "nut specialist".

Later, however, as an untutored broadcaster, I would reflect that humor often comes unannounced from left field. Have you ever sneezed a series of sneezes, not knowing when or whether the next one was coming? I did while speaking to a caller during my evening radio talk show. I probably should have pressed the so-called "cough button" that would have silenced my mike, but I could not foretell how many sneezes were coming and did not want my listeners to think we'd gone off the air. I sneezed five times, a suspenseful pause between each sneeze. *Uh-choo!... Uh-choo!* and so forth.

"That kind of thing," a news director solemnly told me, "is part of your ability to *communicate.* It's hell finding people who can communicate." I suppose I understood what he was saying.

I guess that, to some extent, I had become a flake, as we used to term sports figures who marched to the beat of their own drummer. Most of them did not realize others found them amusing. The memorable sportscaster Howard Cosell, for example, regarded himself with such total admiration that on paper, when I profiled him in 1967 for *Sports Illustrated,* I gauged that readers would find his ego more amusing than repulsive.

"Look at Mantle!" he shouted at me. "He did a half-hour show with me, and he felt like he had a cathartic experience. He felt *cleansed.* Joe Namath! The kid poured his heart out to me." Yet self-doubt did exist in a corner of Howard's heart; it became evident to me only when he confessed, "I am not the greatest man in the world."

I suppose that I myself, when I wore my broadcaster's hat, caused people to smile at times without intending to. Things just happened. In my role as color analyst for Pittsburgh Steelers radio broadcasts (a role I have filled for more than three decades), I sat on two telephone books (both yellow pages, if it matters) that were strapped together with duct tape. I am a fraction of an inch under five-five. The phone books were strictly utilitarian—they made it possible for me to see the game. Now and then, when I've entered the booth and not immediately sighted the phone books, I have become frantic. "Where are my phone books, where are my phone books?" I've bellowed.

"Right there," our producer would calmly say, "on the floor beside your chair."

Stadium workers one season were instructed to move our television monitor from a platform that for years had extended outward from our booth on metal support brackets. The monitor, it had been determined, posed the danger of falling, thereby giving the survivors among the spectators seated directly below us a strong basis for litigation. Now the monitor was placed inside the booth, suspended above my head and slightly to my left. During our first broadcast in the new setup, a terrific catch by a Steeler receiver so excited me that I bolted up from my chair, and yes, struck my head on the bottom edge of the monitor.

"Jesus!" I cried out—across the airwaves. My eyes watered from the pain.

Bill Hillgrove and Tunch Ilkin, my broadcast partners, could not help laughing. But they saw to it that for the next game a strip of protective foam rubber was attached to the bottom of the monitor. Shortly after Three Rivers Stadium was imploded in February 2001, to be succeeded by Heinz Field rising next door, Hillgrove, our play-by-play man, introduced me to a dinner audience as the main speaker and told the gathering:

"I have a surprise for Myron. I'd like to present to him a couple of precious mementos from Three Rivers."

Hillgrove reached for a large paper bag and from it produced my phone books and the strip of foam rubber. Having observed Steeler fans paying as much as $800 for a pair of seats at an auction of Three Rivers memorabilia, I have instructed my daughter that upon my death, she's to auction off my phone books and foam rubber. Now *that's* egotistical.

Of course, most football broadcasters do not shoot out of their chairs screaming into their headset mikes, but I came to broadcasting more or less by accident, a total amateur, and without giving it a lot of thought, remained one. The first time I was shown a ratings book by a co-worker—and of course, ratings might tell you how long you're apt to be employed or how much money to ask for in your next contract—I said, "I may as well be trying to read Chinese." I never again looked at a ratings book.

The point is that soon after entering the broadcasting field, I began noticing that broadcasters who had earned degrees at Northwestern, at Syracuse, at Columbia—universities boasting noteworthy schools of communication—were regularly being shown the pavement. I told myself, "Hey, if your ratings stink you'll go out the door soon enough. Why take the trouble to analyze the ratings book for clues?"

On a February morning in 1968, I answered the telephone in the basement office of my Pittsburgh home and heard a man identify himself as Don Shafer, program director of WTAE, a local radio station. "We're a music and news station," he said, "but we're trying to develop a little bit of a sports image. You're somewhat known around town as a writer for *Sports Illustrated.* We're wondering if you'd be interested in broadcasting a brief sports show in morning drive time—say, five minutes.

"You won't have to leave home," Shafer went on. "We'll put a microphone and all the necessary apparatus right there. When you're traveling on magazine assignments, you can broadcast through the telephone in your hotel room. Before you go on the air, we'll fill you in on yesterday's ball scores and any interesting stories we have from the AP wire. Rattle 'em off and then give us a two-minute commentary—an opinion, an anecdote, anything you choose relating to any sports topic under the sun. You've been recommended highly by a couple of our people who drink with you."

"Listen," I said. "Are you pulling my leg? I've heard my voice on tape, and it's sure as heck not a broadcasting voice." Almost 34 years later, Frank Celizik, an internet columnist for MSNBC, would happen to tune in to our broadcast of a Steeler playoff game while driving the Pennsylvania Turnpike. In his column two days later, he likened my voice to "a tornado going through a junkyard."

"No problem," Shafer continued on the telephone. "We like to think we're a forward-looking radio station, one step ahead of the competition. We think we see a coming trend in obnoxious voices." Shafer's hyperbole brought a smile to my face, though it occurred to me later that he might not have intended hyperbole.

I replied, "Lemme think about it. I'll call you back." I was 39 at the time and reasonably successful in what I perceived to be my life's work. *Sports Illustrated,* in that day the best-written, most literary sports publication in America, retained me under contract to provide first call on my services and carried my name in the magazine's masthead as a Special Contributor. *SI* had awarded that status to just me and one other freelance writer—the erudite, better-known New York socialite George Plimpton.

So I was doing okay, thank you. No, six figures—the equivalent of today's seven figures—were not rolling in, but my wife Mildred and I were living a middle-class lifestyle and building savings, attainments not expected of writers. For example, when I asked my terrific *SI* editor Pat Ryan to improve my contract, she replied:

"Myron, we're already paying you as much money for your pieces as any writer we buy from. Nobody gets more."

Pat did not intend her words as a compliment, but rather as a re-minder that I should keep in mind the low position writers held in the economy. To drive home the point, she named a well-known byline liv-ing in eastern Pennsylvania. He did not enjoy a contract, which would carry with it the comfort of an annual retainer, but he had made his mark with well-crafted prose and choice assignments. Pat said, "He lives in the boondocks in a log cabin. We're not giving *him* a raise."

Well, my wife had given birth less than a month before I received the radio executive's phone call. A few extra bucks would not hurt. Surely my little show would fail miserably or at best run its course in short time. It would be a brief lark. I went upstairs to the kitchen and told Mildred of the phone call.

She said, "Don't do it. You'll embarrass me."

She maintained ever afterward that she had said no such thing, that I later fictiously attributed those words to her because I enjoyed telling friends the story. She said I told the story so frequently that I came to believe it. I am telling you, that kitchen conversation happened. It really happened—I think.

In any case, I returned Don Shafer's phone call and said, "You've got a sportscaster."

More accurately, an ersatz sportscaster.

As I steeled myself for my first broadcast, I studied the microphone on my desk and could not bring myself to believe that listeners driving to work across expressways many miles away could hear my words. I started in yelling. I continued to yell. Shortly before I began writing this book, I mentioned on the air in passing that I would soon attempt an autobiog-raphy, whereupon a note came in the mail from a woman listener named Pat Starn. "Why don't you call your book *Yellin' It Like It Is?*"

How best to describe my voice? Harsh? Abrasive? The first morn-ing I went on the air, the switchboard at WTAE lit up.

"Get that man off the air! I can't wake up to a voice like that!" Such were the calls that poured in for about two weeks. Soon, however, the protests abated as listeners became—how shall I put it?—inured to my voice. Not enraptured by it, but inured.

Before unleashing my first broadcast, I said to myself as a writer, "Well, let's see. How do I go at this broadcasting thing? How do I write these scripts for two-minute radio commentaries?"

Long ago, I had developed my own approach to writing. Writing, I decided, was creating music for the eye. There had to be rhythm—in phrases, sentences, paragraphs—that would engage the reader's visual senses. Every sentence counted lest the reader become bored and decide there were better things to do than finish reading my lengthy profiles of sports figures and others. Broadcasting scripts, on the other hand, should be music to the *ear,* I concluded. They should be conversational, even ungrammatical at times. In high school, I'd had an English teacher who taught that good writing is conversational, and I suppose there have been thousands of English teachers who have preached the same. I think they're fools. Any writer or teacher who fails to sense the difference between conversation and writing for the printed page is better suited to become a school crossing guard.

So in this new task of writing radio scripts, by intent I would strive to write badly well. Radio and television scripts were, and still are, not to be considered quality writing. Thus I would rely upon my writer's instincts to write poorly but do an effective job of it in order to arrest the ear. Content, too, mattered. Commentaries by definition are opinion. But when it comes to sports, you can get an opinion in any saloon or cocktail lounge in town.

"That trade stinks!" "Our owner is cheap!" "Jerome Bettis is over the hill!" Or when Bettis proceeds to gain more than 1,300 yards in the ensuing season, "If the Steelers don't re-sign Bettis, they're not only cheap but outta their minds."

Barroom commentaries, I decided, were a dime a dozen and not likely to gain a listenership. I reasoned that I must be informative or entertaining, and when possible, both. As a sportswriter privy to sources, I had an edge on the barroom commentator and an ability to give my listeners information and perspective the armchair coach normally could not provide. Simple as that. So after the station switchboard quieted down, listeners settled in to pay attention, although my voice and sing-song delivery continued to make their teeth gnash.

Within approximately a year's time, a couple of developments caused me to believe that this sideline to my writing career might last a while. WTAE radio, you see, existed as a meager 5,000-watt poor sister to WTAE television, Channel 4, both of them owned by the Hearst Corporation and housed in the same three-story building. Now, Channel 4 said, "How about doing commentaries for us, too?"

Okay, but more significantly, a rival radio-and-television station, KDKA, arranged a short time later a clandestine meeting with me. KDKA's general manager of radio, one Bill Hartman, dispatched his top aide to have lunch with me at a hotel restaurant miles from the city. (This was my first inkling that broadcast companies, when moving to lure a rival's talent, operate in the sort of secrecy as must have shrouded plans for the Normandy invasion.) KDKA reserved a table shielded by a curtain.

"Here's our offer," Hartman's aide said. He proposed much more money than WTAE was paying me, plus benefits, which at WTAE I was not receiving. WTAE had not put me under contract, so I felt free to say it sounded swell. We shook hands on the deal and arranged to formalize it the next evening with Hartman and a bean counter or two in attendance in a private room at the Pittsburgh Press Club.

That afternoon, I entered the office of WTAE-Radio's general manager, a tall, ruddy man named Geer Parkinson, to give him notice. "Look, Geer," I said. "You people have treated me decently. I'm not going to try to put you over a barrel. I shook on this deal with KDKA, so I'm resigning."

Whereupon Parkinson, his face flushed, rose from his chair and pounded on his desk with a fist. "Goddammit, Myron! We've got money, too!"

Interesting. But I had committed to KDKA and was going to join a radio powerhouse—a 50,000-watt clear-channel station that carried to vast reaches of the country and always had dominated the Pittsburgh market. Hence I reported to the Press Club that evening to sign a contract.

Following routine pleasantries, Hartman abruptly cut his offered salary nearly in half.

"What the hell are you talking about?" I said.

"Let's put it this way, Myron," Hartman replied. "Would you rather bat cleanup in WTAE's lineup or eighth in KDKA's? Eighth in KDKA's is obviously better."

I walked out. Now I had no new job with KDKA and had resigned at WTAE. Whoops.

Next afternoon, my phone rang. John G. Conomikes, the general manager of WTAE television and much more powerful than Geer Parkinson, invited me to his office. There he offered me a fat raise plus a contract with benefits. "Gee," I told him, "that's too good to pass up." Not until some 30 years later did I let Conomikes know that he'd had me where he wanted me.

I recall an evening when I stood beside John at the bar of a Holiday Inn five minutes from the station. Over the years, he and other station executives from time to time had to field nasty letters and phone calls from listeners demanding that I be summarily fired for positions I had taken in my commentaries and talk shows. "You must realize by this time," John told me, "that we will never tell you what you can or cannot say on the air. I know that if we ever tried to, you'd walk right out of the building."

Silently, I thought, "Hmmm. Would I? The dough I'm making ain't bad." I took another sip of my martini and then changed the subject. So give me no awards for integrity.

As you may have noticed by now, unexpected phone calls have had a way of changing my life. In 1970, by which time I had been plying my broadcast sideline for two years while continuing my writing career, I received a call from a longtime friend, Ed Kiely, the Steelers' director of public relations. "You probably know," said Kiely, "that we're moving our radio broadcasts from KDKA to your station this year." Yes, I'd heard.

The Steelers, throughout their history dating back to 1933, had never won so much as a divisional title and were regarded as the town buffoons. Their problem was that club owner Art Rooney did not mind the store. His first affection was for horse racing and horse breeding. He would be off to the racetracks or to his horse farm in Maryland, leaving his various head football coaches with a free hand to make whatever trades and other moves they pleased. "I think that was my whole mistake," Art said to me during a conversation we had only months before I received Ed Kiely's phone call. But by now, Art, to a great degree, was turning over the day-to-day operation of the franchise to his eldest son Dan, who targeted his undivided attention upon it and decided that as a matter of self-respect, the club must move its radio rights away from KDKA.

KDKA, you see, broadcast not only Steelers games but Pirates games as well, and the Pirates came first. When the kickoff of a Sunday Steelers game coincided with a Pirates game, KDKA would broadcast the Pirates, and then, at whatever time their game ended, broadcast the Steelers on tape delay. "Nuts to that," Dan said. He moved the rights to little WTAE, then met with PR director Kiely and the club's young publicity director, Joe Gordon, to throw around names of color analysts.

"How about Cope?" said Gordon. "He already does work for the station we're moving to."

Rooney instructed Kiely, who handled broadcast matters, to contact me. "Would you like to be the color analyst for our games?" Kiely asked on the phone.

"Color analyst!" I exclaimed. "Ex-jocks and ex-coaches are color analysts. What the blue blazes do I know about that kind of stuff?"

"Well," said Kiely, "you've been hanging around our team for years. You know the team. Why not give it a shot?"

"Okay, Ed, I'll try it. But you've got to know up front that if the Steelers are playing well, I'll be thrilled and make no secret to the audience that I'm thrilled, but if the Steelers are stinking out the joint, I'll say they're stinking out the joint." The previous year, 1969, the Steelers, under a new, young head coach named Chuck Noll, had won but a single game and lost 13, so they had great potential for again stinking out the joint. I said, "Ed, I can't have you people leaning on me when you don't like what I say."

"Myron," Kiely replied, "you know us better than to even bring that up."

The Steelers kept their word. To this day, not once has Dan Rooney or any other Steeler official objected to any portion of my color commentary. I'm sure that's been a luxury not universally enjoyed by NFL broadcasters. By way of illustration, had a Daniel Snyder type owned the Steelers, I might have been fired by halftime of my first game. On December 16, 2000, I unwittingly invaded the thin skin of the actual Daniel M. Snyder.

Snyder, a self-made marketing billionaire by the time he entered his 30s, purchased the Washington Redskins in 1999. Now toward the end of his second year as an owner, he came to Pittsburgh to be part of the final game played at 31-year-old Three Rivers Stadium. Snyder had had a rough year. Impatient for a Super Bowl championship, he signed a boatload of expensive, free-agent stars during the off season, but to his great embarrassment, saw his Redskins lose as many games as they won. "The worst team that $100 million can buy," laughed the media.

"Well," I told myself while brushing my teeth a few mornings before the farewell to Three Rivers, "I believe that in the broadcast this weekend, I'll rename the Skins the Washington Red*faces*."

Over the years, as my listeners well knew, I have had a weakness for nicknames. I hung them on athletes and teams alike, either because the nicknames described their recipients or because I simply enjoyed the sound of these monikers as they rolled off my tongue. For example, in the early 1970s when Daniel Snyder was barely emerging from diapers, I took to calling the Skins the Wash Dirtyskins. Their head coach, George Allen, traded away draft choices by the bushel in exchange for crafty old veterans who knew every trick, such as glancing around for fallen opponents in order to step on their outstretched fingers. Ergo, in *my* book the Redskins became the Dirtyskins.

At any rate, by halftime at the doomed Three Rivers Stadium, the Steelers led the Redfaces 17-3 en route to giving them a 24-3 pasting. In the third quarter, when our broadcast broke for a commercial, our producer, Greg Weston, said to me, "A guy from the Redskins, a suit, came into the booth a little while ago and told me to tell you to stop calling them Redfaces."

"What?" I said. "You're kidding me, of course."

"No, I'm just telling you what the guy said. He said you're to stop that Redfaces stuff."

"That is just preposterous!" I told Weston. Coming out of the commercial break, I howled into my mike, "Dear listeners, you're not going to believe what I'm going to tell you." By then, I'd figured out the scenario. Snyder, seated in the visiting owner's box, had been listening to our piped-in broadcast (he could have turned it off) and sent a message by phone to his public relations staff seated in the press box to our immediate left: Get over to the Pittsburgh radio booth and tell that guy to knock it off.

"If that boy billionaire," I now bellowed to our audience, "thinks he can shut me up, he should stick his head in a can of paint."

Hours afterward, when The Associated Press caught wind of Snyder's attempted censorship and that night reported it across the country, Snyder claimed to have been unaware of my goings-on until after the game had ended; it developed that an *oberstleutnant* named Steve Baldacci, who carried the title of Redskins president, was the man who phoned the press box. But given the fact that Snyder had earned a reputation for firing employees by the boxcar, I suspect no underling was going to place that call on his own whim. Surely Snyder had given Baldacci an order.

Whatever the actual facts, Washington newspapers blistered the neophyte owner. *Washington Post* sports columnist Thomas Boswell noted that the Skins, instead of wisely letting this miniature tempest die, sent forth a spokesman to elaborate on the club's position. This, in part, was that I had committed mischief with the team's trademark—Redskins. Secondly, said the spokesman, "Our initial reaction was, 'Gee, is that sportsmanlike to make fun of us because we're losing?' " Earlier in the same season, following a game between the Skins and the Baltimore Ravens at FedEx Field, the NFL had reprimanded the Skins because their PA announcer had boomed to all in attendance, "Ravens fans suck!"

Columnist Boswell, harking back to my recommendation that Snyder stick his head into a can of paint, concluded his piece by declaring, "Like it or not, Myron Cope was speaking for America. And the Redskins should listen." Well, now. Was President Clinton, passing his last days in the Oval Office, reading his sports page and wishing he'd made me a member of his cabinet? I spoke for America. As Terry Bradshaw was fond of saying, "Golly, gee."

As I have mentioned, my career as a football broadcaster began in 1970, the year Three Rivers Stadium opened. I broadcast every game the Steelers played there, missing only the first quarter of one game to attend a brother-in-law's funeral. (I missed only one road game in that stretch of 31 years—a late-September trip to Seattle in 1994 that fell just five days after my wife died.) "How have you lasted in the booth so long," I would be asked by fans from time to time, "while all the other color men are former football players?"

Good question.

Part of the answer traces to a late afternoon spent at Dante's Restaurant, much favored by Steeler players of the 1950s and '60s. This particular day, perhaps ten years before the Steelers invited me to attempt a role as color analyst, I sat at the bar drinking martinis with Ernie Stautner, a fearsome defensive lineman whose bronze bust years later would be placed in the Pro Football Hall of Fame. By the by, we fell to verbally dismembering various Steeler players we judged to be incompetent. I said to Ernie:

"I couldn't diagram a play on a blackboard if my life depended on it, but I've been watching football for as long as I can remember, and I think I can recognize when a football player can, or cannot, run, block, throw, or tackle."

Stautner ruminated a moment over his martini and then growled, "Cope, that's all the fuck you got to know."

To sustain me in times of differences with players and coaches, I never forgot Ernie's words. "You don't even know what a cover two is," I was told one day in the 1970s by linebacker Andy Russell, who captained the defenses of the Steelers' first two Super Bowl championship teams. Russell, with whom I now have spent almost 30 years fiercely debating football issues over dinner, was a tough linebacker and exceptionally brainy, though somewhat slow afoot.

"I do so know what a cover two is," I retorted, "and I also know a slow linebacker when I see one." I could hear Ernie Stautner's voice from the past: "That's all the fuck you got to know."

I ploughed ahead, riding the coattails of four championship teams to a certain amount of prominence. I became, to use a hoary cliché, but one that describes me as well as any, a big fish in a small pond. A *Pittsburgh Press* columnist, Roy McHugh, who years before had been best man at my wedding, happened one day to be introduced to Howard Cosell as a friend of mine. "Well!" said Cosell. "And how *is* the diminutive one?"

"He's doing fine," McHugh replied. "He's in your business now. He's a celebrity."

Cosell set McHugh straight. "In Pittsburgh."

I did not enter the broadcast booth intent upon flogging coaching decisions or stupid plays in order to gain attention; I would have been an imbecile to think that Chuck Noll or his successor Bill Cowher did not know more about football than I could learn if I lived to be 300. Still, no coach is perfect. So I felt obliged, carrying the fancy title of color analyst, to pop off. For example, conservative by nature, I usually objected when the Steelers lined up on fourth-and-short to go for the first down.

"That *dumb kopf* coach!" I would cry out, and often I made a point of saying so *before* the play was run, so as not to be accused of hindsight. "Doesn't that coach know the other team has eleven men on *their* side of the football? These coaches practice short-yardage defenses constantly, then forget the other team likewise is trained to stop that play."

More often than not, I turned out to be right—75 percent of the time, I am modestly guessing. As the great Buffalo coach Marv Levy once said, reflecting upon the predictable urging by crowds to go for it on fourth down, "Confucius once said, 'Coach who listens to fans ends up sitting with fans.'"

As for me, few would remember when the coach proved to be right and I wrong. So I survived, pressing forward, always thankful to have known Ernie Stautner.

Chapter Two

I Never Coulda Been a Contenda

The great majority of sportswriters and sportscasters are men (I cannot speak for the women) who in their youth were would-be athletes. They advanced no farther than the high school varsity, if that far. All one has to do is look at their shapes and sizes to know they turned to sports journalism after their childhood dreams of competing big-time were squashed. Of course, I include myself in this motley array.

Could I have been a fighter?

I was 16 the Sunday afternoon I stood in the boxing gym located in the Hill District, Pittsburgh's largest black section, ready to embark on a career in the ring that would bring me a few bucks. I felt sharp in my trunks, even if my ribs protruded like rows of xylophone bars. I loved the fight game, which thrived as a major sport until television wiped out the small boxing arenas in the 1950s by bringing the fights into living rooms at no charge. Earlier, few cities in America ranked above Pittsburgh as a fight town. Dating from the 1920s, our region produced a remarkable eight world champions over the decades when there existed only eight weight divisions and but a single recognized champ of each. Now, in 1945, World War II was nearing an end, but even through the war, boxing survived on the strength of professional fighters who were either too young for military service or had been classified 4-F, rejected because of physical disabilities. Then, too, a kid who loved attending fights easily could find the "smokers"—cards made up of amateurs under the auspices of the Amateur Athletic Union.

I enjoyed putting on the gloves at the neighborhood recreation center and sparring with pals, but before being invited to the gym in the Hill District, I had fought formally just once. I won a three-round decision over a kid name Peewee Chotiner and was handed an AAU certificate designating me the flyweight champion of the recreation center. Personally, I thought Peewee was robbed.

In any event, one Ralph Martzo, well known in Pittsburgh boxing circles as a coach and trainer, began showing up at our center on Saturday afternoons, having been hired to give us a few pointers. He happened to be watching the day I took on a basketball player named Teddy who stood seven or eight inches taller than I, but who (unbeknownst to Martzo) possessed a glass chin. I put an uppercut on it, and down went Teddy for a short count. Impressed, Martzo approached me afterward and said:

"Kid, I've got a stable of amateurs, but I need a 12-pounder"—boxing lingo for a fighter weighing no more than 112 pounds. "We box in smokers. The promoters give you a wristwatch that you can take to a pawnshop and make a few bucks."

Martzo instructed me to report to the gym in the Hill District the next day when his fighters would be training. Accordingly, I boarded a trolley to the Hill and, for openers, was put to work punching the heavy bag; while doing so, I looked up at the ring and was frozen in shock. Martzo's heavyweight was about to go three rounds against his middleweight. The middleweight would have been a light heavyweight save for the fact that he possessed only one arm.

The heavyweight, Jack Itzel, 4-F, had played football for Pitt and was now about to become the starting fullback for the Steelers. Meantime, he had knocked out approximately 30 opponents in a string of 32 fights, as I remember. Perfectly sculptured, Itzel weighed about 220. His middleweight sparring opponent, one Sailor Jack Kelly, resembled Huntz Hall, an actor who in that era appeared as a punk and bully in a popular film series called *The Dead End Kids*. Like Huntz Hall, Sailor Jack had sandy hair combed straight back, a pale complexion, and sloping shoulders. His most distinguishing feature, however, was that he wore a boxing glove laced to the stump of what had been his right arm.

Oh, I knew Sailor Jack could handle himself, for I had seen him fight in a smoker. Taking into account his nickname, I guessed he had lost his arm in a naval battle, and I suppose the attending physicians at the smokers allowed him into the ring knowing full well he could whip just about any amateur middleweight in town. (Those docs were also blissfully unaware that there would come a day when malpractice suits would become an American pastime.) At any rate, it seemed incongruous to me that, even in a workout, a one-armed man would be pitted against a fighter some 60 pounds heavier who was knocking out almost every amateur who climbed into the ring with him. I turned from the heavy bag to watch.

For a while, Sailor Jack bided his time, constantly rotating his shoulders and eluding Itzel's hooks. Then suddenly, Sailor Jack went under Itzel's right hook and came up lunging with a swooping left that traveled behind Itzel's neck and grabbed it. Pulling Itzel's head forward, Sailor Jack buried his gloved right stump into Itzel's face—and then twisted that stump as though operating a corkscrew. When the two fighters broke, Itzel was bleeding.

So it went for two rounds before Martzo, concerned about a nasty cut developing above Itzel's left eye, told Itzel to leave further sparring for another day. Martzo then turned to me and piped:

"Hey, kid. Go a couple o' rounds with Sailor Jack."

"You talking to *me?*" I asked.

"Don't worry, kid. Sailor will go easy on you."

Oh, sure. I had yet to see Sailor Jack go easy for a single round. "Mr. Martzo," I said, "my fists are kinda raw from punching the bag. Could I take a little more time to get into shape?"

"Sure. Take your time."

I never returned to that gym. Several weeks later, I bumped into Martzo on the street. "Where y' been, kid?" he said. "I can make you a good 12-pounder."

"Well," I replied, thinking quickly, "my dad caught wind of my going to the gym and told me no fighting."

Fast-forwarding now to the Steeler booth in the 1970s, my play-by-play partner Jack Fleming, with whom I would broadcast for 24 years, looked down one day at a melee that had broken out on the field. "You could teach those guys a thing or two, Cope," he said. "You were a fighter, I've been told." I quickly denied the rumor, but every couple of years or so, Fleming would return to the idea, finding mirth in reviving it. It took a toehold in the public's memory, partly because a nasty infection I had contracted in my junior year of college left me with a deformed ear that some took to be a souvenir of the ring. Bill Gleason, a witty Chicago sports columnist, once referred to me in his column as "the Pittsburgh sportscaster with an ear and a half."

Anyhow, unlike the mob-victimized pugilist played by Marlon Brando in *On the Waterfront*, no, I never coulda been a contenda.

Could I have been a basketball player?

I made the roster of the high school junior varsity—the jayvees — but that's as far as I went. I had not yet reached my full height of 5-feet-4 3/4. The basketball coach did not stop me in the hallway to persuade me to come out for the team.

Could I have been a baseball player? I often dropped off to sleep ticking off the names of short infielders who had made it into the big leagues. I reported to a tryout camp the Pirates conducted at Forbes Field once each summer. All one needed to get a tryout was a glove and a pair of baseball shoes. A scout named Leo Mackey, laden with an enormous beer belly and carrying in his jaw a proportionately huge chew, sent me to second base and rapped a handful of sharp ground balls at me. I fielded them cleanly, then was beckoned to the batting cage where I took three cuts and met the pitches not once. "Okay, son," said Mackey. "You can go home now."

Could I have been a football player?

I went out for the high school team, weighing by then about 120. The head coach, a slender, white-haired, kindly man named Bob Irvin, refused to issue me a uniform. He placed his hands on my shoulders and said, "Son, I just can't take responsibility for you."

I played now and then in ragtag football games organized by young men who scoured around until they found 11 or so willing players and then shopped for an opponent. I wore a cardboard helmet and cardboard shoulder pads, the best my dad could afford when he gave them to me as a birthday gift. I also wore long street trousers with football shoes beneath them. In my final game, I returned a kickoff, heading up the right sideline behind ten blockers. When the traffic slowed, I decided to cut to the middle of the field to see what was doing there. What was doing was Jerry Finn, a 6-foot-4, 280-pound tackle who shortly would report on a football scholarship to Clarion College in north central Pennsylvania. He did not even bother to lower his shoulder. He simply ran over me and kept running, pausing only to pick up the football I had fumbled, and trotted into the end zone. About five minutes later, I awoke on the sideline and decided football was for larger men.

Could I have been, even, a dancer?

Well, I studied under Gene Kelly—yes, *the* Gene Kelly, star of stage and screen.

I was no more than ten at the time. Each summer, Gene Kelly's mother brought her sons Gene and Fred to a high school gym that lay just a block from where I lived. All business, she sat behind a table, registering neighborhood kids for dancing lessons to be given by Gene and Fred, both grown young men, and collected 25 cents per lesson. During the Great Depression, mind you, 25 cents was not chump change. After a month or two of lessons, the dance classes culminated with a kermis—a stage production that took place in the high school auditorium, all the dancers clad in spiffy costumes Mrs. Kelly had either sold or rented to the dancers' parents. Furthermore, she knew that the kermis would sell out the auditorium every summer, because after the lead-footed pupils had been gotten out of the way, Gene and Fred Kelly would appear on stage to tap-dance stunningly for about 30 minutes. (Fred, by the way, danced every bit as well as Gene and was a conventionally handsome fellow to boot, but he never became a star; he lacked Gene's engaging smile and twinkling eyes—in short, Gene's charisma.)

My mother took me by the hand and practically dragged me to my first lesson. "I wanna play ball," I howled. "I don't wanna learn dancing." Having no choice, I suffered through the lessons and, for the sold-out stage production, donned top hat and tails, ugh, and carried a glass walking stick. I was merely to be part of a chorus line that would tap dance its way from the wings, each top-hatted male brat flashing his walking stick side-to-side while his left arm intertwined with the right arm of a female wearing a short, frilly dress. My partner was Phyllis Manheim, who (if I remember correctly) lived two doors away.

Five steps or so into the footlights, Phyllis Manheim was stricken with stage fright. She froze in place. I had to tug her through the routine, after which I said, "That's the last straw." The following summer, my mother's insistence on dancing lessons dissolved. I played ball. And later, along with millions of others, I loved hearing Gene Kelly sing and dance his way through *Singin' in the Rain*.

"I studied dancing under Gene Kelly," I occasionally mentioned to make an impression on a girl.

It may surprise the reader to learn that I hold a certain amount of sympathy for professional athletes who endure questions put to them by, in most cases, journalists such as I who have never experienced playing games at a high level. Of course, as the pay in broadcasting became increasingly attractive, many pro athletes went on to careers in the media, and no small number of them conducted interviews that, however brief, were insipid—I mean, their questions reflected the brainpower of a domesticated mongrel. This is never surprising, because the former athlete comes to the media with no formal training and may even wince at the thought that he's become one of the parasites who too often misquoted him. (Sportscasters, like athletes, are interviewed by writers, so I know whereof I speak.) Anyhow, we print and broadcast reporters who have brought no athletic accomplishments to the table take smug satisfaction in watching a former jock uncork an idiotic interview, and I take my share.

Dan Edwards, the Steelers' director of public relations at the time and now a vice president of the Jacksonville Jaguars, phoned me on a Monday preceding an important game the Steelers would be playing on the coming Sunday, a game to be televised by NBC. "NBC will be in town Wednesday," Edwards said. "They asked if you'll come to the stadium and be interviewed by O.J."

O.J. Simpson would be working on one of his weekly features that were carried in NBC's hour-long pregame show. "Okay," I said to Edwards and on Wednesday reported to a conference room at Steeler headquarters where an NBC camera crew had set up their equipment for the interview. A producer greeted me and explained that O.J. was not present but that she (the producer) would conduct the interview. I knew without asking that later in the day O.J. would sit alone before the camera and repeat the questions the woman had put to me. A tape editor then would make it appear that O.J. and I were in the same room.

I dropped into Dan Edwards's office on my way out. "How'd it go?" Dan asked.

"Fine," I said, "but where was O.J.?"

Edwards informed me that O.J. had gone to one of Pittsburgh's elite golf courses to play a round as a guest of Jack Ham, a fellow Hall of Famer. No doubt O.J. had phoned Ham to tell him he would be in Pittsburgh and suggested that Ham set up a game. "You know, Dan," I said, "I had the feeling back there during the interview, that O.J. *never* conducts his interviews—that it's always the producer who does, and that NBC is happy to have him out of the way."

Dan chuckled. Still, I found it a little surprising that Ham and O.J. would be playing golf on a cold day in October, in an all-day drizzle. I found it all the more surprising when, not very long after, O.J. was arrested and prosecuted for double-murder by knife in the trial of the century. His attorneys argued that he could not have wielded the knife to commit those vicious multiple stabbings because he had terribly arthritic hands. I mused that healthy, supple hands are equally important both to playing 18 holes in miserable weather and to stabbing the life out of two previously robust humans. Do you get my drift?

Chapter Three

You Wouldn't Care to Buy a Baby Picture, Would You?

The crew chief, whom I judged to be in his early 40s, sat at the wheel as the four of us made our way southeast from Pittsburgh toward Uniontown, Pennsylvania, a mining town of slightly more than 20,000 that lay a few miles above the West Virginia border. The other two men looked to be in their 30s. Little conversation passed between us as we drove through the frozen wooded countryside. Weather reports, as I recall, pegged the temperature at two degrees.

A vast range of the Appalachians, mud-ugly in winter and towering almost 2,800 feet above us, loomed over Uniontown's farthest border. East of Main Street, narrow streets threaded their way up steep hills crowded with frame houses that continued clear to the edges of the ridges at the top. Mostly, coal miners and their families lived in these homes. Soon the crew chief parked his car off Main and proceeded to carve Uniontown into four slices, each of us to work his assigned section that day and in the days ahead until we had worked out the town.

"Okay, fellas," said the crew chief. "We'll meet back here at four."

Our purpose? To sell baby photos.

Actually, as we pounded door to door, we were selling appointments for a photographer to visit later and, if possible, pose whole families, but if an infant existed in the household there would be no excuse for failing to come away with a deposit from the loving mother. Wearing a necktie and a cheap overcoat, hunched over in the face of a biting wind, I told myself, "My God, this is the First Day of My Future?"

Just two days before, you see, I had marched in the January commencement procession at the University of Pittsburgh, harboring an absolute passion to become a newspaperman. Months before graduation I plodded through the newsrooms of the city's three papers, urging editors to keep me in mind for a vacancy. No suburban papers existed to offer an alternative, because in this winter of 1951, precious few suburbs had been built. At the *Pittsburgh Press*, the city editor—a gruff, white-haired man named Larry Fagan—kept me waiting 45 minutes in an anteroom, then emerged from his newsroom to say, "Kid, go to a small-town paper and get some experience." End of job interview. Fagan had not even taken a seat.

At the *Pittsburgh Sun-Telegraph* I entered hopeful. I knew a vacancy existed in the sports department; besides that, the sports editor's son was one of my college classmates and a friend. Harry Keck, the *Telegraph's* longtime sports editor and boxing expert, rightly considered himself the country's foremost expert on Harry Greb, a legendary middleweight boxing champion and sex-binging high-roller of the 1920s and '30s who had sprung from the streets of Pittsburgh.

A pleasant, garrulous man, Keck welcomed me into his office. He then proceeded to regale me with Harry Greb stories for a solid hour. At last he said, "I'll certainly keep you in mind."

He gave the job to a young man of limited talent who, writing a potpourri of notes from the Pittsburgh sports scene one day, found it newsworthy to include an item thanking a local florist for sending him flowers.

Down the street at the *Post-Gazette*, I gained a toehold. Joe Shuman, the city editor, studied a few samples of my writing—clippings of articles and columns I had shown him from Pitt's campus newspaper.

"Tell you what," Shuman said. "We can use a stringer out there at Pitt."

Metropolitan newspapers employed networks of "stringers" working at small-town papers throughout the region. "Keep your eyes and ears open," Shuman told me, "and bring us a piece whenever you think you've got one." I would be paid 30 cents per line. Not per line of typewritten copy submitted but per line of newspaper type that actually saw print. Soon after, I pleased Joe Shuman with a story about university administrators cracking down on a drunken fraternity party. I earned more than seven bucks on that one. But it quickly became apparent to me, as Shuman discarded one offering after another, that he was not interested in stories about victories won by the university debating team or elections to student council. He wanted more drunken fraternity parties.

Yet as a stringer, I had obtained entrée to the *Post-Gazette's* newsroom. Newsrooms in those days were called city rooms, sprawling the entire length of a floor. Each time I delivered a story, I thrilled to the sounds of the city room, especially if the clock on the wall was nearing four when reporters—this was a morning paper—came in from assignments and beats, filling up deep rows of desks and charging the air with their clattering typewriters. Shouts rang out. "Boy!" the editors and copy readers would cry, and one of the so-called copy boys (actually, males in their late teens or 20s scrounging for a living) would race to fetch finished copy. They would plug it into a tubular container and fire the container through pneumatic tubes that ran clear into the composing room, where the story would be transformed into lead type by rows of men seated at noisy linotype machines. Much later, with the advent of computers, city rooms would fall as noiseless as hospital corridors, and if one were to address a fellow employee as "Boy!" there surely would follow a discrimination grievance. Meantime, in 1951, I hungered to be part of that city room action.

But graduation from Pitt lay less than two weeks away, and still no job offer. The circumstances called for an act of desperation.

"Mr. Shuman," I finally said, having stood patiently beside his desk in the heart of the city room while he penciled changes into a page of reporter's copy. "If you don't hire me, some other newspaper may beat you to it."

Shuman slowly looked up and peered at me over the bifocals that rested at the end of his nose. "Well," he said in his West Virginia drawl, "I believe we'll just prefer to take that chance."

The fact was, all three Pittsburgh papers had come through a strike not long before and were now pinching to make up lost economic ground. There would be few hirings for many months to come. So it was that I climbed those icy, precipitous streets of Uniontown, only to be turned away at one door after another. At one of the first, a miner's wife answered the door nursing her baby. An attractive young brunette, she invited me to have a seat at the kitchen table. She continued to breastfeed while I stumbled through my sales pitch, perspiring from self-consciousness. I lost the sale, a harbinger of things to come.

Mind you, the potential for success was there. Families in those days did not own half a dozen cameras and at least one for videotaping Junior's first attempt to crawl. Most families owned only a rudimentary camera known as a "box brownie" that made foggy still photos. Housewives—the great majority of married couples clung to the belief, can you imagine, that it was important for mothers to stay home to attend their children—did not fear being set upon when answering the knock of a stranger. They welcomed a break from cooking meals, scrubbing floors, and hand-washing laundry. During my own childhood, my mother especially had welcomed the periodic visits from the Fuller Brush Man, his genre being the elite of door-to-door peddlers. Always dapper and smiling warmly, our man would spread open his outsized attaché case with a flourish to reveal a dazzling cornucopia of hair brushes, cleaning brushes, whisk brooms, combs, and sundry other items; he would extol the quality of manufacture by the Fuller Brush Company. Few could turn him away without having purchased at least a comb. "Thank you, thank you, and good day, madam," the Fuller Brush Man would sing, practically whistling with cheer as he made his way to the house next door.

My pitch, when the front door came open, went something like this:

"Good morning. You wouldn't by any chance be interested in purchasing an appointment for a picture, would you?"

I had been born without a drop of salesmanship in my blood. Years later, I would be asked to deliver a eulogy at a funeral service for a wonderful man named Jay Davis, who had been head of sales for our radio station. He not only encouraged his salespersons in a caring manner that won him their affection, but on days when he had particularly enjoyed one of my commentaries or talk shows, he took the trouble to walk to my office and tell me so. "Salesmen and saleswomen," I told the gathered mourners, "are America's life's blood." I meant every word.

But I hated selling, for unaccountable reasons. One summer, during my sophomore year of college, I played second base (good field, no hit) for a fast-pitch softball team called the David L. Lawrence 14th Ward Club. Our navy blue uniforms had been supplied by Davey Lawrence, Pittsburgh's powerful political boss then running for reelection to the office of mayor. We scorched across the city's neighborhood ball fields, finishing the season with 22 victories, no defeats.

But the next year, alas, brought with it no mayoral election. Gone were our uniforms, packed away for the next political campaign. "We're going to have to sell raffle tickets," came the edict from our manager, Jerry Finn—the same 280-pound Jerry Finn who, as earlier noted, ended my football efforts. "We gotta raise money to buy uniforms."

"I'm not selling raffle tickets," I piped up. "That's like being on the bum."

"You sell raffles," replied Finn, "or you're off the team."

I left the team.

In Uniontown little more than two years later, I found no latent talent for salesmanship. At the end of the first day, I had earned three dollars in commissions. The First Day of My Future left me in despair, filled with self-pity. A metal sign hanging from a post I had passed informed me that not long before the outbreak of the Civil War, escaped slaves had trudged over those formidable Appalachians, having heard that Uniontown was a hospitable refuge along the Underground Railroad, as the escape trail was euphemistically named. In a house on Baker Alley, the slaves would find food and a night's lodging.

"Those poor bastards," I told myself. "They certainly had it a lot rougher than me. But on the other hand, they didn't have to sell baby pictures."

I knew, though, why I had come to Uniontown and why I likely would be back the next morning. The stock market crash of 1929 coincided with the year of my birth and brought on the Great Depression. Within five or six years, the small wholesale clothing business owned by my father—Ellis A. Kopelman—would go under. One by one, the retailers who were his customers failed, too, leaving dad stuck with unpaid invoices. His debtors were friends. He could not bring himself to pursue them in court. In fact, they trusted him to the point of asking judges to appoint him bankruptcy referee to settle disputes as they arose between creditors and debtors while the Depression tightened its grip on the nation.

Alas, along with Dad's store, in the wholesale district located on the edge of downtown, went his spirit. Though without a college education, he possessed a computer-like mind. Ask him to multiply, say, 2,063 times 3,120 and he would spit out the correct answer from his head in seconds. Surely he could have been a physicist. He was also a hilarious teller of stories. Relatives and friends who came to visit would collapse with laughter. But dad's business failure made him irascible at times, burdened by the struggle to raise me and three daughters, all older than I.

To make ends meet, he bought a truck and made the rounds of failing clothing stores, buying their inventories for resale to still-existing businesses. He had no sight in one eye as a result of an auto accident, so he had to hire a driver, and the two of them came home with bundles of clothing to be unloaded and deposited on the floor of every room needed. Meanwhile, when idle time presented itself—and mind you, night baseball games had not yet arrived—Dad took me to Forbes Field in the afternoon to watch the Pirates play. He deposited me in a general-admission seat, then took himself behind the top row of the lower third-base grandstand. There, daily, stood a throng of gamblers, prepared to bet on most any development—even a single pitch. Ball or strike? (Owners happily tolerated the gamblers because they paid their way into the park.)

"One hundred to one the Pirates lose," cried a voice one day when the Pirates were down, 10-0. Dad took the bet for a buck. The Pirates roared back, and we ate steak that night. A somewhat better salesman than I would prove to be in Uniontown, Dad went to work for the Metropolitan Life Insurance Company, but not entirely as a salesman. By day, he walked a debit, as the insurance companies called a route. His debit, in the Hill District, took him up hills and tenement stairwells where door-to-door he collected pennies from poverty-stricken blacks—pennies due on the only insurance they could afford: the policies were written to provide for their funerals. Through snow and rain and sweltering summer weather, dad plodded along his debit. Evenings, he pitched relatives and friends to buy life insurance, but the supply of such prospects ran thin. Even after World War II ended the Depression—no, Franklin D. Roosevelt did not end it—by sending unemployed millions to war and placing lucky civilians in defense plants at comfortable wages, there was no money for Dad to send any of us to college.

I was the fortunate one.

Uncle Bob—Uncle Bob Davis on my father's side—had given up his dentistry practice because, I suppose, patients no longer could afford to have teeth pulled. He had wangled a steady job as a state health inspector. As best as I can recall, he inspected barber shops, doctor's offices, restaurants, and the like for sanitation. A mustachioed man with an ear-to-ear smile, Uncle Bob used his political connections to win for me a four-year "senatorial" scholarship, state senators being empowered by the legislature to award small numbers of scholarships to one college or another across Pennsylvania. I got to college on political pull.

I rode the No. 68 trolley to classes and lived at home. But Dad preached two strictures to his children:

1) "You will never have to support me in my old age, and meanwhile, I will not support *you* once you are out of school."

2) "Once you *are* out of school, whether it's high school or college, and so long as you continue to live at home, you'll pay rent."

Hence, Uniontown, and pushing baby pictures—on the Monday following the Saturday I had received my Bachelor of Arts degree. Why had I wound up in this particular job? Memory fails me, but I'm damned certain I did not place a classified ad under "Employment Wanted," saying "Ace Salesman Seeks Profitable Territory." More likely, I had scanned Help Wanted.

History is filled with success stories far greater than mine, of men and women who pulled themselves up from humble beginnings. I know that. Yet if, on that bitter cold Monday in Uniontown, someone would have told me that one day I would mingle with the rich and famous, would be brought back to this very town on at least three occasions to deliver after-dinner speeches and be paid for them, and perhaps would hold in my hands John F. Kennedy's ability to be elected president, I would have thought it preposterous. My God, I'm sounding as though I think I rated a chapter in Horatio Alger.

More about my role—real or imagined—as a maker or breaker of America's first Catholic president, later. For now, as I rode from Uniontown in the dusk, I prayed.

"Dear God," I silently said. "Please, when I get home, let there be a call or a letter from a newspaper editor."

Bingo! Dad said, "You got a call from a man named Gene Cuneo. He said he's sports editor of the *Erie Times.*"

Goodbye, Uniontown. Hello, Erie. That very night, owning no auto, I boarded a Greyhound bus bound north, some 150 miles, to the shores of Lake Erie, eight dollars and change in my pocket. I would learn that Erie was the Bowling Capital of America. Oh, swell.

Chapter Four

Off and Running, Sort Of

As noted, I reported to my first newspaper job not exactly flush and quickly learned it would be a week till payday (at which time I would find that my take-home pay, the amount left after taxes, would come to $38.50 per week), so I resolved to be prudent. With a portion of the eight bucks and change in my pocket, I purchased two pounds of bologna and a loaf of bread to get me through the week. Across the street from the *Erie Times* stood the YMCA. I rented a room for $7.50 per week, persuading the YMCA to trust a *Times* employee until payday.

I soon learned that at newspapers in the 1950s and for ages before, a familiar question asked by one reporter of another was, "Brother, can you spare me a fiver till payday?"

In my ignorance of that custom, and wanting to make a favorable impression, I ate bologna sandwiches in my YMCA room. No problem.

My problem was bowling.

I have hated bowling ever since, as a kid, I worked as a pinsetter in a ten-pin alley. Before automation, you see, pinsetters reset the fallen pins, then leaped onto a ledge to escape pins sent flying by the next roll of the ball. The job left me with a sore back and a lifelong aversion to bowling. Yet here I was in Erie, which boasted of being the Bowling Capital of America.

Each night in the sports department, where only four of us worked, the phones began ringing relentlessly. Bowling leagues and clubs were phoning in the scores, it seemed, of every bowler in town who that evening had picked up a ball. The *Times* the next morning would devote copious space to agate type listing names and scores. One night I awoke in my room bathed in a cold sweat from a nightmare. I had dreamt that I answered the phone and heard a man say, "I'm calling for the Polish Falcons. I've got 80 scores."

Eighty Polish names to take down! The next day I said to the sports editor, Gene Cuneo, "Gene, I know you gave me my first newspaper job, and I've been here only a few months. But if you don't mind, I'd like to see if there's an opening on city side."

A caring boss, Cuneo replied, "If that's what you want, kid, go for it."

Bowling alone had not caused me to lose my enthusiasm for sportswriting. Growing up in Pittsburgh, I was a fan of big-league baseball and football—the Pirates and Steelers—and of big-time college sports played by Pitt and Duquesne University. Erie had minor league baseball and basketball, small college sports, and oh yes, once-a-week professional wrestling. My first week in town, Abe Cohen, who owned an auto-parts store and promoted the wrestling cards, said to me, "Come to the matches any time. You're comped for ringside."

By coincidence, Abe's weekly matches took place on my night off, so I dropped in at ringside. Early into the program, a wrestler hoisted his opponent and (with the opponent's cooperation, of course) hurled him through the ropes. I distinctly remember that the red-haired, sweaty victim, wearing Hawaiian trunks, was billed as Lucky Sumanovich, the Hawaiian Flash. He bounced off the edge of the ring and landed in my lap. I watched the rest of the card from the rear of the arena and never went back.

Well, actually, I did return once, but not to watch the matches. The governor of Pennsylvania had appointed a new state athletic commissioner, whose job it would be to govern all professional boxing and wrestling throughout the western portion of the state and to collect taxes from the promoters. John Holahan, the recipient of this political plum, earlier had been general manager of the Pittsburgh Steelers and, I was reasonably sure, got his new job through the ample political connections held by the team's owner, Art Rooney.

"The new athletic commissioner's in town," Gene Cuneo told me. "Go over to the wrestling matches and interview him."

I shook John Holahan's hand and followed him as he entered a large dressing room that housed every wrestler who would appear on the card that night. Their sharing a single room posed no problem, for little animosity exists between rivals who know the outcome of their bouts have been prearranged. Anyhow, Holahan, a short, pudgy man dressed in a black suit, addressed the room forthwith, announcing:

"Men. I am your new commissioner, and I want you to understand one thing right now. I want *honest* wrestling."

The wrestlers rolled their eyes at one another. I was sure Holahan's declaration was intended for my newspaper story.

Of course, the next morning's headline said "Commissioner Demands Honest Wrestling." But a strange thing had occurred back in the composing room where printers arranged type and photographs on a page-sized block known as a stone. A *Times* photographer had accompanied me to the arena to photograph Holahan, and upon returning to the paper he developed his film and sent it by messenger to a nearby lithographing company that processed the newspaper's photos into metal images called "cuts." Alas, the lithographers had been slow that night to deliver Holahan's cut, so the printer in charge of our sports pages, knowing the presses were waiting to roll, did what he always did when the lithographers did not come through.

He looked for any cut lying around that would fit the hole reserved for Holahan's likeness. The Korean War was now in its second year, and the printer came up with a war map. Appearing below it in the next morning's sports page was the cutline:

JOHN HOLAHAN
Demands Honesty

Well, Erie was not New York or even Pittsburgh, but it was a start.

Having left sports writing behind me, or so I thought, I became part of a two-man team that worked the paper's late-late shift—till three in the morning. My partner and boss was Ed Yates, a tall, congenial, pipe-smoking man. We alone remained in the second-floor newsroom into the wee hours, my job usually being to clean up on minor stories and to walk down the street to the police station to look for new entries into the blotter. (A loud domestic argument could land the noisy couple two paragraphs in the paper.) As summer came on, an unexpected—by me—phenomenon occurred.

A species of mayflies, perhaps half the size of my short index finger, inhabited the bottom of Lake Erie. The locals called them Canadian Soldiers. With the weather warming, they swam to the surface and flew off at night to die wherever they eventually landed. Many landed on Ed Yates and me. They flew through the unscreened windows of the *Times* newsroom, blanketing our desks and hair and even settling down on the keys of our typewriters. Hit a key, squish—you nailed a dead Canadian Soldier.

"Say, Ed," I remarked to Yates. "How come we have no screens in the windows?"

Yates shrugged. "This lasts only a few nights."

I knew the *Times* had a suggestion box for employees, so I popped in a suggestion that screens be installed. When I reported for work the next afternoon, the managing editor, Joe Meagher, beckoned me to his desk.

"I read your suggestion," he said. "You've surely noticed that our windows don't open straight up and down. They slant in and out. The guys who invented the atomic bomb could not design screens to fit our windows."

"Gee, Mr. Meagher," I replied. "That doesn't look so difficult to me."

"Kid," he said, nicely. "I guess what I'm telling you is, we don't put suggestions that cost money into the suggestion box."

The late-late shift could be a drag, with little to do for stretches of time. So it occurred to me to try my hand at fiction, a writing skill I had made the mistake of failing to study while in college. I wrote a short story describing a romance between a professional wrestler and a diner waitress. "Not bad," Yates said when he finished reading it. "Maybe you can sell it."

Okay, where? *Sir Magazine* came to mind.

Back in college, one of several jobs I had worked to obtain walking-around money was that of a clerk manning the counter of a small confectionery in a shabby part of town. The owner, a man called Lefty, tended his store alone until I showed up late in the day to take over. We sold cigars, cigarettes, chewing tobacco, magazines, Mickey Mouse wristwatches, toys, you-name-it, and wrote illegal numbers slips to turn over to the numbers-ring collectors. One of our best customers was a police lieutenant.

From time to time, however, we would be visited by an anti-pornography delegation demanding we remove *Sir Magazine* and a few other similarly brazen monthlies from our shelves. They featured covers showing photos of women posing in two-piece bathing suits.

"*Sir!*" I told myself. "This fiction I've written is no doubt so bad that it might have a chance only at the worst magazine I can think of."

I shot off the manuscript to *Sir's* New York offices, and not long after received a letter, saying:

"Congratulations! Your short story has been accepted. You will be paid 50 dollars upon publication."

My first magazine attempt, sold! Little did I know at that early stage of my career that legitimate magazines paid upon acceptance. "Upon publication" meant the magazine had no intention of paying. *Sir* dressed up my story with a nicely done illustration of a wrestler and a waitress and placed it opposite a page that carried an article entitled, "Is Male Rape Possible?"

No check appeared in my mail. I fired off a letter to *Sir*, demanding my 50 bucks and a second letter threatening to involve the services of my lawyer. I of course had none and could afford none, which *Sir* surely was counting on, as my letters went into the trash.

I had a few days' vacation coming. Still not being able to afford a car, I set off hitchhiking to New York City, a distance of more than 500 miles; thumbing rides was a perfectly safe way to get from here to there in that era. I found the magazine's offices in a brownstone walk-up in Manhattan and demanded to see the managing editor, who turned out to be a woman.

"You mean you hitchhiked clear from Erie to New York just to get paid?" she said after I had told her so and threatened to refuse to leave until I got my 50 bucks. It was a matter of principle.

"Well!" the editor said. "I have never experienced such persistence in a contributor. Do you know what I'm going to do? I'm going to pay you!"

I promptly cashed the check she wrote, then hitchhiked back to Erie. I did not attempt another piece of magazine writing for almost six years.

The telegram from the *Pittsburgh Post-Gazette* said:

HAVE OPENING FOR GENERAL ASSIGNMENT RE-
PORTER. IF STILL INTERESTED, REPLY SOONEST.
                                        SHUMAN

On my final shift for the *Times*, and with Ed Yates's permission, I was going to cheat an hour from my shift in order to comfortably make the 3 a.m. Greyhound to Pittsburgh. Ten minutes before 2 a.m., however, we heard the sounds of our editor-in-chief clutching the stairwell railing and pulling himself up to the second-floor newsroom to disappear into his private office after what I supposed was a night on the town. The paper was owned by the Mead family. John J. Mead, Jr., a tall, white-maned man whose florid face provided contrast for his distinguished white mustache, was editor-in-chief. His brother George ran the business department. My only contact with John Mead in the seven months I worked for his paper occurred whenever he shuffled out of his office to hand me a few bills with instructions to go across the street to the Lawrence Hotel and fetch him cigars. He regularly wrote a column of local items in which he wished one Erie citizen and another a happy birthday and reported where others were vacationing, and I found it curious that he wrote under the pseudonym Jay James but carried a photo of himself at the head of his column. I never understood that.

Now, minutes before I was to head for the Greyhound station, I heard the editor-in-chief loudly beckon me to his office. I glanced at my wristwatch and said, "Oh, shit!"

I noticed that on the wall behind him hung a large photo of him shaking hands with Ed Sullivan, the totally untalented but dominant network television variety show host, who I surmised had visited Erie on a publicity tour. "So you're going to Pittsburgh," Mr. Mead said in a raspy voice. "Well, kid, I'm going to give you some advice. Never mind being just a reporter. Bill Block is the publisher of the *Post-Gazette*. He's an old friend. When you get to Pittsburgh, I want you to see Bill and tell him I sent you. I want you to tell him to put you in the job of assistant to the publisher."

I made the Greyhound with a few minutes to spare, having decided along the way that I would put off the aspirations Mr. Mead's pep-talk recommended lest the *Post-Gazette* throw me out on my ear.

Chapter Five

Mr. Kopelman, meet Mr. Cope

I was Myron Sydney Kopelman when, in the summer of 1951, I reported for my first day's work at the *Post-Gazette.* Joe Shuman, the city editor of whom I have spoken, led me to an unoccupied cubicle at the rear of the city room, and for openers said:

"First thing we've got to do is find a byline for you."

"Pardon me?"

"We've got several Jewish reporters here as it is," Shuman answered, "and on top of that we've got several Germans whose names might be taken for Jewish. Weisgerber over there," he said, pointing to a reporter seated at a nearby desk. "Weisgerber's not Jewish, but our readers might think he is. It won't do to have too many Jewish or Jewish-sounding by-lines."

With that, Shuman reached for a phone book, the white pages. "Kopelman, huh? Let's see if we can find something resembling that." He thumbed his way to the C's, that letter evidently promising a greater supply of Anglo-Saxon names than the K's, which were apt to turn up all sorts of Eastern European names.

"Here's a good one. Cope. Yes, that's it—that's your byline, Myron Cope." Shuman had no idea how fitting his selection was, for in high school my friends had called me Kope, sometimes Kopey, and I wrote a sports column for the high school paper that I dreadfully entitled Kope's Komments.

Today, of course, no editor would dare suggest to an employee that he change his byline for purposes of disguising his or her religion, race, or ethnicity; litigation would follow. But this was another time, and I would soon learn that it was not at all uncommon for editors to follow that course. John Troan, an award-winning science writer for the *Pittsburgh Press* and later the paper's editor-in-chief, recalls in his autobiography that he first joined the *Press* as John Albert Troanovitch, hired as a young re-write man to take down information phoned in by reporters at the scene of breaking news and fashion their information into an article. Reporters' phone calls were directed by the switchboard operator to the city editor, who briefly listened to the gist of the reporter's material and then barked the name of the reporter and that of a re-write man. The latter would slap on a headpiece, greet the reporter by name, and begin rapidly typing notes. One day, Troanovitch's city editor became involved in an annoying phone call from an irate reader. When the conversation concluded, the city editor slammed down his phone and loudly exclaimed, "That sonofabitch!"

Troanovitch, nearby, misheard him and swiftly attached his head-piece, awaiting a reporter's voice. The city editor burst into laughter and roared, "That does it!" He had been mulling over giving Troanovitch a new byline. Not long after, he acted. To this day, John Albert Troanovitch has been John Troan.

Many Americans who wring their hands over divisions that exist today in our society may disagree, but tolerance in America has come a long way since I joined the *Post-Gazette* in 1951. Still, I greatly disliked the surprise Joe Shuman had sprung. I accepted it for two reasons:

1) City-side general-assignment reporters—that is, those who might be given just about any assignment ranging from a breaking news story to a human-interest feature to an obituary—rarely received a byline. Newspapers have changed greatly; today reporters receive bylines atop virtually anything they have written save a one-paragraph weather forecast. To be anointed with a byline in my time, a city-side reporter had to have written a major story or performed superbly under a tight deadline or bought his editor drinks. I had no doubt I would receive few bylines; meantime, perhaps Jack Weisgerber might resign to go into public relations (which he indeed did some years later) and I could return to being Myron Kopelman.

2) I needed the job. It was not that my take-home pay would soar from $38.50 per week in Erie to something over $50, as dictated by the Pittsburgh local of the American Newspaper Guild. This was my escape to the big-time—to a big-city newspaper. Myron Cope it would be, at least for a while.

The *Post-Gazette*, like the *Erie Times*, was a morning paper, oblig-ing some of us to work late shifts, and in the ensuing months I all but pinched myself when I saw Harold Cohen, nationally respected by the theater crowd, come into the office to write his review of a stage play he had just seen, or Donald Steinfirst, a white-haired industrialist whose avo-cation was critiquing music, enter wearing a tuxedo, having come from the symphony or the opera.

About six months after being hired, damn, I was sent back to sportswriting.

"We've adopted a new policy here," the managing editor informed me. "We've decided it's a good idea to rotate some of our people to other jobs. Broaden their newspaper experience. We're moving Normie Greenberg from the sports department to the city-side copy desk to give him a taste of editing news copy." Normie had been a copy boy whom the sports editor had taken a liking to and hired into his department. More-over, Normie and I, being about the same age and size, had taken to hit-ting the after-hours clubs together and had become fast pals. "We know you wrote sports in college and a little in Erie," said the managing editor, "so we'd like you to take Normie's place in sports. It's only for six months, then both of you go back where you were. What do you say?"

"I don't like it at all," I replied, "but do I have a choice?"

To that point, on city side, I had been given perhaps two—three at the most—bylines. The only piece I can actually remember that got one resulted from an evening when I was eating spaghetti in a downtown Italian restaurant. Suddenly I heard a strong, rich voice singing opera back in the kitchen. I put down my fork and spoon and walked to the kitchen where I found a Mexican dishwasher. I interviewed him at once and, yes, received a byline atop my feature story. The publicity, however, did not free the Mexican from dishwashing.

But now, my first night as the new kid in sports, a man in his 70s named Fred P. Alger sat at his desk just a few feet to my left, pecking out a story with two gnarled fingers. He wore a peaked cap, a plaid flannel hunting shirt, and a bandanna tied at the front of his throat. I later heard that as a Marine, Fred Alger had fought in China in 1900 in the Boxer Rebellion and then spent the rest of his working life at the *Post-Gazette* writing about high-school sports. Now, as he pecked away, he failed to take aim at the spittoon sitting at his left foot and fired a shot of chewing tobacco that hit me squarely on the cuff of my trousers. "Mr. Alger," I complained. "Could you be more careful?"

"Goddamn young punks," he muttered.

The second time Fred Alger splattered my trousers, I arose and walked across the street to a saloon that carried no name in its window but was simply known as Benny's, for its proprietor, Benny Samuels. I did not chew tobacco at that time, but I purchased a pack of Mail Pouch. Back in the office, I chewed the tobacco until it was moist, then fired a shot at Fred P. Alger's trousers. We never had another disagreeable moment, and I found I enjoyed chewing tobacco.

My initiation into the sports department, as it turned out, marked my entrance into another world of journalism. Almost the entire sports staff, I judged, had been working there at least 20 years, showing no remote grasp of grammar, let alone any flair for writing. They were likable fellows who in one way or another had obtained a job there. It was just that—a steady job, and you could not blame them for remaining in it. For myself, in college I had aimed to become the complete newspaperman, one who could write grammatical and possibly interesting sentences, edit copy, write headlines that fit into the allotted columns, lay out (design) pages, and work with printers in the composing room as we selectively threw out lines of metal type to make a piece fit into its designated space. Alas, applying myself to all of that turned out to be a disastrous mistake.

Soon after I joined sports, Dan McGibbeny, a colleague with whom I instantly became friends, mentioned to me that Gil Remley—an old-timer who ran the day-to-day operations of the sports department and if working today would be given the title of executive sports editor—had said to him, "Dan, I've got me a newspaperman." Translated, that meant I would be nailed to the inside of the building, exercising all manner of duties except covering stories and writing.

Today, a big-city sportswriter covers one beat—two at the most. Jack Sell, a pleasant man seated immediately to my right, covered the Steelers, plus every sport played by the three universities in town, and tennis and dog shows. But he was not spread thin. A dapper man, Jack would report for work at 4 p.m., place his felt hat atop a coat rack and hang up the jacket of his suit. He would then await phone calls from publicists. Mondays, they would give him a list of their teams' injuries. Tuesday through Thursday, they would update and re-update the condition of the injured. Jack's stories made for exciting reading, if you considered hospital charts exciting. Friday afternoon offered a change of pace. The publicist for the University of Pittsburgh would tell Jack Sell the number of football players the head coach had selected to make a road trip, and the headline clear across the top of Saturday morning's sports page would proclaim:

Panthers Take Seventy to Nebraska

"Why," I once asked the managing editor of our paper, "don't we put more effort into our sports section?"

"Because surveys show it's one of the least-read parts of the paper," he replied.

Little wonder.

I felt a need to write, so before reporting to work I loafed—a Pittsburgh word—at the Steeler offices and at the college athletic offices and wherever sports buzzed, and on my days off watched football practices and attended sports events, admission free to all sportswriters. On my own time (no doubt a violation of Newspaper Guild rules) I banged out stories that Gil Remley liked and printed. I wrote a feature, meaning a piece describing a sports personality, that drew the attention of the *Post-Gazette*'s editor-in-chief, Andrew Bernhard, who thereupon told Remley, "Give that kid more features."

This development greatly disturbed a colleague called Jigger, who covered hockey, hunting, and fishing, and regarded himself as the staff's sole feature writer. Soon after, Bernhard walked to my desk and dropped in front of me a postcard he had received in the mail. "I thought you'd get a chuckle from this," he said.

The typewriten postcard asked:

"Why do you put up with Myron Cope, yclept sportswriter? He's terrible. You should fire him."

I tossed the postcard to Dan McGibbeny and rhetorically asked, "McGib, who wrote this?"

"Jigger," Dan replied at once. Jigger was the only writer I have known who possessed a compulsive tendency to employ the word "yclept," which he seemed to define as "purporting to be"—as in purporting to be a sportswriter.

"Listen," I said to McGib. "You know that new portable typewriter that John Harris gave Jigger for Christmas?" John Harris owned the minor league hockey team, the Pittsburgh Hornets, that Jigger covered. Harris also operated a very profitable string of movie theaters and a traveling ice show, and enrolled just about every department head of all three Pittsburgh newspapers in the Fruit-of-the-Month Club. On the first of each month, baskets of fruit were delivered to their desks. Newspapermen, after all, were low paid, so publishers winked at a certain amount of graft. At the *Post-Gazette,* our television-radio critic annually gave local broadcast stations a list of gifts he wanted for Christmas. In our second-floor city room, reporters would gather at a window to watch with amusement as he and his wife, both having backsides the width of a fireplace, stuffed armfuls of gift-wrapped packages into their Volkswagen bug, carefully strategizing to leave room for themselves. Sometimes we placed bets on the outcome.

"Jigger," I now reminded McGib, "brings that portable to the office. Do me a favor. Next time he brings in that typewriter, type a sampling from it. I'll bet it matches the postcard."

But Jigger at once felt the silent hostility I could not help showing him. He never again brought the portable to the office.

Al Abrams, our sports editor, our boss, stood about 5 feet, 8 inches—a sallow man but one who possessed a presence on the sports scene. His black hair slicked back with pomade, he wore sharp suits, and his daily column carried a photo of himself that bore a slight likeness to the silent film star Rudolph Valentino. Al had absolutely no talent for writing but was smart enough to know it. Each sports editor at Pittsburgh's three newspapers wrote a daily column, prominently displayed, and Al was easily the star among them and a local celebrity. At the *Press*, Chester L. Smith was a witty man and talented writer, but he had fallen into the habit of constantly writing about sports figures he had covered decades earlier or concocting columns from his head rather than leave the office to dig out fresh material. At the *Sun-Telegraph*, Harry Keck virtually made an art form of tedium. One day he received from a reader a package containing the reader's considerable collection of baseball cards, to be looked at and returned. The rage for collecting such cards and other memorabilia had not yet swept across America like an epidemic of smallpox. Children merely waxed baseball cards and skipped them against a wall, as they might skip a stone across a pond, betting pennies on which card would fall to a stop closest to the wall. Would Keck inspect the reader's cards and be impressed, the collector wondered. The next day, Keck began his column by telling of the package he'd received and proceeded to fill the rest of his column with a list of baseball players appearing on the cards. At the bottom, in the event that any reader reached the bottom, Keck promised to continue the list in his next column and did exactly that.

Down the street at the *Press*, Chester L. Smith dropped an anonymous postcard into the mail to Keck. "I have six Carl Hubbell cards. If I send them to you, will you print Carl Hubbell's name six times in your column?"

So Al Abrams was Pittsburgh's premier sports columnist, by default. He attended sports events and loafed in nightclubs where sports figures hung out and collected gossipy notes that, in a time when city population had not yet sprawled into suburbs, appealed to a close-knit urban readership. When Al attempted a full-length essay on a newsworthy issue, he usually lapsed into intolerable dullness, and he surely knew it. From time to time, he would go to a rack in the city room that held about a half-dozen out-of-town newspapers to which the *Post-Gazette* subscribed—papers from New York, Chicago, and other major points—and shopped among their sports pages until he found a column he especially liked. He then tore it from the paper, took it to his desk, changed a sentence here, a paragraph there, and ran it as his column the next day. Technology had not yet shrunk the world, transmitting printed matter across the internet, so believe it or not, so far as I know, Al Abrams's plagiarisms were never found out. More than once, I overheard a fellow employee say to him, "Good column." Al nodded his appreciation.

Having remarked on all this, I may surprise you by saying that as frustrated as I became in Al's sports department, I liked Al. I think he liked me as well, for whenever I walked into his favorite haunts, he'd invite me to join him and his cronies at his table and would say, "How's it goin', cuz?"— "cuz" being a friendly abbreviation for "cousin," employed as a greeting by persons of Lebanese and Syrian extraction. Give him credit, Al worked his job as best as he knew how and succeeded. But my problem was that, like Gil Remley, Al found me most useful nailed to the inside of the building.

When my six-months tour of the sports department ended, Normie Greenberg informed management that he preferred to continue editing city-side copy. Over in sports, I was far from happy, having no beat to work, but at the same time I realized that my interest in sportswriting had been revived simply because Pittsburgh, unlike Erie, possessed big-league and major college teams. So if Normie wanted to stay put, so did I. "Okay, stay there," I was told. Along the way, I managed to anger Gil Remley once and Al Abrams once. One day I informed Gil that although it was a long-standing policy in the sports department that all of us take our vacations in the slow season, winter, I was going to take a summer vacation. "Look," I said. "I can't afford traveling clear to Florida to find warm weather."

Gil blew up. "Nobody here," he cried, "has *ever* taken a summer vacation!" He charged me, brandishing a long pair of copy-cutting shears over his right shoulder. To my relief, he drew up short and settled for saying, "No summer vacations."

Ah, but I had studied the Newspaper Guild's contract with the paper; nowhere did it restrict vacations to wintertime. I filed a grievance, which promptly was upheld. The next year, every member of our sports department took a summer vacation. Now spared the expense of traveling to Florida, I splurged and vacationed in Santa Monica, California. I had gotten on a winning streak in the poker games at the Pittsburgh Press Club.

As for Abrams, no cross words passed between us, but I knew he was hot, and not about my vacation. Early one evening, you see, a very competent, main-bout black middleweight named Freddy Mans sauntered into our sports department. Fighters and their managers visited occasionally, just to pass time and perhaps gain a line or two of publicity. "Freddy," I said, "I've noticed that lately you're catching a lot of right hands to the head."

"Well, sure. It's because I've gone blind in my left eye."

What? How had the athletic commission's doctors okayed this man to fight? If he continued to, the prevailing medical opinion that blindness in a fighter's eye probably would create a "sympathetic" effect upon his other eye might well be borne out and leave Freddy Mans totally blind. He departed the office, leaving me to reflect upon the danger he appeared to be in. I shoved a sheet of paper into my typewriter and wrote the story.

Moments after I'd finished it, Al Abrams walked into the office, as he was apt to at any hour. "Anything doing?" he asked McGibbeny, who that night was in charge.

"Cope's just finished writing a story that Freddy Mans could go blind."

"Lemme see that story," Al said quickly. It so happened that one of Al's close friends, an undersized fight manager named Dusty Bettor from the nearby Mafia-influenced town of New Kensington, owned Freddy Mans. I knew Bettor. Once I had interviewed one of his fighters during the fighter's prefight afternoon steak at Al Abrams's favorite downtown restaurant, Frankie's Bandbox. I excused myself to go to the men's room. Bettor followed me there and stuffed a $50 bill into the jacket pocket of my suit. "I can't take that," I said. Times were changing for the better in sportswriting. It would take time, but graft was on the way out

"Okay, kid," said Bettor, surprised. "No offense intended."

Meantime, Al took my Freddy Mans story and sat down to his typewriter, saying nothing. He thoroughly rewrote my copy. He buried the fact that Mans had lost the sight of one eye, seemingly hoping readers would proceed no farther than they had with Harry Keck's list of baseball cards. Yet some read on, and the embarrassment to the athletic commission was inescapable. The commission terminated Freddy's career. Freddy found employment as a construction worker, and in the years that followed, whenever we saw one another at the fights, he would pass me wordlessly. I felt convinced I had done my duty in his best interest, but today, I wonder. Did I have the right to separate him from the one skill at which he excelled? I really do not know.

Pressing forward under the byline Myron Cope, I took stock. Good bylines *can* make a difference for writers, whether existing on their birth certificates or created by editors. Ring Lardner and Damon Runyon, historic figures in sportswriting, were names that rang sweetly. The *greatest* byline I have ever known—a truly monstrous byline—was that of Phil Gundelfinger, Jr. Standing about 6'3" and wearing glasses, Phil Gundelfinger, Jr. occupied a desk not far from mine, covering golf and bowling. He would not be remembered for gifted prose, but I remember him vividly, and fondly. Gamblers persistently phoned our sports department seeking scores of games they had bet on, even though in the interest of getting our work accomplished, we refused to provide scores. A refusal from Phil, however, was an event. In a voice that would have carried a city block had our windows been open, he would thunder, "We don't give scores!" With that, his face florid, he would slam the receiver of his phone onto its cradle with such a crash that I marveled the phone did not break apart into a mixture of wires, screws, and broken pieces of plastic.

I remember, too, that Phil Gundelfinger, Jr.'s golf beat frequently took him to the area's better courses to cover local amateur tournaments that today would receive scant attention but which in the 1950s were accorded headlines that ran fully six columns. At that time, golf remained largely a sport for the wealthy, and because newspapers deemed it not a bad idea to keep the wealthy happy, Phil made the rounds of plush clubs, batting out his stories and handing them to a Western Union Morse code telegrapher who transmitted them into our office. One day, Phil's story arrived just minutes before the deadline for our first edition, known as the bulldog. Gil Remley quickly handed the copy to me for editing. I immediately saw that one Jane Martin, an accomplished amateur, had continued her dominance of women's golf in Western Pennsylvania. She not only had won another tournament, but with a record-breaking performance had putted out on every hole. ("Putting out" is golf talk that applies to match play in which the winner of a hole has been forced to complete it because his or her opponent has stayed close and not conceded the hole; beyond that, I refuse to elaborate.) Finishing my editing, I hurriedly dashed off a six-column headline for Phil's story and sat back.

About 30 minutes later, the bulldog began rolling off the presses; half a dozen copies were promptly delivered to our sports department. I casually opened the paper to the sports section, began scanning it, and screamed, "Replate!"—that being the order to stop the presses. Words, of course, often carry more than one definition, and sometimes their meanings can be miles apart. My six-column headline, I now had observed, screamed:

Jane Martin Smashes Record, Putting Out on Every Hole

Sadly, the greatest byline I have ever known became victim to the rising cost of newsprint. To economize, the *Post-Gazette* decided to shrink the width of its pages and therefore each column of print. For readers, the change would be imperceptible, but for Phil Gundelfinger, Jr., alas, the Jr. had to go. With it, I think, went a certain amount of bounce, of flavor.

Meantime, as Myron Cope, and almost from the first week I had entered the sports department, I managed to get a steady stream of my stories into the paper by writing them on my own time and during lunch hours. I was receiving byline upon byline because in sports, the complete opposite of city side, virtually every story one wrote was by-lined. Sportswriting by its nature is opinionated or at least interpretive—did the Pirates play well or lousy? Readers want to know; thus it is well-nigh obligatory to let them know whose opinion they're reading. My by-line was gaining a following. Gil Remley sent me to cover college basketball games on Jack's Sell's nights off. Also, he let me have a weekly crack at an actual *column* we published daily entitled "Roamin' Around"—a heading ranking second in insipidity only to my high school newspaper column, "Kope's Komments". Gil assigned each "Roamin' Around" to our various sportswriters, thus the inspiration for its title. Readers seemed to enjoy my "Roamin' Around" columns, so Gil said, "Write two a week instead of one."

But when Al Abrams noticed the change, he told Gil, "Cut the kid back to one column."

As I said, Al was the star, no challengers wanted. Was I angry? Yes. But I shall say it again—I admired Al for his ability to know his own shortcomings and protect his territory. With his gossipy items and plagiarized essays, he remained an oasis in a desert of sports journalism.

I would spend eight and a half years on his staff, and by the fourth year there, I knew I would keep Myron Cope as my byline. Cope was short and somewhat catchy. Besides, the athletes, promoters, and fans who populated the sports circles I traveled had come to know me by my by-line. So be it. Meanwhile, by the time I departed the *Post-Gazette*, I had yet to be assigned a beat, the job promotion all sportswriters who have an iota of writing ambition expect to receive eventually. Without hope of gaining a beat, I left to try my hand at freelance writing, my aim being to sell articles to magazines.

My final day at the *Post-Gazette*, I stopped at Al Abrams's desk to say goodbye on my way out. He reached up and gave me a limp hand-shake and allowed himself a crooked smile. "Kid," he said, "you'll starve. You'll be back in six months."

Chapter Six

On to Magazines and to Saving Jack Kennedy's Bacon

I had just turned 31 and was living in a one-bedroom, furnished apartment in Shadyside, a Pittsburgh neighborhood popular among writers, artists, and lovers of jazz clubs. The fact that I was single, with only my own mouth to feed, had given me the courage to give up my steady paycheck at the *Post-Gazette.* Then, too, I had already sold more than half a dozen articles to national magazines, and it galled me that despite those sales, the newspaper not only had failed to assign me a beat, but had designated me its specialist in, good Lord, Little Leagues. They were just coming into popularity, relieving American children of having to organize their own recreation.

Each evening, in order to be on hand to perform my specialty, I had to take my "lunch" hour shortly after six, alone. When I returned an hour later, all the others would go to lunch, getting the hell out of there before the phones began ringing with calls from the Little Leagues. My job was to take down line scores—inning-by-inning accounts of scoring, plus the names of the winning and losing pitchers and the identities of any kiddies who had hit home runs. Our telephones had no buttons to enable me to move from one extension to another, so when I'd finished getting the facts on a game, I would bound to another desk to answer one of the five or six phones that were ringing away. When at last they quieted, it was my duty to write a few paragraphs citing the highlights of the day's Little League activity. The stars were a constant; regularly, the same six-foot 12-year-olds pitched no-hitters and hit two or three home runs.

"This crap," I told myself, "is worse than taking bowling scores in Erie."

Meantime, without intention, I had begun my drift toward magazines in the wee hours of a morning in 1955, some five years before I departed the *Post-Gazette*. I was standing at the bar in Benny's, the saloon where, remember, I had purchased my first packet of chewing tobacco to answer Fred P. Alger's errant expectorations. Benny Samuels had now hired a bartender to assist him—a limber, balding man whose bashed-in nose gave him away as a former boxer, as if any Pittsburgh sports fan did not already know he was just that. Fritzie Zivic in 1940—before a record Madison Square Garden crowd of 23,190—had won the world welterweight championship by decisioning the great Henry Armstrong in a 15-round battle that was nothing if not grueling. (Armstrong at one time had *simultaneously* held titles in three of boxing's eight divisions—featherweight, lightweight, and welterweight.) Arthur Donovan, the referee the night Armstrong and Zivic fought, allowed both of them to take liberties with the Marquis of Queensbury rules, and it happened that Fritzie Zivic had practically made a science of questionable tactics. Nobody was better at head-butting an opponent or thumbing him in the eye or even stepping on his feet. Fritzie, too, would fire a bolo punch underneath an opponent's protective cup, then say, "Pardon me."

Later, he tried his hand at managing fighters and promoting small fight cards, but because of his spendthrift ways wound up tending bar at Benny's, still in high spirits despite his setbacks. Nightly, he regaled customers with hilariously told stories of fights in which he had abused opponents.

"Your stories," I told Fritzie, "are too good to be wasted here. What do you say we get together for a few hours and put together a magazine article about the art of fighting dirty? Who knows? Maybe both of us will make a payday."

I mailed the manuscript (entitled "You Gotta Fight Dirty" by Fritzie Zivic as told to Myron Cope) to *TRUE, The Man's Magazine*, a solid New York-based monthly. Shortly afterward, I received a letter from the magazine's assistant managing editor saying *TRUE* would pay, if memory serves correctly, $1,200. The contract that came with the letter specified that I would receive 60 percent of that amount and Fritzie, 40. (Of course, I took that to mean that *TRUE* recognized that I had put in many more hours on the piece than Fritzie had.) I promptly telephoned Fritzie to tell him the good news as well as the terms of our split.

About two hours later a lawyer phoned me, saying he represented Zivic. "Fritzie gets the 60," the lawyer said, "and you get the 40. Otherwise, no deal."

What choice did I have? Davis J. Walsh, an aging sports columnist of my acquaintance who worked at various papers in the Hearst newspaper chain, summed up the guiding principles of boxing people in a sentence: "I'll keep the vest and give you the sleeves."

Still, I liked the taste of magazine money. I attempted a profile of a splendid Pittsburgh Pirates pitcher, Bob Friend, who not only won big but was, at the time, a rarity in baseball in that he possessed a college degree and in the off season worked as a stockbroker. I sent the story to the *Saturday Evening Post*, which promptly paid me $1,000 for it. Bob Friend saw to it that I could not throw a party; he sold me $1,000 worth of shares in a mutual fund. One of these days, I told myself, I am going to get a payday that has been neither chiseled nor invested, and I am going to have one hell of a night on the town.

Now, having cut myself off from my weekly *Post-Gazette* paycheck, I knew that to make the rent I could not rely solely on assignments from major magazines. Any check that arrived in the mail was welcome—well, almost any. A phone call came from Lowell Ridenbaugh, managing editor of *The Sporting News*, a national weekly tabloid owned since its inception by a cheap old man named J. G. Taylor Spink. Mostly, his paper carried articles written by newspaper sportswriters from around the country to supplement their income. Anyhow, Ridenbaugh asked me to put together a lengthy piece about Steeler quarterback Bobby Lane and give him enough copy to cover two full pages. All right, done. I then received in my mail a check for $75.

I fired the check back to Ridenbaugh with a note that said:

"Tell Old Man Spink that he should go out and try to find a good-looking whore, and he'll find that she won't lay him for $75."

Ridenbaugh, himself a good fellow, telephoned and said, "I did not relay your suggestion to Mr. Spink, but we're sending you a new check, for one-fifty."

As I said, the idea was to keep busy. As time went on, I acquired a New York literary agent, Emmy Jacobson, employed by a respected Madison Avenue firm, Curtis Brown, Ltd. Emmy could prod editors to keep me in mind for assignments. For example, she phoned one day to tell me Time-Life Books intended to publish a series of American histories—coffee-table-size volumes, expensively designed and expensively priced. She said, "Harold Field is the editor who's been placed in charge. He's hiring freelance writers to write the individual chapters, and I've got you two of them. In one, you're to write a history of the American cowboy. In the second, your topic will be our early sea routes to China."

I piped, "I'm no historian, Emmy. It'll take me a year to research the stuff."

"No, no. Time-Life's research people will provide all the material. You just *write* it."

Okay, by the time I had finished with the cowboys and sent off the chapter, I felt it was time for one of my periodic visits to New York to keep in touch with various editors. First I dropped into Emmy's office. She greeted me by saying, "I told Harold Field you were coming into town, and he said your timing is perfect. He's hosting lunch this very day for about ten or so of his writers and hopes you can join them."

This, mind you, was the hey-day of the three-martini business lunch, a happy ritual that no one embraced more fervently than the publishing crowd. Field had selected an expensive French restaurant and reserved a private room at the rear. As our third martinis were being served, he got down to business.

"I called this luncheon meeting, ladies and gentlemen, because you're having serious problems with your marginalia."

"I'm in trouble," I thought. "What the hell is marginalia?" I kept my mouth shut.

"Myron," Field continued, turning to me. "Your marginalia has been fine. Just keep writing it as you have. I simply wanted you to join us for lunch so you could meet everyone and get a good feel for our project."

I said, "I was *hoping* my marginalia was on track. I'm relieved. Thank you."

A brief discussion of marginalia ensued that utterly failed to dissolve my ignorance; then we ate lunch, enjoyed cordials, and broke up at three o'clock. I guessed that the tab, borne of course by Harold Field's expense account, amounted to at least $200. I'm talking 1960s money.

Back in Pittsburgh, I reached for my dictionary and found but two words alongside marginalia: "marginal notes". For elaboration, I telephoned a friend steeped in literature. Marginalia, it turned out, simply were footnotes that, instead of appearing at the bottom of a page, appeared in the margin adjacent to the material to which it applied. We, as writers of these volumes, had been told the exact amount of space, to the letter, allowed for each note of marginalia and were expected to write no more, no less, and write it with clarity. Hell, I had done a terrific job. Harold said so.

By now I had moved from my furnished apartment into another, larger one-bedroom and even could afford a decorator to furnish it, but much earlier—in fact, no more than a month after I'd left the *Post-Gazette* —I had met a fellow tenant in the three-story building where I lived. Sid Kane was a recent graduate of Harvard, who with his engineering degree had taken a supervisory job on the mill floor of Pittsburgh's Jones & Laughlin Steel Corporation. One day early in 1960, Sid said, "Hey, you want a good magazine story? You'll have to go up to Harvard to do the research."

John F. Kennedy was campaigning for the Democratic nomination for president, bent upon becoming our first Catholic president, but it was his kid brother Teddy whom Sid Kane had in mind. He explained:

"Everybody up there on that campus knows that Teddy Kennedy got help getting through Harvard. The fix was in. Otherwise, he's no Harvard grad."

Well, dear reader, you may recall that in an earlier page I made the brash claim that I just may have held the power to make or break John Kennedy's presidential aspirations. You be the judge.

Having listened to Sid, my first thought was to phone the *Saturday Evening Post*, whose circulation blanketed the nation as no other magazine's and whose quaint Norman Rockwell covers helped make that publication America's magazine. If Sid were right, I would have—given the times—a blockbuster of a story. Mind you, in 1960 America still had a capacity for outrage. Media who covered the White House and Congress rarely intruded into the personal lives of politicians, especially presidents. Oh, they knew about the peccadillos, but even famous athletes were allowed private lives by sportswriters in the know. The supermarket tabloid had not yet been created. Personally, I believe America was a better place for being kept in ignorance of incidental behavior. One rule I followed when out drinking with athletes was: Never quote an athlete if he spoke while drinking. Phone him the next morning and say, "Okay if I quote you on that?"

Sometimes they said, "Sure."

At any rate, it is my contention that America's sense of outrage for years now has been muted by one scandal following upon another, but in 1960 the potential remained.

"What?" you ask. "Voters would have punished John Kennedy if they learned of his kid brother's mischief?" I wrestled with that question.

Might some voters, informed of the fix that was put in for Teddy at Harvard, say, "Well, it's that damned Kennedy family money again!"? On one hand, I would not be invading candidate John Kennedy's personal life, which years later would turn out to be interesting. But with Teddy already a campaign worker (and who but a clairvoyant could know he would become a powerful liberal in the U. S. Senate?), should I not report the family influence that pulled him through Harvard?

In the end, I said, don't make that phone call to the *Post*. I concluded that it was not my place to risk fooling with history by writing an exposé of John Kennedy's brother's campus shenanigans. Could such a story published by America's most popular family magazine have helped tilt a portion of undecided voters to Richard Nixon? You may say, "Get out of here, Cope. Bill and Monica—now that's big-league stuff. But Teddy cheating at Harvard? Get lost."

Yet I'll point out that of 68,374,888 votes cast in the 1960 election, Kennedy won by a margin of only 158,574—a hair more than .002 of the total vote.

And if I am incorrect in remembering the temper of the times in 1960, why did I, a fairly seasoned journalist by then, pass up the possibility of a hefty *Post* paycheck?

By the way, Sid Kane had the right information. The story, dug out later by others, appeared in newspapers after John Kennedy was well into his occupancy of the White House. By then, it was academic—a fleeting story, probably carried by most papers on an inside page.

My being primarily a sportswriter would not have disqualified me from breaking the Teddy Kennedy story. Magazine editors usually did not typecast writers—they simply wanted to know, can you *write* it? From time to time through the years, when suspecting I might be falling into a rut, I requested assignments away from sports. For example, a music piece, a politics piece. I accepted an assignment to explain a mathematics think tank (in Maryland, I seem to remember) but failed miserably. So, too, did I botch a profile of President Kennedy's Secretary of Labor, Arthur Goldberg. Neither the think tank nor Goldberg reached print.

At any rate, my interest in the Kennedy-Nixon battle was keen, so I knew from media reportage that Kennedy, running in the Democratic primaries against Minnesota Senator Hubert H. Humphrey, had to carry West Virginia. Coming off a narrow, unconvincing victory in Wisconsin, he not only needed West Virginia but, as a Catholic, had to show he could win an overwhelmingly Protestant fundamentalist state. And it was widely agreed in West Virginia that to win the state, Kennedy surely must carry Logan County—a political hotbed quickly labeled "pivotal".

As matters turned out, Kennedy carried both Logan County and hence the state. More explicitly, he *bought* Logan right out from under Humphrey's nose with hard cash, as I was to learn.

I wanted to know how he won there. So I persuaded the editors of *TRUE* to foot my expenses for a visit to Logan County a few months after

Kennedy had been sworn into office. *TRUE*, paying better-than-average prices for articles, served up to her macho readers pieces dealing with hunting, fishing, sports, adventures, crime mysteries, and, yes, politics. Its readership was intelligent, all right, but it was not apt to include history professors or political scientists. If the story I was to put together in Logan County were written for one of the intelligentsia publications— say, *Harper's* or *Atlantic Monthly*—I suspect it might have become a source for those writing Kennedy biographies or political textbooks. But, hey, *TRUE* paid better than *Harper's* or the *Atlantic*, so what's to regret?

In any case, and in the hope that Professor J. Sudberry Knowitall, holding a chair in history somewhere, may have wandered into these pages and would be interested in knowing how Kennedy stole Logan County and thus the Democratic nomination for president, I give you Logan County as I found the place in the spring of 1961. I offer it to you with misgivings. For one thing, what has it got to do with my autobiographical meanderings? Secondly, do you care a whit about Logan County? I suppose, however, that as one who worked mostly at the trivial, sports, I have an irresistible need to call attention to the fact that my foremost scoop occurred in the arena of presidential politics where neither newspaper writers nor biographers nor television stations—not anyone—sniffed out the story and made it public. Yes, I'm proud of that. Tolerate me.

Driving to Logan County, I paused briefly in Charleston, the state capital, to acquaint myself with the mores of the mountain folk I soon would encounter. There, a state official told me, "To those people, a vote means something. They'll buy it from you, sell it to you, or do as they please with it."

Indeed, I assure you that the Democratic and Republican politicians who managed the ugly Bush-Gore election battle in Florida in the year 2000 were rank amateurs compared to the politicians of Logan County. On my arrival there, one of them related to me that Teddy Kennedy, acting as an advance man for his brother's primary campaign, had visited the town of Logan, the county seat, and asked a local politician what the Kennedy organization would have to do to carry the county. The politician told him straight out.

Teddy blanched. "Oh, we couldn't do that," he said.

"Well, sonny," snapped the politician, "you asked me, and I done told you."

His advice had been succinct: Buy votes.

Not only would voters expect to be paid, but so would polling-place officers, inasmuch as they accompanied voters smack into the booths to make certain the voters voted the way they had been paid to. Indeed, before electrical voting machines had replaced paper ballots in Logan County in 1954, it had not been unknown for a candidate, after having cast his vote for himself in his home precinct, to learn he had been defeated in that very precinct by a count of, say, 220 to 0.

"Happened to me," I was told by a man who had run for constable but neglected to buy a preacher who was a key election officer in his precinct. "I was zeroed. I went after him to find out why he done me like that, but he run up the street like a bitch in the snow."

Not to belabor the point that money talked in Logan County, I should add that the market for votes was apt to fluctuate clear through election day. A Democrat I spoke to put it this way:

"I've worked precincts in general elections where the Republicans couldn't win a kiss in a whorehouse. But they'd come in anyway and say, 'Five dollars!' Then I'd have to go to seven, and before long, the Republicans would be paying $30, which is more than anyone can pay. But they'd pay it to just a handful of voters and then leave, and the rest of the day I'd have trouble from my voters because I wasn't paying $30. All the Republicans wanted to do was cause me a nuisance."

I wondered, as I increasingly grasped the nature of politics in this county, how Jack Kennedy had reacted when he received Teddy's initial report from the front. As a Boston urbanite, Jack Kennedy had to know he was heading into foreign territory. To him and Hubert Humphrey, Logan County must have appeared at once breathtakingly picturesque and sullenly hostile. The mountains there, unlike the rolling hills of northern West Virginia, lay stacked, one against the other, a maze of gigantic walls whose valleys in many places were scarcely wide enough to embrace a dirt road. Coal, the state's life's blood, was entombed in these hills as nowhere else in West Virginia, but at primary time the mountains put on a face of rich green sprayed with the white of blooming dogwood and the blaze of redbuds. Moonshiners, snugly concealed, tended their stills in happy privacy. Streams rippled beside the roads, tossing their whitecaps merrily lest anyone suspect the pollution they carried from the mines.

Both Kennedy and Humphrey knew, meantime, that only a few thousand votes might well decide the entire state primary, and surely it was difficult for them to know where to turn in Logan County for decisive support; again, the experts were calling Logan pivotal. Raymond Chafin, a pale, balding man who perpetually wore a worried frown, carried the title of Democratic County Chairman, and although his organization had just come into its own, it was generally considered to be the strongest of many factions that typically squared off in Logan County elections. Chafin's stronghold lay in Omar, a coal-mining community. His own right-hand man, Claude Ellis—36 years old, 6-feet-4 and weighing 306 pounds, a cigar-smoking giant who had flattened his share of antagonists but preferred to avoid such exertion—showed no compunction in telling me that Raymond listened when the mining companies talked.

For now, Raymond Chafin had come out four-square for Hubert Humphrey. Time, for John F. Kennedy, was running tight.

The way West Virginia political experts had it figured, even if Kennedy's people paid the Logan politicians the cash they demanded, he would be double-crossed at the polls—the politicians and their followers simply would not accept a Catholic candidate. In the town of Logan— population 4,200—I counted no fewer than 128 clergymen listed in the yellow pages, an entry far exceeding restaurants, service stations, or any other category. I failed to make note of any Catholic priests among the 128, so I am guessing there were none.

With only a few weeks remaining until election day, Kennedy campaigners began weaving their way into the Logan hills. Franklin D. Roosevelt, Jr. came, bringing with him the magic his father's name still carried across West Virginia. Sam Huff and Joe Stydahar, native West Virginians who had won fame in football, came to Logan on Kennedy's behalf. Teddy Kennedy was joined by brother Bobby, sister Eunice, and finally Jack himself.

The Kennedy gang tackled the religious issue head-on, and as the days passed, the natives warmed to the visitors' fighting spirit. While the clan Kennedy, with its brothers, sisters, sisters-in-law and brothers-in-law, may have irritated many voters around the nation, Logan County citizens, a veritable montage of clans, admired the way the Kennedys pulled together. Fine, but admiration went only so far.

A 40-year-old Chicago Irishman named Jim McCahey suddenly appeared in Logan. "He had," I was told by managing editor Charles D. Hylton, Jr. of *The Logan Banner*, "the coolest blue eyes I'd ever seen."

Mind you, I am telling you all this not only because I'm driven to but in part because nowhere in Theodore H. White's celebrated book "The Making of the President 1960" did McCahey get so much as a mention, let alone recognition due him as the actual *maker* of the president. Bill Mazeroski, on the other hand, received a mention. White pointed out that "there is a politicians' rule of thumb, particularly hallowed by Democratic politicians, that no (general) election campaign starts until the World Series is over." Mazeroski, the Pittsburgh Pirates' second baseman, smashed a home run in the ninth inning of the seventh game of the World Series, sending the New York Yankees down to defeat. The time: 3:46 p.m., October 13. Maz, though he did not know it, had given the signal for the Kennedy and Nixon campaigns to begin. But Jim McCahey apparently remained unknown to Theodore H. White.

Big Claude Ellis described to me his first meeting with McCahey, but first, one must know that in the dizzying ebb and flow of Logan politics, Claude had separated himself from his Humphrey-supporting boss, Raymond Chafin, by accepting the chairmanship of the local campaign for Kennedy. A West Virginian high on the Kennedy board of strategy offered Claude the job and found him agreeable; Claude did not mention to me whether any money changed hands.

At any rate, McCahey sought out Claude, who later related to me, "I'm standing on the street with a couple of my boys, and this feller walked up and said, 'I'm Jim McCahey from Chicago, and I'm at your disposal.' I said, 'Well, fine. What can you do?'

"He said, 'Well, I'm a big buyer of coal. I buy from Island Creek Coal Company.' "

Island Creek, as Claude well knew, ranked as the No. 1 coal producer in West Virginia, a monster in Logan County. McCahey was, among other things, president of the Dunn Coal & Oil Company, Chicago; nobody had to drop a load of bituminous on Claude Ellis to make him realize McCahey could be useful. Just as oil cut a wide swath in Texas politics, so did coal interests speak to Logan County politicians in a powerful, if hushed, voice. Might the coal companies, Claude Ellis wondered, give the Kennedy campaign a push?

"I told Jim McCahey, 'You're just what we need here.' I sent him to Island Creek Coal and sent a feller with him to see what I had going for me, and my feller came back and said, 'By God, Claude, they just throwed the doors open for him soon as he showed his face.' Now I knew I was in business."

McCahey worked hard and fast, making the rounds of the county, though when I caught up to him more than a year later, he spoke modestly of the role he had played. He explained that as a businessman volunteer for Kennedy, he had been assigned by the Kennedy hierarchy to the sizable city of Huntington, WV, in Wayne County, but when it was determined the campaign was in trouble in Logan, he was sent there to help out. He told me he made speeches and got permission from villagers to tack up Kennedy posters but that he certainly never tried to influence coal companies. "I do buy coal," he said. "Not a tremendous amount, but some." He admitted he might have visited coal company offices to ask small favors—say, the loan of an auto.

In any event, the election remained seriously in doubt, right up to election eve. During the following year's primary campaigns, I sat with both Claude Ellis and Raymond Chafin in an upstairs suite of the Aracoma Hotel—"Logan's only fireproof hotel," a sign informed guests. Despite Claude's defection to the Kennedy camp a year earlier, he by now had returned to his role as Chafin's right arm. For my benefit, the two of them reminisced, pinpointing the turning point for Kennedy. Had not Chafin and his workers backed Humphrey?

"It was late at night," said Ellis, "with the election only a few hours away, and Raymond was lying on the bed right out there in the other room. His boys gathered 'round, and Raymond laid there with his hands over his eyes, and finally, he said, 'Boys, I got something to tell you, but I don't know how.'

"And they said, 'It can't be all that bad, so go ahead and say it.'"

Raymond thereupon rose from his bed and uttered a two-sentence pronouncement that, with bittersweet pleasure, he now reiterated to me, as though it were akin in historical significance to Lee's surrender at Appomattox. Spoke Raymond:

"Boys, what it comes down to is this: Mr. Kennedy's got to come, or I got to go."

Coal had spoken into Raymond's ear. By dawn, Humphrey placards were removed all over the county, and in their place were Kennedy signs.

The polls opened at 6:30, and by afternoon the front page of the *Banner* reported that "not in the past 20 years has the *Banner* received so many reports of illegal practices at the polls." When the polls closed at 7:30, Kennedy had beaten Humphrey by some 2,000 votes—a whopping margin by Logan County standards.

Raymond Chafin later visited the White House twice. "The president," he said to me proudly, "calls me Raymond."

Earlier, I mentioned that I preferred *TRUE's* paycheck to one I might have received from a magazine playing to the intelligentsia, so please allow me a footnote.

A phone call came one morning from the editor of the *New York Times Sunday Magazine*. Darned if I can remember his full name. He was an Irishman named Jerry—Kelly, I think, but we are going back maybe 40 years. I do know that Jerry was well respected, for he had been an officer of a national association of freelance writers, of which I was a member.

"Myron," said Jerry, "we'd like you to do one of your profiles on Mark McCormack, the golf agent."

McCormack had lassoed both Arnold Palmer and Jack Nicklaus, as well as other golfers, and thus reigned at a relatively young age as the foremost sports agent in America. His Cleveland company, International Management Group, today ranges over sports and television production as a super-heavyweight, certainly not bogged down by having Tiger Woods as a client.

"Jerry," I replied. "Thank you for thinking of me, but no. I know about your magazine. You're making a lot of money on bra ads and ads for expensive china, but you're paying only $500 for a full-length piece. I also know that you assign more pieces than you possibly can use. Then you end up chopping pieces down to a few paragraphs that you run in an assortment of items in the front of the magazine, and the writer gets fifty bucks."

"Well, yes," said Jerry.

"Now it's great for an assistant secretary of state or a Princeton professor of economics to get a byline in the *Times Sunday Magazine*—it's *prestige*. But I write for a living, the hell with prestige. No, I'm sorry."

"Tell you what. I'll pay $500 and guarantee it. Even if we chop down the piece, you get the $500."

I mulled over the offer. "Okay, Jerry, I'll do McCormack. It so happens my wife is expecting soon. I can drive over to Cleveland in a couple of hours, do my interviews, and be back the same night. I can do that for as many trips as it takes. It'll be better than an assignment that takes me away for a week or two. And McCormack," I continued, "will go along with my schedule. The *Times Sunday Magazine*? He'll love it like an assistant secretary of state."

McCormack did love it and asked the date the article would appear. He would be in Sweden on that date, but his secretary could phone him (no fax having yet been invented) and tell him whether my piece was favorable. She would get it to him by air mail as quickly as possible.

I awoke on the designated Sunday morning and tooled over to the neighborhood pharmacy to pick up the *Times*. No Mark McCormack piece. Nothing. Monday morning I phoned Jerry.

"I'm so embarrassed," he said, "that I could not even bring myself to phone you to let you know the piece would not run."

"What are you talking about?"

Well, let's start with the fact that the managing editor of the *Times* was Clifton Daniel, who had married President Harry Truman's daughter Margaret. A Carolinian, Daniel had worked as a World War II correspondent in England and returned to America, I found it curious, with a permanent British accent. Anyhow, at the time I submitted my Mark McCormack profile, stories were still being cast into lead type by linotype operators, after which galley proofs were spiked onto long nails for proofreaders to check and editors to read if they chose. Clifton Daniel, Jerry now explained, had removed the proofs of my article, interested to read it.

He did and then went to Jerry and said, "We cannot publish this piece."

Why not? "The writer," Daniel told Jerry, "describes a meeting in which McCormack and Arnold Palmer negotiated a major endorsement deal with Lincoln-Mercury. Obviously the writer was not there and has described the negotiation through sources. This is secondhand reporting, so we cannot publish this piece."

"My God," I told Jerry. "Does he expect those people to invite me to sit in on their negotiations?"

"I know, I know," said Jerry. "It's ridiculous, but what I'm going to do is send you the entire $500 guarantee."

I hung up the phone and mailed off a copy of my manuscript to the *Saturday Evening Post*. Several days later, I received a check for $3,500. Throw in the *Times's* five hundred and I totaled $4,000—the largest magazine payoff I had enjoyed up to then. I wish I had known Clifton Daniel so that I could have thanked him.

Part Two

Characters Along the Way

Prologue

As the reader by now has seen, my career evolved from newspaperman to freelance magazine writer to radio-television performer. In the second phase, I received tremendous help from the prestigious *Saturday Evening Post*, a magazine that took pride in discovering new writers; the *Post*, in fact, employed "readers" to scrutinize the unsolicited manuscripts that thousands of would-be writers mailed in. By the summer of 1964, three and a half years removed from the newspaper game, I had gained enough favor at the *Post* that the magazine signed me to a contract that provided me with a yearly advance against a given number of pieces and listed me in its masthead as a Contributing Editor, a title I prized but never understood inasmuch as I did no editing.

One day, however, I walked into the *Post's* New York offices and served notice I would not be entering a renewal of my contract. One reason was that the *Post*, as a mass magazine appealing to as many Americans as possible, often assigned me to write about star athletes —superstars as they later became known. These were the athletes most familiar to readers, but I usually found them dull. Had they been interviewed so often they found the attention boring? Whatever, I had a second reason for resigning from the *Post*—its editors were giving me fits by editing from my manuscripts many of the flourishes that in my opinion (perhaps arrived at from writer's conceit) gave my stuff style.

From the *Post's* offices, already beginning to worry about next month's rent, I walked over to Rockefeller Center to say hello to a *Sports Illustrated* senior editor, Ray Cave, who had handled most of the stories I wrote for *SI* between *Post* assignments. *SI* in that day stood as a beacon, calling writers who aspired to lift sportswriting from an ocean of clichés to a higher level of prose. I mentioned to Cave that I had left the *Post*— that I wanted to spend more of my time writing about goofball jocks, even if they were not exactly stars.

"Sign a contract with us," Cave said. "We'll give you all the nuts you can handle."

All right, fine. I would remain in *SI's* stable for six years, but I suppose what I'm getting at is that over the course of my three-part career, I encountered all manner of sports figures; in these pages, however, I am not about to tick off the greatest of this or that sport or to wax ecstatic on the most exciting games I witnessed. I have been a people-watcher, you might say. So I merely offer sketches of a few who, among many, intrigued me.

Chapter Seven

Cassius Marcellus Clay
The Baby With the Big Mouth

On a summer's morning in 1962, Chris Dundee, a short, swarthy Miami boxing promoter, drove me to the Fifth Street Gym in Miami Beach to introduce me to the 20-year-old fighter about whom I would write. Chris's brother Angelo trained Cassius Marcellus Clay for an 11-man syndicate of wealthy businessmen residing in Louisville, KY, Clay's hometown; they had signed him to a professional contract when he won the light-heavyweight gold medal at the 1960 Rome Olympics. Angelo, at the moment, was in Paris to work a corner, so Chris had temporarily been put in charge of the *wunderkind.*

"I bawled him out yesterday for being late," Chris said after we had walked the stairs to the second-story gym and found no Clay, "so he's being deliberately late today."

Twenty minutes later, Cassius appeared in the doorway. "Come over here," called Dundee, "and take that toothpick outta your mouth. I'll smack you."

"These Dundees," Cassius piped, not removing the toothpick, "are crooks."

He stood 6-feet-2 and weighed 196 pounds, a full-blown heavy-weight now, sleek and muscular, boxing his way up the ladder toward an unreasonable goal—namely, to win the heavyweight championship in the next year and a half and thereby become the youngest ever to have done so. (He would fall short by just 73 days.) That morning, it became clear to me that Cassius Clay reigned over the gym's white, black, and Cuban fighters by simply talking them into submission. He jabbered at the Cubans in homemade, simulated Spanish, and they threw up their hands and walked away, shouting, "Niño con boca grande!"—the baby with the big mouth.

The blabbermouth informed me that he would not follow the fiscal path of the great heavyweight champion Joe Louis, who after his career ended found himself horrendously in debt to the Internal Revenue Service and wound up working as a greeter in a Las Vegas casino. Declared Cassius:

"When I'm finished with boxing, I'll have me a roller rink with 700 pairs of skates, different sizes, and lots of pretty girls on the ticket box. I'll have ballroom dances on Saturday nights—girls $1 and men $2.50, because where the girls go, the men got to follow. And I'll have nice pretty girls working back in the kitchen making hamburger sandwiches for 25¢ apiece.

"I'll have me a Cassius Clay Taxicab Line," he tore on, "and get me about 35 or 40 cheap cars, and all my friends who don't have a job will get a job. And I'll have me a pretty pink house because pink is a color the girls like, and they'll pass my house and say, 'Look at that pink house and pink Cadillac outside. That Cassius Clay, he must be something.' "

In the 1960s the battles for desegregation would inflame the South, and Cassius Clay—Muhammad Ali by then—would outrage millions of Americans by defying the military draft, proclaiming, "I ain't got nothing against them Viet Congs." Boxing authorities stripped him of his heavyweight championship; in every state where athletic commissions existed, he was barred from the ring. Politicians and patriots assailed him, war protesters cheered him. As for myself, I wondered. I remembered being told by a military psychologist who during World War II was stationed at a west coast point of embarkation: "Shipping out, the most frightened were often the successful athletes. They dreaded the possibility that harm could come to their bodies."

For three years Ali remained without fights, until a federal judge reinstated his license. But for now, not far removed from his Olympics victory, he was the model of a superpatriot. He recalled to me that after he had won the gold medal in Rome, a Russian reporter inquired of him whether he did not find it ironic that he still would be refused admission to many public restaurants back home. Cassius decided that the Russian was trying to paint America at her worst, for there were five or six other reporters from various nations standing in on the interview. He thereupon looked down his nose at the Russian reporter, he related to me, and replied:

"Russian, we got qualified men working on the problem. We got the biggest and the prettiest cars. We get all the food we can eat. America is the greatest country in the world, and as far as places I can't eat goes, I got lots of places I *can* eat—more places I can than I can't. Lookeehere, Russian—there are good and bad in every country, and if there weren't good and bad we wouldn't have to be talking about Judgment Day."

As a footnote, Cassius remembered the Russian departing, head down, and he, Cassius, saying to himself, "If you don't think we's a great strong country, crank up one of your aeroplanes and load up a bomb and head our way. We'll see."

American Legion posts across America would have stood and saluted him, but meantime, I faced a logistics problem. My plan was to spend five days in Miami Beach, then fly to Louisville where Clay was to box a German trial horse named Willie Besmanoff. Angelo Dundee returned from Paris and explained that he, too, faced a problem. Cassius had a deathly fear of airplane travel. Indeed, at the Fifth Street Gym, he ranted, "Every time I pick up the paper, SIXTY-FOUR DAID! Or SEVENTY-TWO DAID! Cause of accident unknown, but everybody *daid.* I once missed a plane going from Chicago to New York for the Golden Gloves, and the plane blew up over Indiana."

The alternative to flying to Louisville was a 27-hour train ride, of which Angelo Dundee wanted no part. "Look," he said to me. "I need him to have a chaperone. You be the chaperone, and it'll be good for your story. You'll get lots of material." Angelo booked Pullman space for Cassius and me.

Throughout the trip, Cassius jabbered incessantly. At mealtimes he shadowboxed his way to the dining car, causing travelers in coach cars to sit bolt upright as he sang rock 'n roll lyrics along the way. "I'm going to be a great recording artist," he announced, "and be on a lot of ablums." Because he did not possess a good memory for names, he dubbed me Mickey Rooney, a sobriquet by which he would address me in all our future meetings through the years. At dinner in the diner, I was about to attack an appetizing roast loin of pork when he said:

"Poke give me a headache."

"What do you mean, pork gives you a headache?"

"Poke always gave me headaches. Doctors told me poke 90 percent live cell parasites. Poke 90 percent maggots."

I had no idea that Cassius Clay was secretly taking lessons to become a Black Muslim, a cult abstaining from pork, or that upon his dethroning Sonny Liston from the heavyweight championship he would proclaim to all the world that he was, indeed, a Black Muslim and would be known henceforth as Muhammad Ali.

"I appreciate the education," I now told him. "But please, let me eat my dinner."

"You let that poke lay two days, it get up and crawl. The hawg is an unclean animal. Cat, rat, dog, hawg—add 'em up."

Halfway through my dinner, I felt queasy. Meanwhile, across the table, this young man I took to be the only kosher Baptist in the heavy-weight division was eating to beat the band. Earlier, when boarding the train, he had told me train rides spoil his "appeltite" but now he looked up from his meal and said, "Be sure to write in there that I chew and eat twice as fast as the average man. I been through all my chicken, two veg-etables, and a salad, and had me a dip of tutti-frutti and a piece of pump-kin pie, and you ain't half-done yet. Man, you a slow eater."

When I lay down in the bunk of my roomette, Cassius reached over from his own roomette directly across the aisle and pulled aside my drape. "Mickey Rooney! I just writ a poem." He forthwith recited his poem while others in the Pullman trying to sleep wondered if a madman were loose. "I struggled through high school with a D-minus average," he confided to me. "But I was on the track team. Fastest I ever did was the mile in three minutes and fifty-five seconds."

The world record, I pointed out, was 3:54.6.

Now, an aside. I have quoted Cassius Clay *verbatim,* attaching to him a propensity for constantly mangling words and grammar. Some might suspect, therefore, that I am holding him up to ridicule. If so, my re-sponse is twofold. For one thing, writers are supposed to have an ear for dialogue and dialect, the better to capture accuracy and flavor. Secondly, I've long suspected that Muhammad Ali, as Cassius Clay, in his childhood was incapable of learning at a normal pace. A newspaperman friend of mine, Roy McHugh, who covered Ali from the time he was Clay, once remarked to me, "I think he suffers from dyslexia"—the disorder that causes one to see letters and words reversed.

Obviously, Ali possessed a nimble, creative mind, an imagination that indeed might be called brilliant. Nobody in the fight game could charm or enrage the public in the interest of selling fights as he could. Publicity flowed to him worldwide. Meantime, McHugh and I observed that neither of us ever heard of Ali objecting to a single story written about him. In other words, perhaps he could not read his own publicity or found it too difficult to try. To that notion, McHugh added, "When you've written about an athlete and then go to see him again, you usually get an inkling whether he liked or disliked your story, if only from his manner." Neither of us ever received the slightest indication one way or the other from Ali.

Wilfrid Sheed, in his biography *Muhammad Ali*, described Ali as "semi-literate." Sheed noted that in a high school graduation class of 371, Ali ranked 358th and that the U. S. Army, intending to induct him, found from his written examination that he had an IQ of 78. I knew he at least could read a little, for had he not written a poem and read it aloud to me in the Pullman? But assuming our dyslexia theory to be a fact, my guess is that reading was an ordeal for him. Alas, had he been born in a later time, he probably would have been put into special-education classes and gotten rid of his disorder.

At any rate, not long ago I found myself reading a Robert B. Parker detective novel in which Parker's ace private eye, Spenser, was investigating a rumor that one or more players on Tate University's powerful basketball team was shaving points. (Never mind an explanation of point shaving for the benefit of the uninformed; suffice to say it's a criminal act.) Spenser unearthed conclusive evidence that Tate's culprit was none other than Dwayne Woodcock, the most talented college player in the nation and seemingly certain to be the first pick in the next NBA draft. Spenser also discovered that Dwayne, although now in his senior year at Tate, could not read. He was almost totally illiterate. Spenser's beautiful lover, the psychologist Dr. Susan Silverman, at dinner one evening suggested the possibility Dwayne Woodcock might be dyslexic.

Spenser asked, "Can you be dyslexic and be the best basketball player in the country?"

"Probably not," replied Silverman. "Frequently, though not always, dyslexia affects your balance. A standard dyslexia diagnostic test for kids is to ask them to walk a balance beam."

Well! Did not Cassius Clay become the best boxer in the world? Never mind Silverman. I'll stick with the McHugh/Cope diagnosis. Obviously Clay was the exception, his balance unaffected.

Meantime, as I found him at the callow age of 20, he showed a capacity for being downright profound, uttering words worth remembering. I recall an afternoon stroll we took alongside a railroad track in Miami.

I said, "You talk a big game, but what if you never do become champion?"

"I've got to think big," he replied. "Still, if the most I'm ever going to be in the rankings is No. 2 or 3 or 4, that's what I'm going to be. People in hell want ice water, but they can't get it."

Many's the time when I have faced irreversible disappointments that I have found myself saying, "People in hell want ice water, but they can't get it."

Back home in Louisville, Cassius made short work of Willie Besmanoff and continued up the ladder. Two years later I again made my way to the Fifth Street Gym to watch the champion, Muhammad Ali, train. He had spent six months traveling in the company of an entourage of Black Muslims through Chicago, Harlem, Ghana, Nigeria, and Egypt, spreading the word of Allah. His travels had left him overweight, downright flabby, his face puffed up like a pumpkin, and seemingly without his former exuberance. When he sighted me in the doorway of the gym, he sang out softly, "Mickey Rooney!" Following his workout, he descended to the street and climbed upon a shoeshine stand where he piously lectured an elderly bootblack at work on his shoes.

"Why don't you give up that wine and get you a glass of cold soda water? Why don't you get you a glass of cold milk?"

Religion and a Messianic compulsion to serve a purpose had dramatically changed Ali, it seemed to me. I hoped not. We entered a car driven by a Muslim chauffeur, and as we drove from the Beach to Miami, a flash of Cassius Clay reappeared. Spying a friend driving ahead on the causeway, he leaned out the window and frightened the man with a perfect imitation of a police siren.

I felt better about him.

Chapter Eight

Chuck Noll—
The Emperor

In 1969, at the age of 37, Chuck Noll became head coach of the Steelers, having been a little-known defensive assistant for the Baltimore Colts. He stayed in the job 23 years, won four Super Bowl championships, was elected to the Pro Football Hall of Fame in his first year of eligibility, and to this day remains the least understood, if not most misunderstood, of all the great modern-era football coaches.

From the time I became the Steelers' radio color analyst during his second year as head coach, I conducted the weekly *Chuck Noll Show*—the usual coach's radio show in which a broadcaster poses a series of questions the coach answers however he chooses. Such interviews are taped a day or two before game day and played over the air in the pregame broadcast. For Sunday home games, Noll and I recorded his show Friday mornings (and for road games, usually on Saturday at the team's hotel). Fridays I arrived at the Steeler offices at about 8:30 a.m. and went straight to a room known as the kitchen—an area holding perhaps a half-dozen vinyl tables and a counter on which sat two pots of coffee and boxes of fresh doughnuts and sweet rolls. Noll, a thickly built former linebacker and guard for the Cleveland Browns, would already be sipping his coffee, so I would sit with him until an engineer arrived from my station to set up microphones and other recording apparatus in the coach's office. Inasmuch as no other member of the media had regular private access to Noll,

I'm sure it's safe to say I came to know him better than any of my contemporaries. That said, it was slow going.

It took five years until he came to trust me enough to utter an off-the-record comment about his football team.

Five years! I cannot remember what he said off the record, and I suppose he would now sever our relationship were I to break the ancient confidence, but I clearly recall a brief, testy confrontation we had early into my first season as analyst. His regularly scheduled weekly news conference had ended, whereupon he motioned me to join him in the rear of the room. He voiced a complaint. One part of my duties was to broadcast each week a postgame Steeler locker room report in which I interviewed a few players or coaches, fresh from the battle.

"I hear," said Noll, "that you're asking our people questions that can be divisive to our team."

In other words, I was probing my guests to pinpoint or discuss Steeler weaknesses. That season, there existed a sufficiency of weaknesses to send the Steelers down to defeat nine times in a 14-game schedule. Meantime, as I related earlier, my understanding with Steeler management was that club officials would not censor me. "Divisive?" I said. "Can you give me an example?"

Noll gave one (and again, I plead senility, unable to recall it after more than 30 years), whereupon I said, "Where did you hear that?"

"From my wife. She heard your show."

"With all respect," I replied, "your wife gets a poor grade for reportage. Her quotes are very inaccurate."

Noll lifted his head and gazed over mine, silent.

I believed I knew what he was thinking. Occasionally, he had been pressed to specify the fundamentals of coaching to which he subscribed and had said, "Don't worry about things you cannot control. And don't let yourself become involved in peripheral matters."

I think that having challenged me on my handling of the locker room report, he was saying to himself, "This shit is peripheral." He nodded curtly to me and went about his business. Never did I hear another complaint from him.

Oh, I remember a morning when I sat across his desk, taping the *Chuck Noll Show*, and asked an unwelcome question that brought no answer but only the Noll Glare, well known to his players. He narrowed his eyes and fixed me with a look that I imagined could burn a hole through my forehead. Andy Russell, his right linebacker and defensive captain, once remarked, "I can be passing him in the hallway, and if I made mistakes on Sunday, he'll give me the Glare as he passes, and I want to disappear." I met Noll eyeball to eyeball, not flinching, and said to myself, "Don't melt. This kid is three years younger than you, Cope." Finally, Noll spoke. "Start the tape over."

As the record shows, Chuck Noll proved himself to be a brilliant coach, a great teacher of football techniques, a man whose eye for talent fastened in training camp upon low-round draft picks and undrafted free agents whom he would fashion into stars. Tagging along, I would in time regard him and his wife Marianne as true friends one could count on in times of family tragedy—an auto crash that sent my wife Mildred and daughter Elizabeth to a hospital and, many years later, Mildred's passing from cancer.

In the first instance, I was in Dallas broadcasting a Steelers-Cowboys preseason game, when I took a phone call to our booth from a friend notifying me of the crash and telling me the hospital listed Mildred as critical and Elizabeth as serious. In the Steeler locker room after the game, Noll gathered his players and led them in a prayer for my wife and daughter. Devout Catholics, Chuck and Marianne were nothing if not good people, but to the public and much of the media, nationally, he remained an icy, unfeeling martinet. In January, 1975, he took his Steelers to their first Super Bowl, in New Orleans, where he at once engendered seething hostility from football writers gathered from 'round the nation.

At his first news conference, standing on a stage in a hotel ballroom packed with reporters, he grudgingly gave short answers to the questions asked of him. Seated out front, I said to myself, "Oh, no. He's killing himself." Rarely, I think, did Noll enjoy talking football with anyone other than players, coaches, or scouts. Did Einstein enjoy discussing his theory of relativity with the editor of Princeton's campus newspaper? Noll, either because of his reticence or because this was his first appearance on the Super Bowl stage, left the writers snarling.

"Who does that guy think he is?" I heard them saying as they departed. "Condescending" was the adjective they hung on him. In their stories, they ripped him.

As he won Super Bowl after Super Bowl, Noll remained miles from becoming recognized as a football icon, and little wonder. While Don Shula, his former boss at Baltimore, eagerly supplemented his fame as coach of the Miami Dolphins by performing national television commercials, Noll shunned endorsements and the income and exposure the commercials would bring. "They're for the players," he said. One of his close friends, a CEO of a major Pittsburgh bank, at last persuaded him to appear on a billboard advertising the bank's offering of Steeler T-shirts. On his way to work, Noll had to pass one of those billboards daily. I'm positive he gritted his teeth. You never saw him on a billboard again.

Thus did he not only continue to be relegated to the role of giant with little acclaim, but often, if he read out-of-town sports pages, he could find that his name was Chuck Knox. Did Knox, himself an NFL head coach, find himself being called Chuck Noll? I doubt it. But careless writers confused Noll with Knox, not just in the early stages of Noll's head-coaching career but throughout it. Likewise, writers frequently spelled his name Knoll. (Depending upon which definition of knoll you choose, he was being equated, I suppose, with either a hillock or a clod.) Early in the year 2001, nine years after Noll had retired, one of his quarterbacks, Joe Gilliam, died of a drug overdose, prompting the *Pittsburgh Post-Gazette* to carry a column written by a Dallas sportswriter who claimed knowledge of Joe's considerable, but unrealized, potential. The columnist mentioned Noll's role in Gilliam's life and spelled his name Knoll. The mistake was not intercepted even by the *Post-Gazette*'s Pittsburgh editors.

The year before, Jim Haslett, a onetime Buffalo Bills linebacker, had landed his first head-coaching job, hired by a dismal franchise, the New Orleans Saints. Instantly, he transformed them, coaching them into the playoffs, and was named the NFL Coach of the Year. Not long afterward, Haslett said, "To me, the best coach who was ever in the game was Chuck Noll. He never won Coach of the Year, but he won four Super Bowls. That's the most important thing."

Actually, in 1972, United Press International had selected Chuck as its American Football Conference Coach of the Year, preferring him to Shula, whose champion Dolphins went undefeated that year, and in 1989, two years away from his retirement, the Pro Football Writers Association named him AFC Coach of the Year. Oddly, however, he never won a Coach of the Year award in any of the four seasons he won Super Bowls. No coach in NFL history has won that many.

That Haslett should call him the best NFL coach ever was perhaps surprising, for Haslett had neither played for him nor served under him as an assistant. But in the '70s, as a Steeler fan, he had played high school football in a Pittsburgh suburb and college ball at nearby Indiana University of Pennsylvania and later had played against Noll's teams. So Haslett had formed a basis for being in awe of Noll. From closer up, however, I detected an element of Chuck's success that received no notice.

In the 1972 player draft, he selected Joe Gilliam from Tennessee State in the 11th round—an audacious choice, for black quarterbacks in that day were held to be risky picks, probably not intellectually capable. But therein lay one of Noll's hidden strengths. He was color-blind, meaning race-blind. He was, I tell you, just about the only white football coach I spent substantial time with in that era whom I never heard tell a so-called "nigger joke." During those mornings in the Steeler kitchen, he told jokes, all right, and he was awful at reaching and delivering a punch line, but never a racial joke. Belatedly, I would like every black man who played for Noll to know of this—and thus to know that when he looked, for example, at rookie defensive end L. C. Greenwood, a tenth-round draft choice, or at safety man Donnie Shell, an undrafted free agent, both of them long shots to make the team but stars waiting to be developed, Noll asked but two questions: Can this guy play? Can we make him a player?

Who knows? Under a less fair-minded coach, Greenwood and Shell and others as well might have been put on a bus, never to be heard from again.

Contributing to his public image as a steely-eyed tyrant, Chuck lit into the hugely talented quarterback Terry Bradshaw almost weekly in front of the Steeler bench, through the first four years of Bradshaw's career. Bradshaw, coming off the field, would find Noll's face in his, the coach barking criticism. Years later, Noll explained to me, "I was trying to help him gain self-confidence." *You* figure that out. I could not. There are times when I simply leave enigmas to their own thoughts.

At the Pittsburgh airport when the Steeler squad gathered, waiting to board their chartered flight, I found it amusing to notice autograph seekers standing a distance from Noll, hesitating. Would he snap their heads off if they approached him? Some took the chance. He greeted them, to their amazement, with a bright smile and a handshake, and while signing his name, asked theirs and inquired where they lived and what they did for a living. They went away whispering to one another, "He's a nice guy!" as if they'd discovered that Chuck did not dine on nails. On draft day one year, an intern named Stu Chaban was sent to the Steeler offices to act as a gopher for our radio team that was broadcasting the draft. Steeler management had spread a buffet the length of the kitchen, so I said to Stu, "Go get in the line and get yourself some lunch." Later, he returned to our broadcast room carrying a plate but almost dropping it, he was trembling so.

"I was in line right behind Chuck Noll," he explained, "and do you know what he did? He turned around and introduced himself and asked how I was!"

"Did you expect him to slap you?" I asked.

At his weekly news conferences, Chuck presented himself to the media in a crowded conference room, seated at the head of the table. One day a kid named Vic Ketchman showed up. I thought, "If that kid were Jewish, he'd be only a couple of years past his bar mitzvah." I figured him for 15. He had gained admittance because he really *was* a sportswriter — he wrote for a small-town paper, the *Irwin Standard-Observer,* owned by his father. Not bashful, Vic would pose questions to Noll every week, most of them going something like this:

"Coach, in the second quarter Sunday, you punted on fourth-and-one. Would you explain the psychology behind that decision?" Vic may not have been shaving yet, but he was heavily into psychology.

"The psychology?" Noll would reply, always careful to maintain a straight face—oh, maybe furrowing his brow only slightly.

"What I mean, Coach, is, there had to be factors forming a psychological pattern that led you to believe it was the right time to punt, weren't there?"

"No."

Today, Vic Ketchman is senior editor of *Jaguars Inside Report,* the official weekly tabloid of the Jacksonville Jaguars, and knows football as well as any journalist you would care to meet, and I suspect Noll treated him with endless patience because he saw promise in Vic, if for no other reason than that he dared show up and come prepared with, well, avenues of inquiry.

Through the years, Noll thought of himself as an educator—a teacher of football. At the same time, he was a renaissance man, though I would be surprised if he ever thought of himself as one. He read voraciously, attached a small greenhouse to his home in order to cultivate orchids, attended the symphony, boned up on medical texts the better to understand his players' injuries, expressed passionate off-the-record convictions about politics and government, and told me on his occasional visits to my home just a mile away from his that I was not tending to my roses properly. I confess I took advantage of his versatility and used him occasionally as a handyman. For example, I had purchased a stereo as a gift for my wife, Noll having recommended the gift and the store where I could buy it. I have no aptitude whatever for working with my hands and found myself unable to wire up the stereo. "Don't worry," I told Mildred. "Chuck's coming over Friday morning to tape a show"—I had a basement studio where we sometimes recorded his *Chuck Noll Show.*

"How do you like the new stereo?" he asked as he entered our front door.

"I'm sure it'll be fine," I answered, "but I'm having a little trouble getting it to work."

In a flash, unable to resist, he extracted his bifocals from his breast pocket and spent the next 20 minutes hooking up the sound system. How many can claim to have made a Hall of Fame coach his handyman?

Many who approached him to talk football met with terse responses, but on a myriad of topics he conversed enthusiastically. My writer friend Roy McHugh ran into him at a party at clubowner Dan Rooney's house, and with the knowledge that Noll, a licensed pilot, had recently purchased an airplane, lightly said to him, "I'm sure you read that Arnold Palmer just flew his airplane around the world. Are you going to try that and do it faster?"

Noll launched into a 20-minute discussion of piloting. "He practically gave me the history of aeronautics," said McHugh.

Personally, I found that the best way to tap Chuck's football thoughts was simply to allow it to happen. At his news conferences, for example, he sometimes uttered a fleeting, ever-so-subtle jab at a player, but if a reporter knew Noll's ways and paid attention, he picked up on the jab and knew it was deliberate—that Noll had decided it was time to light a fire under the guy. Very occasionally, he was more explicit. Asked to comment on the fact that a running back named Sidney Thornton had been fumbling the ball rather frequently, Noll tersely replied, "Sidney has problems, and they are many." He did not elaborate, but Sidney now had a campfire roaring under his backside. When Noll and I taped his *Chuck Noll Show*, he usually covered for his players' deficiencies but after the taping ended might come clean—off the record. To cite a case in point, I questioned why he was not often playing a tall, muscular, swift receiver whom he had drafted in the second round. Noll parried the question. Afterward, with a look of anguish on his face, he said, "The guy just can't learn pass routes."

He gave up on the player after two short years.

Contrary to his image, Chuck brought great passion to coaching. When his 1974 team headed into Oakland to play for the AFC championship, he was steaming. The Raiders the previous week had defeated Miami in an absolute thriller of a playoff game, and the media was contending that *that* was your Super Bowl—no other game would count. Before kickoff, Noll with fervid emotion told his players they had been insulted all week—that they were better than the Raiders. The Steelers proved it and went on to their first Super Bowl. On another occasion, after a furious battle against the Oilers in Houston, I put a microphone under his chin in the locker room and remarked that Franco Harris had given a downright heroic performance. Tears welled in Noll's eyes.

When Chuck first came upon the Steeler scene, my fondness for nicknames led me to call him Chas (pronounced Chaz) on the air and later in our conversations. Why Chas? In my youth, men named Charles were called Charley or Chuck, or, yes, Chas, which became archaic. Five years later, I would give Chas another nickname.

The Steelers had returned from Miami where they had won their third Super Bowl championship, and the next day, on Monday at noon, they gathered for a public celebration in a downtown parklet called Market Square. Some 5,000 fans, almost all wearing black and gold, jammed into Market Square, some hanging from telephone poles. Two years before, the Steelers had won their second championship, prompting callers to my evening radio talk show to say, "They're a dynasty now, aren't they, Myron? Come on, call them a dynasty."

"No," I would reply. "It takes *three* championships to become a dynasty."

So now, the Steelers had won their third, and a large stage had been erected in Market Square. Players, coaches, and front-office executives stood upon the stage, soaking up the public's adulation. I had been asked to be master of ceremonies. I faced the throng and cried out, "Repeat after me!" I threw up my arms and shouted, "All hail the Steeler Dynasty!"

The crowd threw up their arms and roared as one, a thunderous voice that surely shook the windows of nearby office buildings: "All hail the Steeler Dynasty!"

"Gee," I said to myself. "This feels pretty good. This makes me feel like Julius Caesar."

I shouted, "Every dynasty has to have an emperor! Repeat after me." Again, I threw up my arms. "All hail the Emperor Chas!"

This time, I thought a few windows may have shattered. In any case, from that day forward, Steeler fans called him the Emperor Chas, or simply the Emperor, or even more simply, Emp. After he won yet a fourth Super Bowl the year after he'd won his third, his teams began to decline through the 1980s. He coached the Steelers to the playoffs four more times, but could not get back to the Super Bowl. I have a theory about that. One reason he ran upon rough seasons, I think, was that he could not bring himself to be a politician. Head coaches and assistant coaches, you see, spend countless hours on the telephone, speaking to other coaches around the country to keep friendships alive; a coach always is a candidate to be fired, so it never hurts to have a friend out there to recommend you for a job. In short, do not neglect your politics. I believe Chas did and that indirectly his ignoring the politics of football hurt him.

When he came to Pittsburgh in 1969, he brought with him a splendid staff of assistants, some of whom he had worked with or knew well when he had been an assistant in San Diego clear back in the days of the American Football League. Assistants come and go, of course, but even when some of Chuck's went, the ones who remained recommended men they knew from their grapevine or past experience to be bright prospects. Often these men came from the anonymity of the college ranks, but they could coach, all right. But when the head coach relies too much on recommendations from his assistants, ultimately he gets lemons, who in turn recommend other lemons. Noll, averse to spending time chit-chatting with other coaches around the nation, allowed his contacts to dry up; thus the quality of his staff slipped. As I said, that's just my theory.

At any rate, in his heyday, Chuck went about assembling coaching staffs unlike any in the league. In 1977 I wrote a piece for *Sports Illustrated* in which I examined, man by man, Noll's assistant coaches. Noll himself had played professional football, yet just one member of his '77 staff, running backs coach Dick Hoak, had played in the pros. Not one of them, at the time Noll hired them, had coached pro football. With the exception of Hoak, all had risen from college coaching jobs; Hoak had been hired after coaching one season of high school football. Was Noll the second coming of Major Bowes, who in the days before television conducted a radio "amateur hour" in which he paraded totally unknown performers before the microphone and interrupted many of them in mid-act by ordering a single blow to a tympanum that he termed giving them "the gong"? Apparently not.

"We're after teachers," Noll told me. "Teachers are not necessarily people who have played pro football. You find 'em wherever you find 'em."

Many years later, in 2001, head coach Bill Cowher had a staff of 13 assistant coaches, eight of whom had played professional football. Of that number, offensive line coach Russ Grimm, new to Cowher's staff, had enjoyed the most distinguished playing career—he played guard in the famous Washington Redskins line, known for their size as "the Hogs". He and his teammates won three Super Bowl rings. In Grimm's first year as a Steeler coach (he'd come to Pittsburgh from the Washington staff), Grimm fashioned an excellent line that helped take the Steelers, to the surprise of most everyone, clear to the AFC championship game. Along the way, starting left tackle Wayne Grandy remarked:

"The one thing that Russ brings is a certain amount of trust. You know of his career, you know where he comes from, you know of his Super Bowls. So when he walks in the door, you listen....You know that whatever he's telling you, he's been there, right out there on the battle-field."

Chuck Noll, I'm guessing, would have said, "Who cares? Can the guy teach?" *My* guess is he can.

Okay, where do you find the outstanding teachers? Noll knew where not to find them. He scouted college players by dropping in at spring practices and hated hearing a coach bark, "I *told* you not to do that!" Telling was not teaching. "Teaching," Chuck said, "is doing it and doing it and doing it—and selling it. The most important thing you have in coaching is a fight for the mind."

Flabbergasting critics, he hired Woody Widenhofer, age 30, to coach his linebackers. Widenhofer would be giving orders to all-pro linebacker Andy Russell, who 11 years earlier had been the University of Missouri's Most Valuable Player while Widenhofer was a callow Missouri redshirt. What sense did his hiring make? Noll scoffed at the question. "Just an interesting sidelight for sportswriters," he said.

Still, in linebacker meetings, when Woody caught Russell blowing a play on film, he spoke tactfully. "Andy," he would say, "you're too good a player for that to happen." Whereupon the testy middle linebacker Jack Lambert, professing horror that the ex-redshirt dare criticize his Missouri MVP even mildly, would shriek, "Oh, my God! Did you two have a spat?"

Woody rose to the title of defensive coordinator and eventually went on to college head-coaching jobs, but Noll surely wasted no time mourning his departure. Sportswriters have branded Noll's successor, Bill Cowher, a hard, unfeeling boss because a succession of his assistants have moved away to other—often better — jobs. Noll welcomed movement, convinced that staff stagnation produces inbreeding and misses out on fresh approaches.

His critics suggested he hired college coaches in order to collect yes-men. He needed no yes-men. So sure of himself was Noll that when he became head coach of the Steelers he appointed himself offensive coor-dinator and quarterbacks coach, even though all his coaching experience had been on defense. "I felt I had to learn more about offense," he said. The headmaster would educate himself as he built a team. The teacher would teach himself.

If indeed an eventual loss of contacts in the sport diminished his staffs, one must understand that his constitution allowed little or no room for politicking. But I shall not go on analyzing a man difficult to analyze. Instead, and just as an aside, I'll point out that Chuck never gave me any indication whatsoever that he disliked or approved of me calling him Chas. Nor has he ever, to this day, given me so much as a hint that he disliked or approved of me anointing him the Emperor. Although sportswriters during my growing-up years made it a constant practice to refer to athletes, coaches, and baseball managers by their nicknames, sportswriters in the 1960s (for reasons I shall examine in a later chapter) began to shun nicknames, and for the most part still do. Rarely did a writer call Noll the Emperor. But he may well have wished I never had hung the moniker on him, for when he ran into two straight losing seasons in 1985 and '86, a columnist or two started calling him the Emperor—snidely.

That he never expressed to me an opinion of the nicknames I gave him should not be surprising. Do you think he would concern himself with peripheral matters?

Chapter Nine

Terry Bradshaw— Lovable Liar

In the summer of 1974, NFL players struck the league's training camps, leaving Terry Bradshaw and the Steelers' backup quarterback, Terry Hanratty, to walk a picket line on the road that ran along the training camp at St. Vincent College in Latrobe, PA. Rookies, however, reported to camp, and among them was Joe Gilliam, who immediately attracted attention with his whip of an arm. A week into camp, Hanratty took stock of this development and said, "I better get my ass in there." Another week passed, whereupon Bradshaw, who was going into his fifth season but had not yet achieved a level of consistency that would guarantee him his starting job in the face of the rookie's surprising challenge, likewise abandoned the labor movement. Indeed, in the days just before the Steelers were to open the regular season, Coach Chuck Noll announced that Gilliam would be his starting quarterback.

A little after eight the next morning, Bradshaw burst into the office of Steeler publicity director Joe Gordon crying, "Where's Dan? Where's Dan?"

Terry was frantic. He had not been able to find Dan Rooney, the boss, in his office. "Dan usually doesn't get in till around nine," said Gordon. "What's the emergency?"

"I screwed up! I really screwed up!"

"What are you talking about?"

"I got two phone calls last night from reporters. One of them was a local guy, some Pittsburgh reporter, and the other was calling from San Francisco. They both wanted to know how I felt about being demoted. I told one of them, 'If I'm not gonna start, I'll demand to be traded. I want outta here.' And I told the other guy, 'Everything's cool. I'm not gonna make a fuss about this. I'm sure I'll get my chance.' "

"Go on," said Gordon.

"Well, I meant to tell the Pittsburgh guy that everything's cool and tell the San Francisco guy I want to be traded, but I did it the other way around."

In other words, his strategy was to play the good soldier and create no stir in the local sports pages but give the San Francisco reporter a lively story, because who in Pittsburgh would read it? Of course, a story printed in San Francisco could travel almost instantly across the country via wire services, but Terry had overlooked that possibility, his accommodating nature being to give a writer way out there in California a fresh angle. Alas, he had dropped his bomb right at his own front door.

As matters turned out, Bradshaw got his chance to start, but not until the seventh game of the season, after which he remained the starter as the Steelers made their way to their first Super Bowl championship. Meantime, the day after Terry had barged into Gordon's office, Gordon ran across a maxim in a publication he happened to be reading: "You'll never be sorry for what you don't say." He enlarged the maxim to the size of a small poster and attached it to his office wall.

"See that poster?" he said, the next time Terry wandered into his office. "I put that up there for *you.*"

Terry guffawed but went on his way undeterred,

A strapping, yellow-haired, down-home Loosiana boy, he navigated a course through big-city media in a fashion that reminded me of Dizzy Dean, a St. Louis Cardinal baseball pitcher who emerged from rural Arkansas in the 1930s to become an immediate big-league sensation and a 30-game winner by his third full season. Television did not exist at the time. Baseball teams traveled from city to city by train, and at each stop there would be a reporter waiting to get the amazing rookie's life story. "What's your full name, Diz?" one would ask, and he would say, "Jerome Herman Dean." To the next sportswriter he would give his name as Jay Hanna Dean. He served up a variety of birthplaces—Lucas, Ark.; Holderville, Okla.; Bond, Miss. Later, pressed to explain why he distributed his birthplace among three towns, he replied, "I got friends at all three places." And he explained to a sportswriter, "Ol' Diz just wants to give each o' you boys a scoop." Eventually, a sore arm finished Dean's career, so he turned, as Terry Bradshaw would do following arm trouble, to broadcasting—in Diz's case, radio, where he managed to enrage high-school English teachers across the country by saying, for example, "That durned runner slud into third base and made it!" Terry, with CBS Television and later with the Fox network, has succeeded immensely more than Dizzy Dean did, but his *modus operandi*, it seems to me, resembles Dean's: Go in there and just say whatever pops out of your mouth. I gather it's worked well enough, given the fact that he's run through three wives—a Miss Teen-Age America, an ice-show star (JoJo Starbuck, who once sat beside me on a Steeler flight reading a Bible) and a lady lawyer—without having had to declare bankruptcy.

In 1970 the Steelers made Bradshaw the very first selection in the NFL draft in the oddest of circumstances. They and the Chicago Bears had won but one game the previous season, the Bears' lone victory a walloping of the Steelers. Both teams finished in a tie for incompetence, so they flipped a coin for the first pick. The Steelers won the flip and to absolutely nobody's surprise chose Bradshaw, who though he had played for a small-college team, Louisiana Tech, could propel a football so hard it might chop cotton if thrown low through a field.

I remember being there a day or two after the draft when the Steelers flew Terry from Shreveport, LA, his hometown, to an evening news conference at The LeMont, a plush restaurant atop the Mt. Washington section of Pittsburgh that offers a glittering view of the downtown skyline—a nighttime view I have found to be unmatched in any American city I have visited. Though Shreveport certainly was much more than a whistle stop, Terry struck the assembled media as every bit a respectful rural southern hayseed, and I imagined that when he took in the view from The LeMont he said, "Hoo-eee!" Joe Gordon, however, imagined otherwise.

"It was a cold night," he remembers, "and the newspaper photographers posed him out on the restaurant's fire escape so as to have the skyline view for a backdrop. He was shivering. I think he was thinking, 'What have I gotten myself into up here in the north? What's going to happen to me in this place?' "

But one liked him at once. When he stood before the microphone, he conveyed nothing if not enthusiasm and found himself at no loss for words. "I'm here to lead the Steelers to the NFL championship," he proclaimed. Too, he gave us a nice little serving of Bible Belt upbringing by remembering to thank the Almighty profusely for his good fortune.

Two seasoned Steeler players, curious to get a feel for their new quarterback, had slipped into the crowd of reporters and club officials. When the news conference broke up, linebacker Andy Russell and center

Ray (the Old Ranger) Mansfield, introduced themselves to the prodigy. "Come on," said the Old Ranger. "We'll show you a little bit of the town."

They invited me as well, so there were four of us who took a table in a downtown nightclub that hummed. Terry ordered a vodka and tonic (or was it gin?), accepted a huge cigar from Mansfield, fired it up, and smiled as if in hog heaven. "This fellow," I said to Russell and Mansfield, "will fit in."

I don't recall any customer in the nightclub recognizing him, let alone asking for an autograph, but of course that would change. A few years later, still struggling to find himself on the field and having recently married a Pittsburgh girl, Miss Teen-Age America, he took her to the Holiday House, a ballroom-sized club that featured nationally known entertainers. As Terry and his wife were led through the room to their table, the customers booed. From that point, he became virtually a recluse.

A shame, I thought, because if ever a young man enjoyed having fun, it was Terry. He thrived among people. Accommodating? Whether coming off a victory or a wrenching defeat, he showed up at his locker to face the reporters racing at him in waves. I sometimes stood on the rim, just eavesdropping.

"The turning point?" a voice would shout.

"When I saw Swann breaking loose over the middle, and I said, 'Golly, gee!' and fired her in there."

The first wave of reporters would disperse, to be replaced by a second wave. "The turning point?" came the question again.

"Hey, when you see ol' Stallworth wide open on the sideline, where else you gonna go?"

Beyond dishing out fresh angles to this writer and that, Terry's imagination—not unlike Muhammad Ali's, come to think of it—hurtled him into the sphere of the outrageous. Early in the week of Super Bowl XIV in Pasadena, where he would win his fourth ring by whistling a 73-yard touchdown pass to John Stallworth and then, two series later, throwing a 45-yard pass to Stall that set up another touchdown, I traveled to the Rams' hotel to take in the usual media interviews extravaganza. In the ballroom, every Rams player had been placed at his own circular table that bore his name on a sign so that the horde could identify him. I sat down at quarterback Vince Ferragamo's table. A darkly handsome fellow, Ferragamo had enjoyed a surprisingly good season, and in fanciful Hollywood fashion the Rams had publicized him as an off season medical student at the University of Nebraska. In the course of several innocuous questions posed to him by the six or so reporters seated around his table, I said, "Okay, so who's going to win the game?"

The Rams were 11-point underdogs, but Ferragamo said, "Oh, we'll beat them. Sure, we'll beat the Steelers."

I headed back to the Steelers' Newport Beach hotel, where I was staying. I ran into Bradshaw making his way through a crowded lobby and told him of Ferragamo's prediction. He became livid. "He said that? He really said that?" At 4 o'clock that afternoon, I went live with my evening radio talk show—it was 7 o'clock in Pittsburgh—from the Steelers' locker room as the players trailed in from the practice field. Unexpectedly, I heard Terry calling out to me.

"Hey, Myron Cope, here I am, your new friend Vinnie Ferragamo, who gave you your scoop today that the Rams will upset the Steelers. I just thought I'd drop in here to the Steelers' locker room to shake hands with your boys and wish 'em good luck. But it's a shame they won't win their fourth championship."

Sensing Bradshaw was embarking on one of his flights of fancy, I played along. "Well, if it isn't Vinnie Ferragamo himself! Do sit down here and give us an interview."

Terry made himself comfortable at a microphone and said:

"I just want to tell all those Steeler fans in Pittsburgh that we are not only gonna whup their team but if they send me a request with a stamped, self-addressed return envelope, I'll be happy to send them an autographed, 8x11 glossy photo of me, Dr. Ferragamo, wearin' my surgery gown. You can't believe how good I look when I go in there to operate."

There was no stopping Terry. He went on like that for at least 30 minutes. Although his Louisiana drawl was well recognized in Pittsburgh, one woman listener telephoned the radio station to shout, "Who does that Ferragamo think he is, anyhow?"

Clear to the final week of his football career, when the handwriting was on the wall, Terry Bradshaw remained ready for a laugh—ready to step out on the diving board and execute a belly-whopper into preposterous situations. I'll tell you about the time I introduced him to a couple of myna birds, but first, we must back up. In 1982, in the training camp of his 13th and next-to-last season, he had thrown an off-balance sidearm pass that cause a jolt of pain in his arm—a muscle strain near his right elbow was the diagnosis. As the season continued, the pain worsened. At season's end, he returned to his cattle ranch in Grand Cane, LA, and consulted a Shreveport surgeon, who recommended surgery, calling it minor.

I remember speaking to the Steelers' orthopedic surgeon, Dr. Paul Steele, who said to me, "What Terry's got in that arm is like a rubber band that's frayed. He's been throwing those cannon shots all these years, so there's been a lot of wear." The Steelers, I took it, decided surgery was no answer —maybe the rubber band would stay intact for another season or two. But in March Terry opted for surgery. He checked into Doctors' Hospital in Shreveport, and then went to rehab at a place called, believe it, the Shreveport Bone and Joint Clinic. It may have been the best rehab clinic in America, for all I know, but I somehow equated the name with Gus's Body Shop. Those of us who called Terry to inquire about his progress were told, "Doin' swell! Threw 30 yards to my therapy guy in the parking lot today."

In fact, when he showed up for spring mini-camp, Terry could not throw more than ten yards. He sat out the entire first 14 weeks of the 16-game 1983 season. The Steelers nevertheless somehow managed to demonstrate playoff possibilities until Terry's struggling replacement, Cliff Stoudt, went ker-plooey, and they lost three in a row. They were heading into New York to play the Jets at Shea Stadium in week 15; winning was a must. Chuck Noll rolled the dice and named Terry his starting quarterback. Whereupon a bird-keeper, a total stranger to me, phoned me from Toronto to inform me that he owned two myna birds that possessed magic healing powers.

"I guarantee you, they will heal Bradshaw's elbow," the bird-keeper assured me.

"Fine," I said. "I think I can get Terry to undergo the treatment, but you pay your own expenses to get here."

Terry, whooping with delight, said, "Let's do it."

We convened in a conference room in the Steeler offices, a television crew from my station poised to capture medical history. The two myna birds—green and feathery, as I remember—each sat in its own cage, squawking. Their Canadian keeper removed one of them, instructing Bradshaw to hold his right arm akimbo, at which point the man placed the bird on Terry's elbow.

"Ooooo," said Terry softly, into the camera. "I can feel the *power*! Yes! I feel the power of the myna bird. Myna bird, can you do something about my alimony payments?"

In the hallway outside, I was told later by a Steeler official, the vicious linebacker Jack Lambert paused to glance into the conference room. "That fucking Cope," he muttered, "is turning this place into a circus."

But whaddaya know? At Shea Stadium, Terry right off the bat took the Steeler offense on two consecutive long drives that he finished with touchdown passes to jump the Steelers in front, 14-0. His second touchdown pass, a ten-yarder to receiver Calvin Sweeney running a slant pattern into the middle, was one he had to snap off to beat a Jets blitz. It was the last pass Terry Bradshaw ever threw. Less than a minute into the second quarter, he removed himself from the game, his Hall of Fame arm gone forever.

The Steeler victory that ensued gave Bradshaw's team the AFC Central Division title. Whether the myna bird helped reduce Terry's alimony payments, I have no idea.

I must remind myself that a huge portion of the football fans who watch Bradshaw's NFL studio work, some of them enjoying him while others dismiss him as a clown, are not old enough to have seen him play. Trust me, the man was a phenomenal athlete. For one thing, of course, he had that wondrous arm. Only a couple of years ago or so, I asked Chuck Noll if he had ever been tempted to install the so-called West Coast offense, which for a long time now has been popular in one form or another; essentially, it's based on throwing short passes to receivers in hopes of springing them for long gains. "Actually," Noll replied, "we fooled around with it for a few days in practice. The problem was, our receivers were having to catch those short bullets from Terry and they were complaining about bruises on their chests."

Terry, however, was much more than an arm. He played anywhere from 215 to 230 pounds and, when at 215 one year, was clocked as the fastest player on the squad. Strong? When he scrambled wide, the cornerbacks who came up to tackle him took the worst of the collision. He was mule-strong and eel-slippery as well. Many were the times I saw two, three, four pass-rushers pounce on him in the pocket, even to the point where he disappeared completely from view. Seconds later (and bear in mind that the referee's whistle was slower in those days) he would emerge to fire a pass or run for big yardage.

His arm at last gone at age 35, he proceeded into a hugely profitable broadcasting and public-speaking career, but for many years brought recriminations from Pittsburghers upon himself. Their complaint? "You're avoiding our town as if you hate us." The great Steeler teams of the '70s, unlike today's championship teams that in this era of free agency see their players come and go, had been kept largely intact. Squad reunions would follow in the years to come, but where was Terry Bradshaw? A no-show.

In Pittsburgh, you should understand, the Steelers are a religion, practically a church. When they play well, they're revered. When they play poorly, the parishioners are of a mind to throw rocks through the stained-glass windows. Terry certainly in his early years had experienced the fans at their worst; one Sunday afternoon, he was helped off the field injured, and the crowd cheered. Chuck Noll had frequently barked in his face. Often the fans called him a dummy. But when Terry at last took charge of his football career, Pittsburgh fans elevated him to deity status. Why, then, did he seem to be putting Pittsburgh behind him? Letters to the editor poured in to the newspapers. Did Moses, having delivered the Ten Commandments from Mount Sinai, tell the Hebrews, "It's been nice knowin' you. You guys head for the Promised Land, but I'm outta here. Don't bother to write."

As Terry traveled the nation on speaking engagements, he would tell media in whatever town, "What do I owe Chuck Noll? I made it in spite of Chuck."

But he remained the same old Terry. A week later he was apt to tell another city's media, "Hey, I *loved* Chuck."

Many of my listeners, when traveling around the country, clipped newspaper articles and sent them to me. From Nashville, where Terry had spoken to a convention of music-industry people, came an article quoting him as saying that after the Steelers had won their first Super Bowl and taken part in a motorcade celebration, fans along the parade route booed him. Same thing after the Steelers' second Super Bowl victory, Terry claimed. When they won their third, Terry said, he told Noll, no way I'm going to ride in the parade.

He had not been booed during the first two motorcades. He received a hero's welcome. After reading the clipping from Nashville, I at once phoned Joe Gordon. "Joe," I said, "if I remember correctly, you guys did not stage a parade after the third Super Bowl."

"Nope. He's imagining we did."

Why, then, has Terry shunned the town that he once owned? I have a theory, perhaps too simple. He was just busy, and did not want to take the trouble to return. Also, he had moved on, fixed on his future, and could be excused for being unwilling to live in the past. If such was the case, his indifference to Pittsburgh and Steeler memories nonetheless went a little too far. Moon Mullins, a guard, had been his best friend among his teammates. In the off season one year, Terry had embarked on a national nightclub tour posing as a country-western singer and had taken along Moon as his "stage manager." Years later, Moon, by then a successful businessman, told me with great disappointment, "I phoned him not long ago, but he never returned the call."

Again, it's not easy being in demand. Things slip. At any rate, Terry did appear at one Steelers reunion in Pittsburgh. I happened one night to be aboard a riverboat where I was to speak to the membership of a local fraternal lodge. "You going to be at the Steeler reunion at the Convention Center this weekend?" a man asked me.

What reunion?

I checked it out the next day and found that indeed a glittering array of Steeler stars from the 1970s was to gather at the Convention Center. Terry would be among them. But the "reunion" had not been organized by Steeler management. A card-show promoter had signed up the players and advertised their impending appearance as a reunion and beckoned fans to come and get autographs. In the days immediately following, checks paid to Steeler heroes for $10,000 and $20,000 bounced in banks around town like tennis balls, but Terry Bradshaw, I learned, had gotten $100,000—up front. So much for his having been a dummy.

Hang in there, Terry. You're having a great run.

Chapter Ten

The Rev—Praise Be
Our Motivators

Speaking of Terry Bradshaw, I might mention that even as I was writing about him, I opened the *Post-Gazette* one morning to come upon a full-page advertisement that blared:

ATTEND AMERICA'S MOST POPULAR BUSINESS SEMINAR
SUCCESS MAGAZINE'S SUCCESS 2001

Attend the blockbuster event praised and acclaimed by CNN, USA
Today, TIME, PEOPLE, The Wall Street Journal
and The New York Times
All Speakers Live and in Person

Directly beneath that clarion call ran a row of photographs of seven live-and-in-person speakers—they included Terry—and farther down, beneath their uniformly smiling faces, appeared a larger photo, this one of Bill Clinton, who less than three months before had left office embroiled in wholesale controversial pardons he had issued at the 11th hour to crooks. What's more, he and his wife were besieged by insinuations that they had attempted to steal furniture from the White House on their way out. Clinton now headed this lineup of inspirational luminaries who would appear in just a couple of weeks at Mellon Arena, which seats 17,000 for hockey. Wanna be motivated to succeed in your job? Clinton and company, the message seemed to be, will motivate you till your hair stands on end. The cost at the door was $225, "but you will receive an unbelievable special early registration price of only $39" for the afternoon session only. Here's your chance to listen to *winners*, the ad trumpeted.

I phoned a friend who knows about such things. "These speakers carry a big ticket," I said.

"Those promoters know what they're doing," my friend replied. "They've probably sold large blocks of tickets to corporations, to begin with. My guess is they'll draw about 8,000 people, which is plenty."

Motivational speeches by celebrities have been a lucrative pursuit in America for close to 50 years, starting in the 1950s, I'm guessing, and later booming into stupendous fees for the biggies of sports, network television, industry, Wall Street, you name it. Hey, Terry, rumble. You were a winner, why should you not have something instructive to say to those who aspire to be winners? My friend Rocky Bleier, who ran in the backfield alongside Franco Harris for the great Steeler teams of the 1970s, ever since has made his living delivering motivational speeches from one end of the country to the other. In the Vietnam War he had lain in a jungle, severely wounded, and had prayed to God that if He somehow got him out of there alive, he would try to do good if given an opportunity. Not long ago, Rocky and his wife Jan traveled to the Ukraine and brought home two abandoned little girls, ages two and three, whom they adopted. "My God, Rock," I told him, "you're 55 and starting all over again?" He shrugged and smiled. He was making a payment on his promise to God. Surely, an audience can be motivated by such a man as Rocky Bleier.

As for me, without being critical of traveling motivators, I simply recuse myself on the basis that I, personally, have never felt in need of motivation by microphone. Chuck Noll, as he built the Steelers into an NFL dynasty, put it this way: "I want self-starters." Give him the player who knew he had to give an honest effort, and he would take that player over one who needed pep talks. In my case, motivation was supplied in full by a desire to do credit to myself and give me and my family economic comfort. Nothing complicated about that. No other motivators needed. And if I were a corporate executive, I would think twice about paying $25,000 to Rick Pitino, a basketball coach, to deliver a speech. I do believe that if instead I paid a $2,000 Christmas bonus to each of 12 secretaries, I would have a dozen secretaries in my company giving total effort, and if you don't think 12 dedicated secretaries are a major plus, you have never had a secretary.

At any rate, it's my safe guess that the first American athlete to discover the profitability of crisscrossing the nation preaching the fundamentals of success was the Reverend Bob Richards, an ordained minister in the Church of the Brethren. He was best known as a pole vaulter who won an Olympics gold medal in 1952 and another one, at age 30, in 1956. At 17 Richards had been shipped off from his home in Champaign, Illinois, to Bridgewater College, a church school in Virginia. The Brethren sect apparently found him to be precocious, for at 18 he was "licensed" to preach and worked his way through college—after Bridgewater, the University of Illinois—by filling as many as three pulpits at once. Eventually, Richards became pastor of his own church in Long Beach, California. The job paid only $6,000 per year, but the hours seemingly were flexible, inasmuch as he was able to travel the country competing in track-and-field meets, which in the 1940s and '50s drew huge crowds in many American cities. Headline writers across the nation challenged their own capacity for alliteration, splashing their sports pages with such headlines as

POLE-VAULTING PARSON TOPS 15 FEET
or *VAULTIN' VICAR STEALS SPOTLIGHT*
or *DECATHLON DEACON TAKES TITLE.*

Track and field remained an amateur sport, governed by the Amateur Athletic Union, which in turn was ruled by Avery Brundage, a tyrant of long standing. Promoters of meets were permitted to pay the athletes travel expenses, all right, and indeed slipped them illegal cash payments on the side. But the Reverend Bob knew he had the oratorical talent to capitalize on his fame in a more meaningful way. Studying his upcoming schedule of meets, he booked himself into pulpits and banquets at just about every stop. Brundage and his fellow AAU officials bristled, for their rules strictly forbade amateurs to profit from their reputations, even to the extent of accepting a speaking fee. In Richards's case, however, they pretended not to notice.

"To crack down on a minister," he was to tell me years later, "would have been to put them in a terribly embarrassing spot." So saying, he smiled from ear to ear, teeth gleaming. It was a savage smile, one that he enjoyed flashing whenever he took particular relish in relating a personal triumph.

The bottom line, meantime, had been that by linking speaking engagements with his travels as a pole vaulter and decathlon contestant, he had invented the speaking tour for American athletes. And, you should excuse me, the Vaultin' Vicar set the bar high for those who would follow.

Traveling with him for somewhat less than a week in 1968, when at 42 the Reverend Bob stood at the peak of his motivational game, I heard him cry out to halls full of salesmen, "I want to set you on fire! I want to get you to *go*, to *act*." Shutting his eyes tightly, he paused for effect. Then, his hands knifing through the air, he tore on, invoking football imagery. "You've got to go through that line. The salesman is on the field! He's out there in the middle of the fight!" On stage, Richards paced back and forth, bobbing and weaving, his forehead glistening with perspiration as he proceeded, crescendoing, to the climax of his oration. "No matter what you've done, stretch for somethin' beyond! And lastly, if you want to succeed, put God in your life. . . . Put faith in your life and you've got enthusiasm. Get with it! Feel this dynamic force surge through you and you will win the great race of life!"

Audiences invariably bolted to their feet, cheering. Having evoked that very response in a dinner speech to sales executives at a country club one evening, Richards sat down, whereupon the dinner chairman stepped to the microphone and intoned, "We have been in the presence of one of the great human beings of our time."

Away from the mike, however, the Reverend Bob was another man, one whom I enjoyed more than I did the motivating preacher, given my indifference to fiery pep talks. Let me introduce you to the other Reverend and you may enjoy him as I did.

Sports Illustrated sent me to join Richards in Evansville, Indiana, where the day I arrived he would address a salesmen's dinner, then drive a rental car the next day to French Lick for a speech to college students and arise the *next* morning at 6:30 to motor two hours to Louisville to appear on a television show in which he would follow a trained cockatoo. Wheaties, the Breakfast of Champions, had Richards under contract as an advertising spokesman and therefore regularly sent him to TV appearances. "Do you really eat Wheaties every morning?" a lady interviewer pressed him in this instance.

"Seriously," he told her, "I do enjoy them and have eaten them for 30 years."

Once out of the building, he conjured up an answer he would have preferred to have given the lady interviewer when she cast suspicion on his Wheaties habit. In a mock stage voice, he crowed, "For the first five years, of course, I held my nose and gingerly put one flake at a time on my tongue and then hurriedly washed it down with a bourbon and water." We passed a monstrous yellow statue that guarded the front of the television building—a sculpture of a hefty nude rising off her haunches while brandishing a clenched fist in the air. "The title of that statue," mused the Reverend, "is *How Many Times Have I Told You Not to Come into the Bathroom When I'm in Here!*"

For ten years now, Richards had been pitching Wheaties to the nation in television commercials, his picture on the cereal's box. General Mills, "The Makers of Wheaties," had been looking for a Wheaties Man to bring its product out of a sales slump and had first offered the job to Bud Wilkinson, an eminently successful football coach at the University of Oklahoma. But the president of the university, you will be amazed to know in this age of million-dollar shoe contracts given college coaches, refused Wilkinson permission to pitch cereal and coach football at the same time. Ergo, General Mills turned to Richards and at the time I traveled with him was paying him $75,000 per year, an immense fee for a former athlete in 1968. In addition, The Reverend told me he was picking up $1,000 per speech, bringing his total income to $125,000 a year, enough to live in style. He related that back home in La Verne, Calif., where he lived with his wife and three children, he owned a Mercedes-Benz 300SL, a Mercedes 300S, a Chrysler station wagon, and a Cadillac El Dorado, which he purchased after roaring up to the showroom on a Harley-Davidson motorcycle, wearing a black leather jacket. He informed me he also owned 20 truck trailers, minus cabs—40-footers that were sitting around waiting for him to discover how he could put them to use.

Meantime, with the still-trim, flat-bellied clergyman pitching away, sales of Wheaties soared and dominated the market. Muscular, curly haired, and sharp-featured in a wholesome way, he paraded across America's television screens, bursting with Wheaties-provided energy. For example, he would appear in a TV commercial standing alongside a swimming pool and plunge not into water but into a heaping bowl of Wheaties topped with strawberries and cream. "Did you know," he mused in yet another commercial, "that enough bowls of Wheaties are poured each year to fill the Rose Bowl up to the 56th row?" Couch potatoes—the term as yet had not been coined—in some cases reacted with hostility to Richards's brilliant smile and boundless vigor. A Chicago research chemist, trying to envision the Rose Bowl filled with Wheaties, stalked to his typewriter and irritably demanded of Richards, "How much milk is required to go with all that cereal?"

Likewise, the Reverend's image on boxes of Wheaties that also bore pictures of various star athletes the Breakfast of Champions had taken to signing up brought letters to General Mills from smart alecks. "This year," wrote one, "I happen to be rooming with a fellow who eats Wheaties at an incredible rate. As you might expect, the Wheaties box is always to be found on our kitchen table, and as a result I have been forced to stare at Jerry West for more months that I care to recall. Why not try other champions for a change? For example, champions in the world of philosophy? The top line might read: W. V. Quine, metaphysician from Akron, or Father Joseph Owens, C.Ss.R., neo-Thomist from Toronto."

At the time I hooked up with the Reverend Bob, I had just begun to dabble in radio and shortly would find myself pitching products in local commercials. In time I, too, would discover myself in demand as an after-dinner speaker (I came cheap), but not being a man of the cloth, I felt no compunctions about grabbing the money. On the other hand, The Rev, as he was referred to at General Mills's advertising agency, came under fire from clergymen around the country. But when I verbally frisked him for signs of hypocrisy, he made no bones about his quest of material things. "What the hell are we talking about if religion isn't motivation, if it isn't life?" the Rev demanded to know. "Religion should make you happy, it should make you successful, it should give you love. It's a solution to problems." Okay, okay.

Meanwhile, the energetic minister had it in mind to make a killing with a movie that he himself had written and intended to produce. In his travels he carried along his script, entitled *A Young Man's Journey*, and plunked it into my lap while we flew from his television appearance in Louisville to Erie. One passage that caught my eye depicted a character that Richards had named Dr. Complex—a candidate for the presidency of the United States. Out on the campaign trail, Dr. Complex proposes an easing of hostility by the American military toward China. Arguing that nuclear missiles are phallic symbols, he then suggests that our generals can be rendered less belligerent by giving each of them a Chinese mistress.

"I get across my points through the ludicrous," Richards explained to me.

At the airport in Erie, he landed in the laps of a welcoming committee from the Sales and Marketing Executives Club. On the fringe of the committee stood an attractive little black-haired woman who clearly carried a burden on her mind. She explained that a crisis existed at the high school in a prosperous suburb where she lived. Students were fooling with drugs and booze. "It's really serious," said the woman, who gave her name as Joanne. Would the Reverend Bob *please* speak to the student body the next morning? Shoring up her appeal, Joanne pointed out that she ate Wheaties constantly.

"I've got to drive to Grove City, PA tomorrow," Richards hedged. At the Louisville airport earlier that same day, it so happened, he had done an imitation of high school audiences, screwing his face into a sour expression and sprawling indolently in his chair; he had said, "The hardest audience in the world is a high school audience. They look at you as if to say, 'Okay, Buster, move me. I'm here only because I have to be.'" The Rev told Joanne he would see if visiting the high school was possible. First thing the next morning, Joanne phoned his hotel room to renew her plea. Answering to his conscience, he relented, but at breakfast he earnestly said to me:

"You see, the thing about this is that one speech does no good on this kind of problem. You've got to get with these kids for a while and work with them and play with them to accomplish anything."

Indeed, I often felt that judges who handed out probation to famous athletes and ordered them to visit schools to lecture pupils on the consequences of errant behavior were boneheads. What could such athletes accomplish in an hour? What sort of role models were they? At any rate, Joanne, as a member of a neighborhood organization called the Parent Action Club, briefed Richards en route to the high school in her station wagon. "Our program, our approach to these children," she said, "is, 'Look, you can't run for president on LSD. You can't be president on an LSD campaign.'"

"That's pretty good," said Richards. "Why don't you give the speech?"

"I have a confession to make," Joanne piped, lowering her eyelids demurely. "I don't really eat Wheaties."

"No wonder you're so short," Richards snapped.

From the stage of the school auditorium, he regaled a packed hall of 700 children with stirring sports stories interlaced with jokes and admonished them to make something of themselves. Astutely, he barely mentioned the problem at hand. The entire audience hung on every word, the little junkies and elbow benders indistinguishable from the rest. He received a roaring standing ovation. Driving on to Grove City in a rental car, he became distracted by a flatbed truck up ahead carrying a huge, cone-shaped load under canvas. "That's the dope they just hauled out of the high school," he said.

As we pressed on toward Grove City College, a Presbyterian institution whose students he would address, we paused for lunch at a roadside diner. The Rev knew this country well, for it was one of many rural American landscapes where he had cut his teeth speaking to high school audiences in one small town and another. At the lunch counter, a stout, gray-haired customer recognized him and said, "Do you still go to the high schools?"

"No, sir," Richards replied. "I decided to save the salesmen. But today I'm going down to Grove City to save the Presbyterians from the abyss of a flaming hell."

Arriving there, he was greeted by the president of the college, a stubby red-faced man named Dr. J. Stanley Harker, who said, "I'm sure we're going to hear a splendid speech tonight."

"Well, don't expect too much, the money you Presbyterians pay," the Rev replied, deadpan.

His was the grueling life of a speaker in a day when it took a lot of speeches to afford Mercedes autos. Constantly on the road, he was not permitted the luxury of being sick, for the tickets that had been sold and the dinner reservations that had been made dictated that he show up. But in his more serious moments, he expressed to me the conviction that his message of inspiration and motivation reached people. He fondly recalled a man stopping him in the lobby of an Indianapolis hotel and saying, "Mr. Richards, you once gave a speech at the penitentiary, and because of what you said, I'm on the outside today."

So I ask, could you knock the Rev?

No professional speaker, I suspect, bats 1.000 out there in the world of babble-for-pay. Most nights you have it, some nights you don't. Moreover, unsuspected traps occasionally lay in wait. As a sideline to my broadcast work, I have delivered hundreds of speeches—usually after-dinner talks before associations of business or professional persons. (I'm like the Rev—get someone else for your high school banquet.) Now and then, I am asked to provide a motivational speech, but my answer is, "Look, I'm not the man you want. I just try to entertain. My material is light stuff, drawn from my experiences. Hopefully, I'll leave 'em laughing, and usually I do, but I'll tell you what—I can work into my talk about five minutes of motivation, if that's enough." Even for just five minutes, I suffer when striving to lift people's aspirations; my heart is not in it. But as one who is looking for audience laughter, I never know what lies in store at my next engagement.

For example, some years ago an advertising firm named Dudreck DePaul & Morgan phoned to tell me that a client—a Pittsburgh company that ranked as the world's largest manufacturer of tear gas—soon would be hosting a convention of the International Association of Chiefs of Police, whose members would be traveling in from various nations around the globe. The convention would take place at Seven Springs, a popular ski resort an hour or so from the city. John DePaul, a partner in the ad firm, said to me, "Are you interested in being the main speaker at their dinner? You know—about 45 minutes of light entertainment."

"Will the chiefs understand English?" I asked.

"I'm told most of them will."

Having accepted DePaul's invitation, I arrived early—about 5 p.m.—at the ski resort and sat down at the hotel bar. Ten minutes later, DePaul approached. "Myron," he said, "we've had a problem here today."

"Problem?"

"Yes, the chiefs of police were riding up to the top of a mountain for tear-gas demonstrations, and it seems the guy operating the chairlift loop ran into difficulty with a clutch or something." In short, the procession of cable cars heading upward had begun to lurch violently as if directed by centrifugal force. Police chiefs had been thrown from the chairlift like so many Idaho potatoes.

"The last count I heard," said DePaul, "was that we've got eight in the hospital. Pretty serious stuff. Broken legs and whatnot. Nobody dead, though."

I confess my first thought was a selfish one. "And I'm supposed to make people laugh tonight?"

"You can do it, Myron."

Next, I entered the banquet hall—strike two! It was an expansive room, and though crystal chandeliers hung from the ceiling, I observed at once that I would be working a dimly lit room. Such rooms, I had learned, subdue audiences. If you're looking for laughs, a bright room is much better, especially if dinner is preceded by a cocktail hour during which many in attendance can get themselves a little oiled. Puts 'em in better humor.

At any rate, minutes before the tear-gas dinner was to advance from dessert into the program, John DePaul again approached. He whispered, "See that woman in the print dress down the dais to your left? She's from England, and she's the president of this police chiefs' outfit. I almost forgot to mention to you that if there's one thing she can't stand, it's anything *resembling* an off-color story."

Strike three! Eight in the hospital, a darkened room, and a prude in charge. Filthy stories are not part of my repertoire, but when speaking to an adult gathering I find that one or two *mildly* off-color stories amuse even the clergyman who has given the invocation. At any rate, there went those stories. Never had I perspired through a speech as I did that evening. I laid an egg the size of a crate of tear-gas canisters. Days later, DePaul related to me that following my remarks, a couple of chiefs had repaired to the hotel bar, probably driven by my performance to attempt to salvage the evening, and "got themselves blitzed," as DePaul put it. They then climbed into a rental car intending to explore bars along the nearby roads. They tore through the front gates of the resort and spun out of control, narrowly missing a pond, their car ultimately heaving onto its side, demolished. At least *someone* had had a worse night than I.

Again, a public speaker never knows what fate awaits him. Thus I had Dudreck DePaul & Morgan to thank for yet another unforgettable engagement. This time they had booked me for a luncheon of the Laurel Valley Advertising and Public Relations Club at a hotel in the next county. Before lunch, I said to Al Dudreck, "Give me the landscape, Al. Okay if I get a little off-color here?"

"Are you kidding?" he said. "These are advertising and PR people. If you want, you can even use material you save for men's stags."

I certainly did not go that far and would not have done so even had there been no women in the audience. But I gave 'em a few moments more rowdy than my usual fare and felt pleased, driving back to Pittsburgh, that everybody had enjoyed themselves. Well, not quite everybody. Two days later I opened my mail to find a letter that began:

"You should be ashamed of yourself. I have never had to listen to a speaker whose mouth is as filthy as yours."

At the time, you see, the Catholic Church had just given permission to nuns to put away their habits at appropriate times and wear dresses. I phoned Al Dudreck and said, "Why didn't you tell me a nun"—the public relations director for a Catholic girls' college—"was in the audience?"

Al chuckled and replied, "I can't know everything."

When I turned 60, I reduced my schedule of nightly radio talk shows from five a week to two and with more evenings free would be able to accept an increased number of speaking engagements. The thought even crossed my mind that I could go national and rake in some of those five-figure checks floating around out there for the taking. On the road with the Steelers in Washington one Saturday evening, whom did I run into but a former Washington Redskins director of public relations named Mike Menchel, who had moved on to become vice president of a major Washington speakers' bureau that arranged bookings across the country for big-timers. "Whaddaya think?" I asked Mike. "In Pittsburgh I've worked audiences that consisted almost entirely of out-of-town guests brought in from all over by Pittsburgh corporations, and it didn't seem to make a difference that I was strictly a local yokel. I got 'em going."

"Send me a tape of one of your jobs," Mike said.

I owned no such tapes, but I had an engagement coming up that was perfect for the purpose—a luncheon audience of several hundred out-of-towners in the ballroom of a downtown hotel. From my radio station, I hired a very competent radio engineer, Thad Mazur, and asked him to wire up the ballroom with speakers and produce an audiotape of my performance. "Take care that you capture the laughter from every corner of the hall," I told Thad. But when he contacted the hotel manager for permission to set up his apparatus, the manager said, "That's fine, but union rules here require that Myron pay a hotel engineer to be part of this job."

All right, done. I showed up for the luncheon 30 minutes early to make certain the two engineers had everything in order. I found seated at a table beside Thad the hotel engineer, a corpulent fellow dressed in an undershirt and possessing no teeth in the front of his mouth. He explained to me that he would capture all audience responses from the left side of the ballroom and that Thad, manning his own gadgets, would capture responses from the right.

Back at the radio station hours later, Thad played the tape. Half a tape, I should say. The toothless hotel engineer had drawn a blank from the left side of the room, and much of my speech was inaudible as well. I hoped that with the money I had paid him, he purchased a shirt.

"Let's try one more time," I told myself. This time I would make sure I went first-class — I hired a video production company, which charged me approximately $1,500, as I recall. Looking at my speaking schedule, I had two dates coming up soon: A dinner speech to the Western Pennsylvania Association of Funeral Directors and, not long afterward, the annual dinner of the Kiwanis Club of Indiana, Pennsylvania. Which to choose for my videotape?

The funeral directors, I mused, could be a lot of fun. Just the fact that they make their livings in such a lugubrious business should make for funny material. And after all, they're just businessmen like any other association of businessmen, right? Wrong. They turned out to be, well, funeral directors. I now owned an expensive videotape in which no more than five people in the room laughed. The next week at the Kiwanis dinner, wouldn't you know it, I knocked 'em dead.

The hell with it, I decided. I'll just leave those fat paydays to my friends Terry Bradshaw and Rocky Bleier, and to Greg Gumbel, Elizabeth Dole, George Will, the White House furniture burglar, Cokie Roberts, and by all means to the cycling champion Lance Armstrong, whose agent, I have just read, says Armstrong's speaking fees range from $150,000 to

$225,000, the only problem being that the cyclist can find time to accept only three or four such engagements a year. Those corporations, or groups, he turns down surely scramble frantically to find a speaker as expensive, lest the money they intended for Armstrong burn holes in their pockets.

Chapter Eleven

Who's That Guy in the Mirror?

One who is in the business of writing magazine profiles—or for that matter, biographies—of public figures often finds he is introducing his subjects to themselves. None of us sees himself, or herself, with perfect accuracy. We think we know ourselves, all right, but the pictures others have of us may differ slightly or even greatly from the one we ourselves have imagined. Consequently, it was not unknown for a prominent figure I profiled to open the magazine and find a person he did not entirely know and even disliked at first glance.

After I profiled Roberto Clemente for *Sports Illustrated* in 1966, he did not speak to me for approximately a year. At about the same time Clemente began saying hello again, Howard Cosell fell silent. I had profiled him for *SI*, as well. Following my fairly normal procedure, I had spent about a week in New York, interviewing both him and others who knew him, and then spent about two weeks back home in Pittsburgh writing the piece. During that stretch, Cosell telephoned me at least three times, and each time his greeting went something like this:

"Well! And how is the masterpiece coming along?"

"It's coming along fine, I guess. It's getting there."

"Good! You surely must know that this particular piece will elevate you to the zenith of your career. Never before have you contemplated such richness of material to work with. Done with competence, this piece will cause your colleagues to blink at your brilliance. Press on."

At that time, as a radio and television sports commentator and documentary narrator, Howard had become known to millions of Americans, but he had not yet climbed the final step to become a household name. For example, no major magazine had accorded him profile treatment. *SI* was now taking care of that omission, so I found it understandable that he scarcely could wait to read about himself in that publication. When my story at last appeared, however, Howard did not at once reach for the phone to tell me that yes, indeed, I had reached the acme of my profession. I was not surprised.

The second paragraph of my 5,000-word article said:

"Cosell fondles a martini at a table in the Warwick bar, across the street from American Broadcasting Company headquarters. His long nose and pointed ears loom over his gin in the fashion of a dive bomber swooping in with fighter escort."

This probably was not the image Howard saw whenever he checked himself in a mirror. On the whole, I gave him favorable treatment, which he had earned, but I imagine he experienced rough seas reading about this fellow Cosell he did not completely recognize. No, unlike Clemente, he did not refuse to speak to me for a year. I estimated it would take him about three days to be on the phone, and sure enough, it took just that. In my mind's eye, you see, I could visualize his tall, ungainly figure striding up Fifth Avenue, passers-by calling out to him, "Hey, Howard! Saw you in *Sports Illustrated!*" Recognition would be the bottom line. If he received it, he would decide he liked my piece, after all.

"Just as I told you," he now trumpeted when he phoned, "my personage has been the vehicle by which you have traveled to the zenith of your career."

Returning to the matter of Roberto Clemente, I should point out that of all the superb players who performed for the Pirates over their 120-year history, he caught my fancy as only two others had. The first was Honus Wagner, a thickset shortstop who played in Pittsburgh the first eighteen years of the 20th century and today would be long forgotten by the general public were it not for the fact that his statue stands outside the Pirates' PNC Park and also because a baseball card bearing his likeness and advertising a tobacco product brought $1.2 million. (Every now and then, someone makes the news by unearthing a similar Wagner card, which in short order is deemed to be worthless.)

Of course, I never saw Wagner play, but I had reason to admire him. As a teenager I worked as a vendor at Forbes Field. Wagner, by then in his 70s, had long been employed as a coach by the Benswanger family, who owned the team and kept him in uniform as a matter of showing respect for his contributions—for example, a .328 lifetime batting average—to the franchise's history. His coaching duties, however, were mostly vague. You saw him on the field only when, during batting practice, he trundled bow-legged around the diamond, stooping over his huge belly to pick up loose baseballs and dump them into a sack he carried. It's hard to explain, but I found every step he took entertaining. Meantime, he often was the first to show up in the Pirate dugout, arriving well before the players themselves emerged from their clubhouse for practice. I suspect he showed up early knowing that a few young vendors, including me, would race to the dugout to hear him spin baseball tales from another time, punctuating them by firing shots of chewing tobacco at the dugout floor. We were crazy about the old man.

Earlier, in the latter 1930s, a Pirate right fielder named Paul Waner had become my boyhood favorite. He's now mostly remembered by occupants of nursing homes and those of us who may be headed there. A wiry man who stood 5-feet-8 and weighed little more than 150 pounds, he ran like the jackrabbits he had chased in his Oklahoma childhood; he played his position exceptionally well, and at the plate drilled doubles and triples with total nonchalance, never lifting his bat from his shoulder until the pitcher released the ball. What's more, he daily reported to the ballpark drunk or hung over. Journalists did not write of his drinking until after his career had ended, but Thomas E. Schott, a historian who described Waner in a recently published book, *Pittsburgh Sports*, reiterated Waner's problem. "There is abundant evidence," wrote Schott, "that he was a full-blown alcoholic throughout his time with the Pirates and beyond. He kept a flask sewn in his uniform, which he would nip on while in the outfield."

Also, Waner suffered from an astigmatism but eschewed eyeglasses on the field. In a conversation with the memorable manager Casey Stengel, Waner admitted that glasses brought pitches into better focus and gave him a more accurate view of the size of the ball, but without glasses he saw the ball "about as big as a grapefruit. . . . I like the big blur because I just aimed for the middle of it."

One day, my dad returned from a Pirates game and handed me a ball—he had caught a foul off Waner's bat. I was positively thrilled. Unaware that collectibles decades later would become an American craze, I raced up the street carrying my baseball glove and calling out to neighborhood friends that I owned a big-league baseball. Within ten minutes or so, we had a game of street ball going. We beat that ball till its threads unraveled.

Roberto Clemente, a folk hero to many Pirates fans, arrived on the Pittsburgh scene in 1957, by which time I had become a sportswriter. Judging from callers to sports talk shows, letters to the editor, and other unscientific measures, Clemente ranks as the Pirate public's preeminent favorite not only of his time but to this very day—above even the immensely popular slugger Willie Stargell, probably because Roberto died a hero's death on a mission of mercy. Indeed, Pittsburgh's enduring affection for him is measurable. On September 7, 2001—more than 28 years after his untimely end—the Pirates stood in last place in the National League's Central Division, 28 games out of first, and were playing at home against the Cincinnati Reds, who themselves lay 26 games out of first. What reason did a fan have to attend such a game? Well, a standing-room-only crowd of 38,683 jammed PNC Park. Pirates management had made it known that every fan in attendance would be given a seven-inch ceramic Roberto Clemente bobblehead doll.

On New Year's Eve, 1972, Roberto had boarded a plane in San Juan, his purpose being to deliver relief supplies to victims of an earthquake in Nicaragua. It was a jalopy of a plane he rode, and it plunged into the sea minutes after takeoff. His baseball legacy was that starting with his sixth big-league season he had hit well over .300 in 12 of his remaining 13 years—this in a time when the major leagues were usually as awash with superb pitching as they are lacking in that commodity today.

Yet Roberto's reputation, at least among his fellow players, carried one blemish: You could not count on him to show up in the lineup. Frequently, he begged off, complaining of injury or illness.

Teammates grumbled. If I remember correctly, it was the nonpareil second baseman Bill Mazeroski who decades later explained, "It wasn't just a matter of suspecting he was not hurt or sick. It came down to the fact that a Clemente at 50 percent was better than anyone else we could put out there."

When I traveled to San Juan in the winter of 1966 to research an *SI* profile of Puerto Rico's baseball idol, I of course intended to ask him his response to rumors that he was either a hypochondriac or one who faked injuries to play the *prima donna*. I took a cab to his handsome, Spanish-style house high atop a hill in the suburb of Rio Piedras, where from his veranda at night he could take in a glittering view of all San Juan, clear down to the bay. It was, however, late morning when I knocked on his door and said, "How are you, Roberto?"

"How *am* I?" he replied. He wore a gold oriental pajama top, tan slacks, and battered bedroom slippers. For purposes of answering my routine greeting, he walked to his 48-foot living room and lowered himself onto the carpet, sprawling on his right side and flinging his left leg over his right. On his face he wore a tortured grimace. He was about to show me how he must greet each new day in his life.

"Like dis!" he cried, and then dug his fingers into his flesh, just above his upraised left hip. He explained that he had a disk in his back that insisted on wandering, so when he awakened he was compelled to cross his legs, dig at his flesh, and listen for the sound of the disk popping back where it belonged.

"No, you cannot hear the disk now," shouted Roberto. "It is in place now. But every morning you can hear it from here to there, in the whole room. *Boop!*" Boop? Certainly, boop. Not only one boop but two, for there was another disk running around up in the vicinity of Roberto's neck. For that one, he explained, he required his wife Vera or whoever was handy to manipulate his neck muscles until the sound of the boop was heard.

All this herding of disks, I would quickly learn, was but a nub on a staggering list of medical attentions Clemente had undergone during his big-league career, which at the time was approaching its tenth year. Relatively small at 5-feet-10 and 185 pounds when able to take nourishment, he possessed smooth black skin, glistening muscles, and perfect facial contours that suggested the sturdy mahogany sculpture peddled in Puerto Rico's souvenir shops. I found him at age 31 looking back upon a career orchestrated by the clicking of X-ray machines, the scraping of scalpels, the trickle of intravenous feeding, and the scratching of pens upon prescription pads, all mounting to such a *fortissimo* that Roberto seemed a fit subject for graduate research. The moment when he first set eyes on his wife was the story of his life: He spied her, he related to me, in a drugstore, where he had gone to buy medication for an ailing leg.

Having picked himself off the living room carpet and deposited himself into a chair, he told me, "I played only two innings in the winter league this year"—his participation was much in demand by his countrymen and was a debt he felt he owed them. "I was having headaches, headaches, headaches, so I had to quit." His voice rose and swept out across the veranda and transported down the Puerto Rican hillside all the heartfelt melancholy ever sounded in sad Spanish song and story. "My head still hurts. The pain splits my head. The doctors say it's tension. They say I worry too much. I've tried tranquilizers, but they don't work. My foot is killing me. I got this tendon in my left heel that rubs against the bone, and I cannot run on it at all. I'm weary, I tell you. All the time, it's go here, speak there, do dis, do dat. Always, always, always. When I go to spring training, that's when I take my rest." Not to overlook another significant malady, Roberto mentioned insomnia, noting that nightly he lay awake worrying that he would be unable to fall asleep.

"When I don't sleep," he said, "I don't feel like eating and I lose weight."

Had he tried sleeping pills, I wondered. Yes, he answered, but they kept him awake all night.

Opera companies have performed *Parsifal* in scarcely more time than it took Roberto to get ready for bed. When the Pirates were on the road he memorized the layout of his hotel room. Where was the door, to the right? Was the window to the left? Four paces or five? "Suppose I have a nightmare and jump up. 'Hooo!' I'm screaming, and I rush through the window and my room is on the twelfth floor."

Did he have nightmares, then? "No," said Roberto.

But his point was, he *might* have a nightmare sometime, and besides, when he memorized his room he carefully noted the exact position of the telephone. Suppose it rang. He would be able to pick up the receiver without opening his eyes. When forced to open his eyes, he lamented, it frequently happened that tears welled up in them, making it perfectly impossible to fall back to sleep.

Enough, already. What did I have here, a world-class hypochondriac? I sought out his personal San Juan physician, Dr. Roberto Busó, who said, "I wouldn't call him a true hypochondriac, because he doesn't go to the extremes of just sitting down and brooding." Far from it, Roberto galloped across outfields making spectacular catches and with a bat in his hands was all over the batter's box, spinning like a top when he swung. For all his exertions, however, he *was* perpetually unfit because, as Dr. Busó went on to explain, he possessed a low threshold of pain that caused him to take minor ailments for crippling debilitations. "If his back hurts," said Busó, "he worries, and then it becomes a vicious circle, leading to more things. If he runs a little diarrhea, he worries that he has a serious stomach difficulty." Yet among his Pirate teammates and opponents as well, his reputation suffered because he was seldom able to come up with a good, visible injury—say, a nice compound fracture with a bone sticking through his flesh.

X-rays and even invasive surgery done in answer to his complaints failed to turn up fractures or even chips floating in his elbow. Roberto perceived, not entirely without justification, that white American ballplayers and management dismissed ailments claimed by Latins and American blacks as figments of their imagination. In any case, Clemente's most exotic infirmity struck him after the 1964 season, when he fell desperately ill in Puerto Rico. Dr. Busó afterward was not certain whether his patient had contracted autumnal malaria barnstorming in Santo Domingo or had picked up a systemic paratyphoid infection from hogs on a small farm he owned, but Roberto himself knew what he had. "Both," he told me.

I genuinely liked and admired Clemente—not only was he a ballplayer headed with certainty toward the Baseball Hall of Fame, but also he demonstrated a strong sense of morality, ruing increasing break-downs in behavioral standards and actively and compassionately promoting assistance to Puerto Rican youth through sports. His work in Puerto Rico lives on in the form of the Roberto Clemente Foundation, guided by his widow and their two sons, Roberto Jr. and Luis. I devoted much of my *SI* article to Clemente's abundant favorable attributes, but of course I felt bound to address his uncommon absorption with infirmities, real or imagined. As it turned out, I had had no need to probe him. He obsessed with matters of health from the moment I had knocked on his door and asked, "How are you, Roberto?" Personally, just looking at his physique and watching his continuing feats of brilliance, I had the notion he could play in the big leagues till the age of, say, 45.

Anyhow, there existed little question in my mind that when he would see himself depicted in the pages of *Sports Illustrated* as a valetudinarian, he would bristle. Teammates who long had suspected him of hypochondria or, even worse, malingering, would pick up the magazine and find fresh ammunition, and he would know they had. Lest there be any doubt he would dislike my story, *SI's* editors made his reaction a given by illustrating the piece with a full-page drawing of Roberto, labeling every component of his anatomy about which he had complained.

As I said, he did not speak to me for a year. I suspect, however, that his wife knew him better than he knew himself and was not angered by my profile of him. The last time I saw Vera, at a charity dinner, she went out of her way to give me a big hug.

What was it, I wondered, that gave Howard Cosell pause when he read my depiction of him in SI? Why had he required a few days to decide he liked my piece? Was it that he came across as an outrageous braggart, an Egotist of the Year? I reported that a man who worked closely with him and liked him had told Howard, "You are not an insufferable egotist. You are a sufferable egotist." Cosell seemed shocked. "Do you really think I'm an egotist?" he said, wounded.

But no, I doubt he was brought up short when he saw himself cast by me in that light—he considered himself overwhelmingly superior to any competitor in the field of sports reportage, be it broadcasting or print, and would say so throughout his career. My guess is that he was troubled, briefly, by my suggesting that while he postured as the most fearless reporter, commentator, and interviewer to have come to sports broadcasting, he was at the same time a fraud on the loose.

Dick Young, the lead sports columnist of the *New York Daily News,* had it right when he told me, "Howard asks better questions than the other radio and TV interviewers, but he hokes up his questions so that actually they sound better than they are. *Now truthfully*—it's always 'truthfully,' as if it's a question the guy on the other end has been ducking — *people insist that you*—people don't say it, they 'insist' it—*that you cannot take a punch, Muhammad Ali. Now truthfully, can you take a punch?"*

Indeed, Cosell dominated news conferences by grilling the principals almost as if they were courtroom defendants charged with felonies. For example, answering NFL Commissioner Pete Rozelle's call for a major news conference, Howard flumped onto a folding chair in the first row of the media seating, placing himself within range of cameras and microphones. Rozelle sat on a sofa, flanked by Dallas general manager Tex Schramm and Kansas City owner Lamar Hunt. Rozelle announced that the National Football League and the American Football League were about to merge. Soon Cosell's voice clamored for Rozelle's attention like pots and pans falling off a shelf. He demanded to know if the AFL, represented by Hunt, had forced the merger by secretly making huge offers to NFL stars. "You *know* that it's true," he told Rozelle.

"No, I do not know that it's true," the commissioner replied evenly.

"I know that it's true," Cosell barked.

He turned to Hunt, demanding a confession. Hunt equivocated.

"You mean you're negotiating for your league without knowing what your league is doing?" Howard persisted.

"I've tried to answer your question," said Hunt, painstakingly courteous. Bespectacled and mild in appearance but famously wealthy, he apologized. "I don't mean to be abrupt," he said.

"It's not a question of being abrupt, Lamar," Cosell broke in, his voice threatening to shatter Hunt's eyeglasses. "It's a question of being evasive at a time when the American people are entitled to know the truth!"

The American people lost, but Howard Cosell had won another news conference. Dick Young, the columnist I spoke to, suggested, "You've got to treat Howard the way he treats you. You've got to throw his same flamboyant crap back in his face." Perhaps so, but the men he interrogated would be risking a heavy price in public relations. Howard boasted of having staged relentless campaigns against football coaches, baseball managers, and front-office bosses.

Just as he couched routine, expected questions in accusatory words and phrases, so did he grandly congratulate himself for achievements that went with little or no notice. I tagged along with him one afternoon into a glass-enclosed ABC radio studio where he would serve up his daily four-minute sportscast. "I can break the story now!" he proclaimed in his nasally acerbic voice. (I should talk.) He thereupon let his listeners know that Charley Finley, the owner of the Kansas City Athletics baseball team, was at it again, stealthily laying plans to move his franchise to Oakland. Having exposed Finley, Howard concluded his sportscast and shouted at me, "That, you see, is a sports show. . . . I broke the story!" There was no holding him. "Now that show was a contribution, journalistically."

The *Times,* I told myself, probably would have given the scoop two inches.

Yes, as I later thought about it, I supposed that Cosell initially had disliked my story because it had zeroed in on his journalistic excesses, which he himself may not have recognized as excesses. But just as was the case in my profile of Roberto Clemente, I amply described his strengths —for example, his courage on the way up when his outspoken syndicated radio comments caused ABC salesmen and top brass to wail that he was alienating advertisers and affiliate stations. His withering opinions of manager Casey Stengel and the New York Mets may well have been the reason the Mets and their flagship station, WABC, parted company following the 1963 baseball season, but Howard refused to quiet down.

In 1970, more than two years after *Sports Illustrated* published my Cosell article, Roone Arledge, the head of ABC sports, persuaded the National Football League to play Monday-night games and made Howard part of the three-man team—Keith Jackson and Don Meredith were the other two—that would hold forth in the television booth. Jackson served as play-by-play man, and Meredith, the former Dallas quarterback, brilliantly provided folksy humor. Cosell, as he would throughout his Monday-night stint, frequently drove viewers to distraction with observations they either found belittling of their favorite team or simply stupid. I myself felt he lacked a real feel for the game—that he got by nicely on nuggets of information or opinions that coaches and players passed on to him but could not intuitively spot a talented player in the raw stages of development or sense strategy forming on the field.

But there was no mistaking that he *made* Monday-night football through his sheer presence. In fact, he made Monday night. Beano Cook, who would become a nationally recognized expert on college football but at the time served as chief sports publicist for ABC, credits Cosell with transforming Monday nights from nothing evenings when Americans recovered from weekend activities into social events where they gathered at bars or at homes to watch NFL football. They railed at Cosell but hung on his every pompous word.

He retired from the booth following the 1983 season, but nobody at ABC or at NFL headquarters made a serious effort to stop him. He had taken to reviling the NFL as a monopoly in flagrant violation of antitrust law. Also, he had created an uncomfortable relationship with the horde of ex-jocks swarming into broadcast booths by generally branding them as idiots. I did not agree, but in my thoughts I granted him good cause for his poor opinion of them. In Monday night football's second year, ABC had replaced play-by-play man Keith Jackson with bland Frank Gifford, a former New York Giants star, and Cosell was stuck with him thereafter. Whenever someone asked me if I had a hero in the world of sports, I replied, "Frank Gifford. Never have I known a broadcaster so bankrupt of talent to last so long and make so much money."

On the evening that followed the first Monday night telecast ABC carried without Howard in the booth, I took an hour-long poll of listeners to my radio talk show—had they *missed* Howard? The next morning, I phoned to tell him of my poll and to say that all but one caller had indeed missed him. "What else would you expect?" he replied. He then launched into a ten-minute diatribe, denouncing the NFL for flouting antitrust laws. When he finally stopped to draw a breath, I said, "Howard, I just thought my poll might make you feel good. It was nice talking with you."

In 1994, *Sports Illustrated* marked its 40th anniversary by republishing, issue by issue, the 40 "classics" its editors had singled out from the pack. I felt highly honored that they chose my profile of Howard Cosell. But as you may have inferred by now, the designation "professional writer" to me meant you got paid for your work. I diplomatically reminded an *SI* editor that his company was in the business of putting together each issue with a view toward keeping the magazine prosperous. We agreed upon a fee of $1,000.

Thanks for the interviews, Howard.

Chapter Twelve

Half the Steel Curtain

Three times a week, Chuck Noll ordered contact drills for his Steelers of the 1970s. Head-butting drills, the offensive and defensive linemen called them. One could measure the ferocity of such drills by the dents in the players' helmets. Once they strapped on those helmets, the offensive and defensive lines became enemies, for who enjoys receiving a blow from the man opposite him?

Assistant coaches fueled these battles that played out eerily on the turf of a stadium empty of fans. "We beat you! We beat you!" defensive line coach George Perles would crow at the offensive line, even when the offensive line had stood off his men for five seconds. Perles, a squat buffalo of a man, beamed when he perceived successes, a perfect candidate in girth and glee to wear the Santa Claus suit at a Christmas party. Ray (the Old Ranger) Mansfield, the Steelers' starting center, reflected upon Noll's staff of gifted assistant coaches and said to me, "All those field generals out there! They don't care if the whole practice is screwed up, long as *their* outfit looks good."

From those drills grew the Steel Curtain, the toughest and most talented four-man defensive line I have seen. Three of them—left end L. C. Greenwood, left tackle Joe Greene, and right end Dwight White—would win four Super Bowl rings before the '70s ran their course, and right tackle Ernie (Fats) Holmes would win two before he ate his way off the team. In 1969, Noll, in his first year as the head coach of a hapless Steeler outfit, had drafted the little-known Greene, from North Texas State, on the fourth pick of the first round. The Steelers conducted their draft that year from a suite on an upper floor of an old downtown hotel, the Roosevelt. From the street below, a handful of fans shouted, "Who's the first-round pick?"

A functionary stuck his head through an open window and yelled, "Joe Greene."

"Joe *who?*" the fans shouted back.

Greene became known as Joe Who—but only until he strode into training camp and terrorized veterans. Before he suffered a nerve injury in his neck in his sixth year, he held forth as the greatest defensive tackle I have seen play the game. Once the injury occurred, opponents decided they could double-team him—put two blockers on him—instead of *triple-*teaming him. In 1987, his first year of eligibility, he was elected to the Pro Football Hall of Fame, and I broadcast the induction ceremony from Canton, Ohio. Afterward, I said to Don Smith, the director of the Hall, "That bronze bust of Joe scarcely bears a resemblance." Smith shrugged off the comment, either disagreeing or thinking he did not care to pay the sculptor for a re-do. So much for enshrinement.

L. C. Greenwood, a lanky, quick-as-a-rattler player, for years now has been nominated for election to the Hall but has been turned away, possibly because fully 11 Steelers, including Noll and president Dan Rooney, from the Steeler Dynasty have been inducted and the Hall's board of selectors has turned its attention elsewhere. L. C. belongs. Meantime, what with Greene and Greenwood having been celebrated in articles and football books, I find my perverse nature leading me to devote attention to the lesser known half of the Steel Curtain—Dwight White and Fats Holmes.

On a Sunday evening in January of 1975, the Steelers flew to New Orleans to play Minnesota in Super Bowl IX, their first visit to the big game. On the plane, White complained to the head trainer of pain in the side of his back. "I'm really sore," he said. Noll had put his team through intensive preparation the previous week, a cold week, his plan being to ease off the week of the game. On the plane the trainer, Ralph Berlin, plastered an adhesive pack to White's back to generate heat. The traveling party landed in New Orleans and dispersed to their hotel rooms. Presently Berlin's phone rang. "I'm in Dwight's room," said Joe Greene. "You better get down here. Dwight is sick."

There would follow the most courageous performance I have seen on a football field.

Players, coaches, and front-office men called Berlin the Plumber, an irreverent but affectionate reference to his medical skills. A chunky man who seemed always to carry a cigar in the corner of his mouth, he had played football at Iowa State, where while having an injured knee attended to, he was told by the trainer, "You're the sorriest player I've ever seen. Why don't you help me out in the trainer's room?" I once asked him how he came to be known as the Plumber. To my surprise, he said, "You named me the Plumber. When Noll first came in here with all his assistants, they'd ask me, 'What about this? What about that?' I told them, 'Don't ask me, I'm just the plumber.' You got wind of it and named me the Plumber on your radio show. The plumbers' union gave me a gold card and made me an honorary plumber."

Okay, the Plumber rode the elevator down to Dwight White's room and found him on all fours. "He looked like a St. Bernard," Berlin told me. "I said to Joe Greene, 'We'll take him to a hospital.' We located a station wagon and put the back seat down so Dwight could crawl into the wagon and stay on all fours."

The nearest hospital fell short of being another Mayo Clinic. "It was like a MASH unit," Berlin recalled. "People in the emergency room who'd been stabbed, that sort of thing. We put Dwight on a gurney and told the nurse we were with the Pittsburgh Steelers. She said, 'You'll have to wait.' "

While they waited, lengthily, two nurses recognized Greene and approached him for autographs. He blew up. "We gotta get outta here!" he told Berlin. The Plumber thereupon phoned the New Orleans Saints' internist, Dr. Charles Brown, who directed him to take White to a hospital favored by the Saints. Meantime, the Plumber phoned the Steelers' traveling secretary, Buff Boston, who tracked down the Steelers' orthopedist, John Best, heartily enjoying the night at the bar of the Pontchartrain Hotel. Shortly thereafter, Dr. Best—a broad-shouldered man in his 60s and standing about 6-feet-4—barged through the emergency room, searching for the bed upon which White had been lain. A nurse stopped him. "You can't come in here!" she snapped.

Dr. Best, whom Steeler players had nicknamed John Wayne, identified himself and said, "Get the fuck outta my way!"

Doc possessed a booming voice that in routine conversation could be heard 50 yards away. Once, on the morning of a Steelers game, I watched him check out a player's injured knee. He squeezed it. The player let out a yelp. "Har! Har! Har!" roared Doc, and yes, his laughter actually took the form of a series of hars. "That doesn't hurt, does it?" What Doc lacked in bedside manner, he more than made up in surgical skills. He saved Rocky Bleier's Steeler career by repairing a foot torn by shrapnel in Vietnam—a wound army surgeons had worked on without much success. At any rate, Best now located Dwight White, flat on his back. Doc seized him by the shoulders and sat him up with a jolt.

"You sonofabitch!" Doc thundered. "I've waited all my life for the Steelers to be in a championship game and maybe even win it. Don't you dare die on me now!"

Soon after Best issued his ultimatum, the Saints' internist, Dr. Brown, arrived and diagnosed White with severe pneumonia complicated by pleurisy, a lung infection. Three nights later, Wednesday, the Steelers' own internist, Dr. Dave Huber, flew into New Orleans and first thing the next morning hustled to check out his extremely sick patient. White, known as Mad Dog, at age 25 was a round-faced black man who ran the gamut of human emotions from compassion to anger to hilarious whimsy, and none of them in moderate doses. The season before, the talented humorist Roy Blount Jr. had attached himself to the Steelers for an entire football season and written *About Three Bricks Shy of a Load*, the best football book I have read. Of Dwight White he wrote, "As an announcer of himself to hotel desk clerks, he was expansive: 'That's me. The man who walked the water and tied the wind, come to bring good to your neighborhood. You can see me free till Sunday.'" Dwight would go on to become, at this writing, senior managing director of a financial services firm and never changed an iota, but now, from his hospital bed, he told Dr. Huber, "I want out of here. I want to practice." In fact, he insisted he be discharged.

Ralph Berlin drove him directly to practice and saw a defensive end who not only had lost considerable weight but also demonstrated no stamina whatever. "He could not lift a leg," Berlin remembers. Noll told the Plumber, "Take him back to the hospital. Pump him full of antibiotics. Whatever."

Early the morning of Super Sunday, Berlin's phone rang. "Come get me!" barked White. Obtaining permission from Dr. Best, Berlin fetched White from his hospital bed to the team's pregame meal at the hotel. "He managed to eat a little bit," Berlin remembers, "but he looked awful. He was just drained, and I don't know how much weight he'd lost."

Once at the stadium, White had his ankles taped and put on his game pants. Dr. Huber—a tall, husky man who surely had played football, though I never thought to ask—studied his patient and said, "What are you intending to do?"

"I'm going out there and warm up."

"You can't do that," Huber replied.

Doc Best piped up. "He's been a big part of this team. Let him go out. He'll just pass out on the field, and that'll be the end of the argument."

Dwight, however, survived the warmups and upon returning to the locker room confronted Noll. "I want to play, and I want to start." Noll glanced at Huber for an opinion, but Best intervened. He said to Huber, "Let him play. How long can he last, one series?"

White played virtually the entire game. He cannot remember that early in the fourth quarter he sat out a few plays, huddled under blankets, Drs. Best and Huber hovering over him. Quickly, he returned to the field and played on until the Steeler defense took the field for the final two plays, victory assured. How difficult had his ordeal been? "You know what?" he said to me not long ago. "It was all kind of a blur."

For a Super Bowl, the weather was ugly—46 degrees at kickoff and damp to the point of being bone-chilling for spectators. Nonetheless, the pneumonia patient played on, series after series, as the Steelers beat the Vikings, 16-6, with a ferocious demonstration of defense. Was it in the Vikings' game plan to test Dwight? The media, of course, had reported him missing from practice all week, save Thursday. Steeler management had vaguely attributed his absence to "a viral infection," irritating the press corps, who wanted specifics but got none. The Steelers' refusal to elaborate probably did not constitute an attempt to downplay the severity of Dwight's illness in hope of deceiving the Vikings. Vikes coach Bud Grant had to suspect that Mad Dog was as sick as, well, a dog. Steeler management, in my analysis, had been evasive simply because NFL teams had become leery of going on record with medical particulars. Dick Butkus, the great Chicago linebacker, at the time was suing no fewer than five doctors employed by the Bears. The Steelers would issue no details of White's illness that might be hurled back at them in a courtroom.

Of their first eight running plays, the Vikings ran seven to the left, where Fats Holmes and Dwight had dug in. Three times Dwight stopped the hard-running Dave Osborn in his tracks—Osborn lost a yard the first time, gained nothing the second, and gained only one the third. Not until Minnesota's final series of the first half did quarterback Fran Tarkenton give up and begin directing his ground plays to the right instead of the left. Those three tackles by Dwight in the end amounted to his total for the game, but it so happened that no Steeler made more than four, simply because the Pittsburgh defense stuffed Minnesota so thoroughly that the Vikes were able to run only 47 offensive plays, which can happen when you're making only nine first downs. Twenty-one times the Vikes ran the ball, producing a total of but 17 yards. Dwight White had held up his end of the Curtain.

Had he so much as thought about taking himself out of the game for a play or two to gather his strength? "Nope," he says. "What I remember, though, was that our players kept asking me in the huddle, 'How you feeling?' It was annoying."

At lunch not long ago, Ralph Berlin told me, "He was as sick as any player I've ever seen." After the game ended, the word got out that he had lost 18 pounds in the hospital.

Anyhow, and for whatever reason, Berlin at lunch remembered a time when he and Dwight had posed together for a photograph. Both of them removed their dental plates and smiled broadly for the camera. "When I got my print of the picture," the Plumber recalled, "Dwight signed it. He wrote, 'We have bridged the gap.' " Together, they had done just that in New Orleans.

On a Saturday night in December, 1975, slightly more than 11 months after Super Bowl IX, I stood alongside several reporters at the bar of a Los Angeles hotel. I had flown that day from Pittsburgh to broadcast the next day's Steeler game against the Rams. Close to ten o'clock, I said, "Gents, it was a long trip, and I'm tired. I'm going to retire early." I walked up a short flight of stairs to the lobby and pushed an elevator button. At the same time, a number of players filed into the lobby, having returned from dinner at various restaurants to make their 11 o'clock curfew with time to spare. An enormous black man approached me and firmly placed a large, meaty hand on my shoulder. "Cope," said Ernie (Fats) Holmes, "let's go down to the bar and have a Courvoisier."

Fats weighed about 300 pounds in an era when 300-pound football players remained rare. He favored Courvoisier, a French cognac, and was known to swill it down like beer. Also, players throughout the NFL knew him as, well, temperamental and no man to trifle with. Pondering his invitation for about two seconds, I looked up into his small, beady eyes and said, "Sounds good to me, Fats."

Phil Musick, a sports columnist, sidled up to me as I stood alongside Fats at the bar. "I thought you were tired and going to bed."

"I am tired," I replied. I then related the invitation that Fats had issued in the lobby and explained, "If Fats had said to me, 'Cope, let's go down to the bar and have an enema,' I'd be down here having an enema."

From his right-tackle position in the Steel Curtain, Fats half-defeated his opponents before they threw their first block. He lined up and straightaway announced to the man opposite him, "I'm gonna kick your ass." Mind you, in the 1970s trash talk as yet had not become the personal, self-advertised style of those many who would later embrace it—in fact, the term had not yet been coined. So when Fats relentlessly insulted his opponents and their mothers and wives as well, he alarmed them, largely because his reputation for unpredictability had preceded him. Early in his Steeler career, after the football season had ended, he set out in his car for his home in Texas and seemed to be in a hurry. On the Ohio Turnpike troopers swung onto the highway in pursuit. Fats pressed the pedal to the floor. The troopers, gaining no ground, radioed for a police helicopter, which arrived and followed Fats overhead. Annoyed by the unexpected intruder, Fats reached for a handgun he carried in his car. He stuck it through an open window and fired a shot into the air—to give him the benefit of the doubt, a shot meant only as a warning (as when a warship fires across an enemy vessel's bow). Alas, the bullet penetrated the bottom of the copter and nicked the pilot in his foot.

The troopers might have pursued Fats unsuccessfully clear across Ohio, but one by one his tires blew. He soon was driving on wheels. So he abandoned his car and fled into a patch of woods. The troopers captured him, but they could not handcuff him because their cuffs would not fit around his wrists.

Now before I continue Fats Holmes's Ohio Turnpike episode, I feel obliged to put it into perspective. It was trivial compared to the alleged murders, drug deals, money-laundering, and woman-beatings we have come to expect in our sports pages these days. Moreover, encountering Fats now and then over the years, I have found him to be a totally jolly, God-fearing citizen. In 1999 the Steelers convened a 25th-year reunion of the squad that had won the club's first championship in Super Bowl IX. Dan Rooney threw a splendid party at a downtown hotel and invited each man to rise and briefly tell the others what he'd been up to lately. Fats became expansive. Easily weighing more than 400 pounds by now, he smiled from ear to ear as he extolled the fellowship to be had from football, the memories to be cherished; he went on to express the hope that all his teammates were as fortunate as he to have the good Lord Jesus looking over him. Finally, the former guard Moon Mullins began lightly booing. Others joined in and rapped their water glasses with spoons. Still smiling, Fats looked upon them with affection and took his seat.

Among the gathering sat Buff Boston, the Steelers' longtime traveling secretary, contract negotiator, and troubleshooter. Perhaps he was remembering a meeting with Fats in a jail cell. The Ohio police had incarcerated Fats in Youngstown, whereupon Rooney dispatched Buff to the scene. Buff entered Fats's cell just as Fats had been served dinner. "You hungry?" Fats asked.

"Not especially," Buff replied.

"Well, if you want, you can have my meal. I ain't gonna eat this shit." Possibly it was the first meal Fats ever turned down.

Rooney, of course, engaged a lawyer for Fats and sent Doc Best to attend Fats's hearing. Courts in those days were more lenient than now, and besides, many Steelers fans resided in Youngstown and were rooting for Fats to be set free. Thus Best, though his profession was bones, not minds, persuaded the judge to release Fats into his custody, promising to place him in Pittsburgh's Western Psychiatric Hospital for care. Fats's first day there, Buff visited.

"How long I got to stay here?" Fats asked with annoyance. "All the people here are crazy."

In the end, his Ohio escapade surely strengthened his game, for it doubled his ability to strike fear into his opponents' hearts. Nor did his own teammates take him lightly. Jack Lambert, who feared no man, nevertheless gave Fats a wide berth. At a bachelor party Fats's teammates threw for him just before he married, he suddenly became vexed—for some forgotten reason—with Bennie Cunningham, a 6-foot-6, 270-pound tight end. He pointed a finger at Bennie and said, "I want you to go stand in the corner." Bennie went to a corner of the room. He stood there throughout the party.

Even George Perles, Fats's defensive line coach, took care to avoid Fats's wrath. One weekday, after the team had taken the field for practice, Ralph Berlin found Fats seated at his locker wearing his football uniform and over it, as was commonly the case for him, a rubber suit for sweating off weight. "Why aren't you out there on the field?" the trainer asked him.

"I'm not gonna practice," said Fats. That day, he had argued with the front office over an advance in pay. His anger had come to a boil.

"Fats, you better get out there."

"No. I ain't gonna practice."

Berlin shrugged and headed for the field. Perles spied him and said, "Where's Fats?" Berlin told him that Fats was on strike. "Go back there," said Perles, "and get his ass out here." Berlin returned to the locker room but could not budge Fats from his stool and had no more interest in debating Fats than he might have in climbing a volcanic mountain in the face of a pending eruption. Back on the field, he said to Perles, "Fats ain't coming out." Perles surely could speak with the voice of authority if he himself went to the locker room and *ordered* Fats to get his ass onto the field, but the coach weighed the possible risks of intervention—namely, that he might end up requiring Berlin's services as a trainer. He sent Berlin back to the locker room a second time, and later, a third. Finally, Berlin said to him, "Look, I told you he's not coming out. You want him out here, *you* go get him."

Instead, Perles practiced his line sans Fats. The next day Fats, apparently having gotten the front office to bend, called off his strike.

Probably, on the previous day, Perles should have sent Joe Greene to get Fats. Greene, who had come from college football nicknamed Mean Joe Greene, was the only Steeler Fats feared. On the morning of home games, a stereo blared music through the locker room, but Jack Hart, who carried the title of field manager, routinely turned off the stereo a half-hour before the squad took the field for warmups. One Sunday morning when Hart switched off the stereo, Fats lumbered across the room and switched it back on. Hart said, "Ernie, you know it's orders the stereo is turned off"—and once more turned it off. Fats again turned it on. At this point, Joe Greene arose from his stool. He tore the stereo's wiring out of the wall. That was that.

Another time, in the midst of a game played on a cold winter day, Joe became exasperated with Fats, for Fats had taken to freelancing instead of playing the prescribed defensive schemes. "You're not playing the defense," Joe screamed at him. "Get off the field!"

Fats sheepishly retired to the bench. Perles hollered at him above the din of the crowd, "Why aren't you on the field?"

"Joe told me to get off. I'm not gonna go back in till Joe tells me it's okay."

When the defense came off the field, Joe was steaming. Perles gingerly approached him. To calm him, Perles put his left hand on Joe's shoulder and with his right rubbed his belly as one might caress a dachshund that has flopped on its back with its legs in the air. "Now, Joe," he said, "we need Fats on the field. Tell him it's okay."

Joe relented. Fats returned to the action.

As I mentioned earlier, Fats Holmes ate his way off the Steeler roster after having played only six seasons, but he had been a force in the NFL and is remembered as a charter member of the Steel Curtain. Hey, it was his nature to eat heartily and gain weight, and he had fought the battle by practicing in that rubber suit, even on sweltering days in training camp. He even attempted a diet. One Sunday morning on the road, he sat down to the team's pregame meal at the Steelers' hotel, the first player to arrive in the dining hall. He joined Buff Boston and Ralph

Berlin, who customarily ate before the players showed up. "I'm on a diet," Fats announced. "I'm starting a diet today. I'm having only a salad."

Forthwith, he walked to the buffet and picked up a huge bowl of salad that was meant to serve a procession of players. He liberally doused it with dressing and sat down to his meal. So much for Fats's diet.

I have had a genuine fondness for the Fat Man, as Ernie was also known. In a battle against the hated Browns in Cleveland, Browns defensive end Turkey Jones made a play on Terry Bradshaw that for old-timers lives in infamy. He lifted Bradshaw high into the air and violently planted him upside-down on his neck as if driving a spike into the hardened turf. Afterward, at the Cleveland airport, an ambulance carried Bradshaw onto the tarmac where all of us in the traveling party stood waiting for Terry to be transferred to the team's plane. He had been strapped to a so-called spine board, on which he lay as medics removed him from the ambulance. "Let me have him," Fats told them. He wrapped his mighty arms under the spine board, arched his broad back, and alone carried the big quarterback up the stairway into the plane. On instructions from team doctors, he gently carried Terry the length of the aisle to the plane's farthermost reaches where the arms of seats had been retracted to create a makeshift bed.

Years later, when Fats Holmes returned to Pittsburgh for that 25th anniversary of the Steelers' first championship team, he told his teammates he loved them. He meant it.

Chapter Thirteen

On Football Coaches

I like football coaches. I can think of very few among the many assistant and head coaches I've known over the years with whom I've felt ill at ease. True, I've known some who were schemers or phonies or job-jumpers who asked loyalty of their players but did not hesitate to break a contract when a better one lay elsewhere. Bill Parcells received the break of his life when New York Giants owner Wellington Mara and General Manager George Young promoted him to head coach. In time he would rank among the great NFL coaches, yet after he won Super Bowl XXV in his eighth season, he secretly schemed to jump to the Atlanta Falcons, whose owner, Rankin Smith, in the end decided Parcells was too expensive. Parcells moved around and won big and made good copy for reporters, but I forever thought of him as a man I would not care to have working for me.

As nearly as I can pin down the reason, I have liked the vast majority of coaches I've known because, while under constant pressure to produce or hire a moving van, they remain earthy and as forthcoming as their job allows them to be, and they probably would rather coach than be Bill Gates. Joe Walton comes to mind. He was head coach of the New York Jets for seven years—he pitched a strong seven, as baseball writers say of a pitcher who had to be relieved—and then signed on in 1990 as offensive coordinator with the Steelers. He brought with him his Jets playbook. During training camp, in a room where coaches and media gathered for a cold beer following afternoon practices, I noticed that almost every day, Walton and his new boss, Chuck Noll, huddled in a corner, locked earnestly in conversation. Clearly, Noll felt he had found a brilliant coordinator.

Joe lasted two years, leaving when Noll retired. Players had complained that his playbook confused them. In a late-season game his second season, the Houston Oilers were pounding the Steelers, 31-6, whereupon Joe ordered quarterback Bubby Brister—once a starter but now a backup—into the game. Bubby refused to go in. "I ain't nobody's mop-up man," he told Joe. Gone from the Steelers, Joe traveled up the road to Robert Morris College, a small school that had not fielded a football team but now wanted to. The suburban campus lay not far from Beaver Falls, PA, where Joe had grown up. He would be home and doing what he loved to do—coach. Once the boss of an NFL team, he would field a team in Division II's no-scholarships category.

He immediately won five straight national championships. I ran into him not long ago at a golf tournament fundraiser he hosted and said to him, "Some of the Steeler players said they couldn't understand your playbook. I suppose you simplified it when you took over at Robert Morris."

"Nah," Joe answered. "It's the New York Jets playbook. My college kids have no problem. The Steelers had no problem. It was just that Brister couldn't remember the formations."

Coaches must coach till it's time to go fishing. Never mind that only a few of them achieve their dream of being boss. Tony Dungy worked 15 years as an NFL assistant until he became head coach of the Tampa Bay Bucs and in his second season there took the Bucs to their first playoff appearance in 12 years. While he had waited for his big break, sportswriters across the country periodically championed him, as if saying to themselves, "It's time for a Tony Dungy column." They blasted NFL owners for failing to hire Tony to fill head-coaching vacancies, writing that the only possible reason for his being repeatedly passed over was that he was black. Perhaps that was true, but I wondered. I had my own theory.

Tony had been a coaching prodigy. He was only 25 when Chuck Noll made him a Steelers defensive assistant and just 28 when Noll promoted him to defensive coordinator. Here, surely, was a promising football mind destined to be an NFL head coach. But in his fifth year as coordinator, a new linebackers coach moved in. He brimmed with ideas and caught Noll's ear. "Come on, Tony," I remember silently rooting. "Assert yourself. Don't let this guy take over."

At season's end, Noll informed Tony he would be demoted—he would coach only defensive backs. Understandably, Tony declined to hang around and suffer embarrassment. He moved to Kansas City to coach the Chiefs' defensive backs and eventually regained his coordinator status with Minnesota. While he fashioned formidable defenses with the Vikings, I could not help but think that word travels on the football grapevine—Tony had let the linebackers coach steal Noll's ear. Was he head-coaching material or a wimp? In time, he answered the question, but the grapevine may have delayed his rise to the top for years.

When he at last made it, Tony coached Tampa Bay to the playoffs in four of his six seasons, whereupon the thanks he received from his employer, club owner Malcolm Glazer, was notice he'd been fired. Apparently nothing but a Super Bowl could satisfy Glazer and three of his sons, each an executive vice president of the team. They had secretly negotiated to bring Bill Parcells out of retirement. I took pleasure in the events that followed. Tony in just eight days became head coach of the Indianapolis Colts, and Parcells soon after decided to stay retired, leaving the Glazers groping 35 days for a coach (and looking for all the world like the NFL's Idiot Family of the Year) until landing Oakland's John Gruden by shelling out a king's ransom. My own view of Tony Dungy's firing was biased, of course. Earlier, during his final season in Tampa, a Pittsburgh sportswriter told me he'd phoned Tony for help on a story and that Tony had said, "Tell Myron I said hello. How's he doing?" A geezer of a broadcaster who likes most coaches appreciates their remembering him.

Meantime, until genetic science proves otherwise, no formula for fashioning a winning coach exists. Successful coaches bring with them varying temperament—Dungy low-key, Parcells acerbic, Bill Walsh brazenly convinced of his own genius—as well as a range of methods, operating styles, and convictions. During the Steelers' spectacular run in the 1970s, I fell into a conversation about the coaching profession with Bud Carson, the team's highly regarded defensive coordinator. He brought up the role of the offensive line coach. "In my whole lifetime," he said, "I have not known three great offensive line coaches." Clearly, Carson viewed Dan (Bad Rad) Radakovich, his colleague on the Steelers staff, as a gem among the breed. "You must be willing to stay involved with fundamentals," Carson went on, "but for most people, fundamentals are boring. Rad does a *helluva* job."

Fundamentals, as opposed to teaching assignments and schemes, are the teaching and reteaching of the mechanics of getting the job done. Having heard Carson's praise of Bad Rad (his players had given him the name by way of protesting his biting candor and the long meetings he put them through), I sat down with Rad. "Fundamentals?" he bristled. "I don't believe in the word fundamentals. I've never in my life used the word."

"I'm confused," I said.

"If you're not teaching assignments, people say you're teaching fundamentals, but I'm teaching assignments *and* how to accomplish them. And that's all there is to it."

Okay, okay. One coach's semantics is another's disgust. Radakovich, by the way, is an important reason Joe Walton's college team won five straight championships. After coaching four college teams and seven NFL teams, Rad at age 57 became Joe's defensive coordinator.

As I approach the 2002 season, my 33rd year in the Steelers' booth, I find it remarkable that I have covered only two Steeler head coaches—22 years with Noll and going on 11 with Bill Cowher. In a business that sends capable coaches flying out the door after one or two losing seasons, the Steelers remain an organization in which Dan Rooney prizes stability. In 2000 his team finished 9-and-7 and missed the playoffs for the third straight year, but Rooney said, "I thought Bill Cowher did a terrific job."

Noll, from the day he retired and accepted the vague title of Administration Advisor, has made only rare visits to the Steelers' offices and has scrupulously avoided uttering a word that might be interpreted as being critical of his successor. Comparing the two, however, is an inescapable exercise, so let's start with eyes and mouths.

When displeased, as I have written, Noll would fix a player with "the glare," his eyes narrowed, his lips a slash on his face. Dejan Kovacevic, a *Pittsburgh Post-Gazette* sportswriter, nicely described Cowher in his angry moments. He wrote, "The jaw juts out, the eyes widen, and the mouth curls downward into a bitter arch."

I once found myself on the receiving end of the Cowher look. On a Friday afternoon, he and I had finished taping *The Bill Cowher Show* in a small office at the Steeler complex. Lately I had fallen into a habit of voicing smart-aleck opinions and waiting for Cowher to agree or, as was mostly the case, disagree. I had strayed from the policy I followed throughout my years of conducting both *The Chuck Noll Show* and *The Bill Cowher Show*—"It's not *The Myron Cope Show*. You'll have your say, Cope, on your own broadcast time." On this particular Friday, Cowher headed back to his office but suddenly reappeared in the doorway of our taping room. "What the *hell* is this?" he bellowed. "Every week, I come here to tape and have to argue with you over crap. Every week it's not a goddam show but an argument!" Sure enough, his eyes grew saucer-like.

He was, of course, dead right. "Your point is well taken," I said. "Do you want to retape the show?"

"No, I don't want to retape the show!" he flared, the famous long jaw aimed at me like the butt of an ax handle. His voice brought Ron Wahl, the public-relations chief, from his nearby office, alarmed. Wahl stood silent as Cowher turned on his heel to leave but suddenly pivoted to reiterate that he was sick and tired of arguing with me over crap. Is it not instructive to know what confronts a *player* when he's come to the bench after having gummed up a play?

Actually, Cowher's capacity for raw emotion serves him well. In each of his first six years as the Steelers' head coach, he took the team to the playoffs, tying an NFL record set by the little giant Paul Brown. The next two years, the Steelers lost more games than they won. There were many reasons, but one, I suspected, was that Cowher seemed bent on modifying his personality, and not surprisingly. In November of 1998, en route to his first losing season, his team lost to Tennessee in a game in which he had yanked his quarterback, Kordell Stewart, and replaced him with Mike Tomczak. Steaming, the coach appeared for his obligatory post-game news conference, but a relatively new wrinkle had been added to this ritual: The Steelers the year before had struck a deal with a television station to televise these news conferences live. Right off the bat, a reporter asked an obvious question. Would Cowher bench Stewart and start Tomczak in the next game?

"No," was Cowher's short, emphatic reply. Reporters pressed him to elaborate and here came the jutted jaw, the mustachioed downswept mouth, the saucer eyes, and contentious answers. For the reporters, this was nothing new, but for the unwashed public watching the telecast, a monster had suddenly appeared. Horrified callers jammed the talk-show lines. The *Post-Gazette* splashed the story across page one, with close-up photos of Cowher's wrathful countenance. The next season, 1999, Bill— as a consequence, I thought—pursued a behavioral modification program. For one thing, he tempered his demeanor on the sidelines, where he knew he was on prominent display. "I'm a father," he told me by way of explanation not long ago. In other words, how might his three daughters, the two eldest in their teens, be affected when seeing him portrayed as a raving bully?

Nonetheless, I thought him mistaken to tone down his persona in the wake of that televised postgame confrontation with the media. Other NFL coaches had exploded at reporters with equal fury and exceeded Cowher by including unlimited profanity. Besides, is it Cowher's fault that God, or genes, gave him a face made for the ultimate in anger?

In the season of 2000, he returned to being his passionate self and returned his team to winning. "When you're winning, people can accept your temper," he said. Hell, they find it charming. At any rate, Rooney must have decided the reversion looked good on his coach. He had Cowher under contract for two more years but extended the contract three additional years.

Cowher had grown up in Crafton, an old middle-class suburb on the edge of Pittsburgh, and had often heard my radio and television shows; maybe, when he came home in 1992 to coach the Steelers, it was his familiarity with my work that at once made him feel comfortable sharing off-the-record insights. "This puts me five years ahead of Noll's timetable," I told myself. A retired baseball writer and longtime friend, Charley Feeney, made it his standing policy to interrupt sports figures when they said, "Off the record . . ." Feeney would say, "Hold it. I don't want to hear it. If I hear it, I can't print it. I might hear it from another source and be able to print it." Personally, I welcomed Cowher's off-the-record comments, as I have those of other coaches, because such confidences provide a better understanding of my subject matter, making it possible to deliver a more intelligent broadcast.

At any rate, I have found Cowher to be, unlike Noll, an uncomplicated man who brings as firm a hand as Noll's was to a complicated job. He often reads Patricia Cornwell thrillers before retiring but is largely a couch potato who sits ready to soak up just about any sporting competition television offers. He even watches billiards. Hot dog! The BCA Open 9-Ball Championship, Men's Final, is coming on at nine on ESPN2! He was Kansas City's defensive coordinator when the Steelers hired him in January 1992, and I assume that wherever he'd coached, he periodically visited Pittsburgh (where his parents and two brothers lived) and maintained at least a cursory knowledge of, say, the city's political leadership, if only from glancing at a newspaper. At a luncheon I toastmastered three or four months after Bill returned home to stay, he took his assigned seat on the dais next to an elderly lady seated to his immediate left. She happened to be the mayor of Pittsburgh.

"I'm Bill Cowher," he said, introducing himself.

"I'm Sophie Masloff," she replied. "Nice to meet you."

"What do you do for a living?" Bill asked.

No, I doubt that he stays abreast of China policy or global-warming issues.

In further contrast to Noll, Cowher has performed a lucrative TV commercial or two and retains an agent. Noll retained no agent, nor did his negotiations, unlike Cowher's, ever prompt a single newspaper story.

The media simply took it for granted he would coach the Steelers as long as he cared to coach. My guess is that a mere handshake with Rooney would have suited him fine, but whenever Dan Rooney thought it appropriate he would suggest a raise and hand Chuck a new contract to sign. In terms of business style, Cowher, en route to earning in the neighborhood of $3 million a year, has come off as a mercenary when compared to Noll. But hey, Noll was the last breath of fresh air before free agency came to the NFL in 1993, more than a year after he had retired; free agency not only spawned legions of mercenary players but at the same time spurred coaches to hire agents and grab as big a slice of football's pie as they could capture. Bill Cowher simply is in lockstep with the times.

Besides, his job is more difficult than Noll's was. At dinner with Chuck not very long ago, I asked him, "Could you have coached in this era of free agency?"

He winced. He did not answer the question but simply said, "By the time you teach these players to play football, they're apt to be gone."

Football, of course, is an entertainment industry and as such expects its coaches to huckster the product. For example, the NFL for decades now has commanded all head coaches to conduct a news conference once per week throughout the season; I imagine most of the coaches would rather lunch on assorted cooked insects than present themselves to the media for, say, 45 minutes, but duty calls, because the weekly ritual not only cultivates publicity but brings in revenue as well. Teams sell radio and television broadcast rights to the news conferences and tack up banners advertising banks or other sponsors on the wall behind the coach so that cameras hopefully do not miss them. By the time Bill Cowher arrived on the Steeler scene in 1992, the weekly news conference had deteriorated into a mish-mash of worthwhile information-seeking questions mixed with unwelcome posturing by broadcaster types. Hey, had not Sam Donaldson become big-time by firing fractious questions at U. S. Presidents in front of the cameras?

At any rate, in the season of 2001—a mostly happy adventure during which the Steelers advanced clear to the AFC championship game—I noticed early at Cowher's news conferences an abrupt change in him. From out of left field in his tenth season came a new Cowher seated behind the table at the front of the room. In previous years he had been something of a Mr. Malaprop, butchering the English language from time to time. For example, he frequently employed the word "deter" but pronounced it "deteer". Reporters silently snickered. Other gaffes arose. While taping his pregame radio show one Friday, he spoke of a bench warmer who was making the most of opportunity. "You never know," he said and dipped into baseball lore. "Wally Pipp took a day off from a Yankees game, and Babe Ruth replaced him, and Pipp never got his job back."

"Bill," I said. "It wasn't Babe Ruth. It was Lou Gehrig."

Bill arched an eyebrow but said, "Nah, it was Babe Ruth."

But now, in 2001, there appeared at the head of the room an articulate master of the news conference routine. So far as I can recall, I heard not one "deteer". On the receiving end of a question he did not care to answer, he might smile and say, "I leave the answer to your imagination," and, lightly applying a needle, add, "I know you have a very good imagination." He knew the first names of maybe half the gathered media—no small achievement for a head coach—and addressed them by name. Of course, when a coach is winning big as Cowher was that season, aggravating questions diminish. The next season could be hell.

Still, Cowher had long believed in learning from his mistakes and clearly had taken stock of testy brushes he'd had with the media in earlier news conferences and remodeled himself. At his final news conference, held two days after a shocking loss to New England in the AFC championship game, he concluded by congratulating the media on a job well done and saying he had enjoyed working with them. I'd guess not everybody in the room bought the diplomacy, but a little civility never hurts.

Meantime, given the fickle nature of NFL owners, many coaches live every season on the edge of being fired. These days, some of those who win have adopted a rule of thumb: Don't stay in one place too long. In other words, jump to another club while you're winning and remain attractive. Cowher, however, will have coached the Steelers 14 years if he serves out his latest extension. "I'm home," he says. "I can go over to Crafton and have a beer with my dad on the front porch. And I have an owner who has patience. Dan knows it's difficult to stay on top every season."

Football lore has it that when Charley Bidwill owned the Chicago Cardinals (later the St. Louis Cardinals and still later, the Arizona Cardinals) in the 1930s and '40s, his head coach requested a pay raise. "Hell," said Bidwill, "do you know how many guys would love to have your job? I can open the front door right now and yell into the street, 'There's a vacancy here for a football coach!' and 50 guys will come running." Bidwill's head coaches, however, came and went, hired and fired. In the 16 years he operated the franchise, he employed seven of them. For Dan Rooney, by contrast, stability is fundamental. "It's good for the public, it's good for the players, and it's good for the coaches," he says. Are you paying attention in Tampa, Glazers? My own view is that if I owned a football team, I, like Rooney, would remain patient through disappointing seasons, for the simple reason that one never knows what he's getting when a new man sits down at the head coach's desk.

Chapter Fourteen

Coach Cope
I Almost Had it Right on Kordell

From time to time over the years, football coaches have addressed me as Coach Cope. They've mostly conferred the title upon me good-naturedly, but in my argumentative moments I suspected sarcasm in their tone. Actually, I once coached a football game—a college game—with nearly devastating effect upon my opponent.

"Let's have lunch," John Majors had said on the phone one spring day in 1974. "We'll go first class, go up to The LeMont on Mt. Washington." Majors the year before had moved from Iowa State to become head coach at the University of Pittsburgh and at once had invigorated a pathetic program, thanks in great part to a dazzling 160-pound freshman tailback named Tony Dorsett, who would take Pitt to the national championship, win the Heisman Trophy, and go on to superstardom with the Dallas Cowboys.

"What's up?" I asked Majors.

"Tell you when we get there," he replied mysteriously.

He also invited Bill Currie, a droll sports anchorman at rival KDKA-Television. When we were seated, Majors went straight to the point. "Our annual spring intrasquad game, the Blue-Gold game, is coming up Saturday after this. Coach Cope, I want you to be head coach of the Blue team. Coach Currie, you coach the Gold team. We need to get more people out to the spring game, so maybe you guys can have some fun with this on the air and pump up a little interest in the game."

"What does it mean, being head coach?" I asked.

"I'll be in the press box," Majors said. "Of course, I'll have my coordinators running the two teams. But you guys can come out to practice Wednesday and put in one or two plays and then stand on the sideline Saturday looking important."

Wednesday, I put in a spread formation—receivers spread sideline to sideline. I was ahead of the times. Spread formations would not become common for years to come. Meantime, I saved my most devilish surprise for the pregame locker room pep talk, which I intended to dominate. Majors had put his defensive coordinator, Jackie Sherrill, in charge of my Blue squad, but alas, Dorsett was assigned to Currie's Gold. At any rate, my Blues gathered 'round in the locker room, and Sherrill informed them I had a few words to say. I stood up and asked Sherrill, "Who are our two fastest receivers?"

He named a couple of compact, black fellows—one named McCray, the other I cannot remember. "Men," I said to them, "when Dorsett and his offense go on the field, I want both of you to stand next to me, one on either side. When they give Dorsett the ball, and if we see him break the slightest bit into daylight, I'm gonna yell, 'Go!' And you two race onto the field and clobber him high and low." Sherrill's face turned ashen. "You can't do that!" he hollered. "That's illegal!"

"Sure it's illegal," I said. I whipped a rulebook from my back pocket. "It's a 15-yard penalty tacked onto the foul. I'd rather give 'em 15 more yards than watch Dorsett go all the way."

Sherrill, his mouth open, found nothing to say. He realized I had studied the rule. I had a play that just might end Dorsett's sophomore season before it was to begin. Hey, I'm a competitor.

The first series Dorsett played proved uneventful. The second time our opponents' offense took the field, no Dorsett appeared. The public-address announcer intoned to the fans:

"Tony Dorsett will be unable to play the remainder of today's game. He has a stomach disorder."

Sherrill, of course, had phoned my secret play to Majors in the press box, where Majors acted decisively. In the end, Bill Currie's Gold squad, sans Dorsett, defeated my Blue squad, but my special play would be remembered as the plan of the decade, in my own mind.

While I am indulging myself, allow me to say that if Coach Cope all these years has known a single thing about football, it is that he can recognize brilliance when he first sees it. "Well," you might say, "what's the big deal about that?" True, but you would be surprised how many coaches, talent scouts, and media fail to widen their eyes at first sight of brilliant talent and do not pay attention until the talent has amassed enough statistics to make a special impression. On a sunny September day in 1985, Coach Cope sat with his wife in the stands at Pitt Stadium, watching Pitt defeat Boston College. Off the bench came a solidly built freshman tailback named Brian Davis, 195 pounds. He had been hotly recruited from Washington High School, just south of Pittsburgh, but thus far had remained a reserve. Soon into the Boston College game, he carried the ball into the secondary and then left tacklers empty-handed by executing a magnificent 180-degree spin for a decent gain. A few more carries and Coach Cope said to Mildred:

"Good Lord! What Pitt has here is a big Tony Dorsett!"

By game's end, Brian Davis had gained 100 yards, and when I picked up the Sunday sports section the next morning I expected to read about the first sighting of a future All-American. But I found no sportswriter going out on any such limb. At a news conference a few days later, I said to a few newspaper friends with whom I felt free to argue, "What's wrong with you guys? You brushed off the Davis kid."

We'll see about him, they said.

We never did see about him. As matters turned out, Davis had a shortcoming. He had absolutely no use for books or classrooms. He played sparely that '85 season and was dismissed from the university. He disappeared, to where I know not. Brady Keys, a long-ago defensive back for the Steelers, once told me, "Myron, there are who-knows-how-many guys standing on street corners in Los Angeles who had more football talent than I can dream of having."

Brian Davis could have made a fortune in the NFL. Coach Cope does not *know* so, but he has never had any inclination to question his supposition.

I greatly respect coaches and football scouts, yet at times they dumbfound me. In 1999 Kurt Warner at age 28 suddenly emerged as a dynamite quarterback who that season would pass the St. Louis Rams to a Super Bowl championship. His saga is well known. In a nutshell, he had played three seasons in the Arena Football League and worked as a stock boy in a supermarket. Finally, in '98, the Rams took him on board but consigned him to the sideline as a third-string quarterback. The next summer, only because starter Trent Green went down injured in the preseason, Coach Dick Vermeil gave Warner his chance. It was, however, not until the seventh week of the regular season that I was able to watch the instant sensation play a game—the Steelers had a Monday-night game coming up, so I tuned into a Sunday telecast of a St. Louis game.

Warner showed a strong arm, all right, but I said to myself, "Look at his release. How did all those coaches and scouts miss that release?" Yes, I still followed the dictum Chuck Noll had given me in the early 1970s: Look for the release. How's the release? How, I wondered smugly, had so many coaches and scouts failed to put Warner's release together with his arm strength for so long?

One ounce of smugness leads to another, so I remember the wee hours of a morning in the 1950s when I sat at a nightclub ringside table with the establishment's owner, Lenny Litman. Litman operated The Copa in downtown Pittsburgh and knew the nightclub business inside-out. While we listened to a young, scarcely known male vocalist perform, I said to Lenny, "That guy's terrific. He's gonna be big."

"Nah," said Lenny. "He's a bum."

Within months, Johnny Mathis was packing 'em in around the country. I mention this only by way of giving the reader ample reason to say, "Enough already, Cope."

Okay, all of my conceited tributes to my instinct for talent bring me to Kordell Stewart.

In 2001—and contrary to practically all expectations for Stewart and his team—he quarterbacked the Steelers clear to the Super Bowl's doorstep, the AFC championship game (which alas, they lost to the New England Patriots, the eventual Super Bowl champs). Coach Cope, dammit, you had had it right on Kordell, you had stood your ground for two years against the howling masses, but why did you not have the fortitude to stick to your guns?

In 1997—Stewart's third NFL year and first as a starter—did Kordell and the Steelers not advance to the AFC championship game, in which they lost by only three points to Denver? For the next two seasons and somewhat more, however, Kordell would flounder pathetically, throwing passes too high, too low, or too wide and seemingly unsure of his ability to run through defenses with his blazing speed and taffy-twist maneuvers. Terry Bradshaw back in the early 1970s had been ridiculed pitilessly by the multitudes—they wrote him off as a dolt or, following another spate of interceptions, phoned talk shows and, while imagining themselves to be great wits, suggested Bradshaw's problem was color-blindness. Still, the abuse Bradshaw suffered was child's play compared to that heaped upon Kordell as his career declined. The difference was that no internet existed during Bradshaw's early Steeler years—no cyberspace into which rumor-mongers could fling false gossip. Kordell's heterosexuality came into question. I cannot count the number of times strangers approached me and said, "I have a cousin"—alternatively, an uncle, nephew, or friend

— "who's a cop and *told* me the police discovered Kordell in a lover's lane with a guy." Kordell felt compelled to address the Steeler squad to declare, so it's been reported: "I believe in Adam and Eve, not Adam and Steve."

I pulled for Kordell. He had come upon the Steeler scene as a second-round draft pick, a young man possessed of a broad, engaging smile, a sense of humor, and an articulate manner. I have had a habit of uttering a sound—"um-hah," as nearly as I can spell it—that has been one of my dilatory tactics that buy a second when I'm mulling a comment or question. Whenever I put my mike under Kordell's chin for an interview in my postgame locker room show, he would smile hugely and say, "Um-hah!" More to the point, my answer to his detractors was succinct:

"He has a load of natural talent, but pure and simple, he's lost confidence in himself. He's aiming the ball, not slinging it. Whatever the reasons"—and mind, a revolving door of offensive coordinators was operating against him—"he has no swagger. If he regains his confidence, he'll be fine."

Oh, that I had continued my defense of his potential. I might have looked sharp. But in the summer of 2000 I gave up. Still seeing him play erratically through the preseason, I joined the mob, concluding that the Steelers could no longer take their chances with him. Indeed, they opened the regular season starting Kent Graham—a journeyman free-agent quarterback signed in the off season. Not until Graham went down early with a hip injury did Kordell return; he at once began to make his move. Of his 11 starts, the Steelers won seven, and late the following season, 2001, his teammates elected him their Most Valuable Player while others across the country elected him to the Pro Bowl. Coach Cope, you had championed his potential, but along the way, you faltered. A surgeon, no matter his past successes, cannot congratulate himself on a job well done when he has operated on the wrong knee.

Teresa Varley is a diminutive woman, an assistant editor of *Steelers Digest*, the team's weekly tabloid, and from time to time writes question-and-answer pieces—Q-and-A's, they're called in the business—about one Steeler player or another. Perhaps it is odd, but Teresa seems able to evoke from her brawny subjects introspective comments that daily newspaper reporters and columnists fail to elicit. Thus when the 2001 season and the two playoff games that followed had ended, Varley asked Kordell to trace the marked improvement that the Steelers' newest offensive coordinator, Mike Mularkey, had drawn from him. She mentioned that in the previous winter when Bill Cowher had promoted Mularkey from tight ends coach to coordinator, Mularkey at once made it his business to visit Kordell at his off season home in Atlanta. Kordell reflected on that visit.

"The first thing he asked me was, how am I doing? I told him, pretty cool. He came back and said, 'No, how are you doing?' "

Kordell sensed the drift of Mularkey's question, for Mularkey had been witness to the punishing gamut Kordell had traveled. "Mike was knocking down the walls," Kordell said, explaining that he himself had come to trust nobody. He told Mularkey, "Just allow me to play the game the way I know how." To Varley he now said, "If it wasn't for Coach Mularkey, I don't know where I'd be mentally. What he did was take me out of the solitude."

At a news conference that followed the 2001-02 season by just a few days, Bill Cowher noted in passing that not only had the onetime failed quarterback started every regular-season and playoff game but had not missed a single practice. So far as I know, nobody in Cowher's audience mentioned this fact in the newspapers or on the air, but I'll safely guess that no other quarterback in the NFL matched Kordell's durability. How does one put a value on such a factoid? I am tempted to classify Kordell's comeback, all told, as a triumph of the human spirit, but the encomium more properly suits Churchill's leading the British through the German blitzkrieg or a quadriplegic regaining interest in life.

All right, will Kordell Stewart, as he nears his 30th birthday, build upon his Pro Bowl season? I suppose so, but I cannot be certain. I may have been the last among the media to lower myself from his bandwagon, but my mistake in doing so deprives me of my former certitude. In fact, now that I retreat behind modesty, I recall that my self-proclaimed eye for talent failed me in an earlier instance. I once put a question to Mario Lemieux, the incomparable 6'4" hockey star, during the prime of his career. Taking into account his breathtaking athleticism, I asked, "Would you agree with me that if you had grown up in Canada playing football instead of hockey, you would have made a terrific tight end in the pros?"

Mario's eyes twinkled, but he replied, "No. No way."

"Why not?" I persisted.

"Too slow. My speed is just average."

What! This from a man who with huge strides tore past opponents game after game, leaving them reaching desperately with their sticks to slow him down?

"Do you mean to tell me," I said, "that when you take off your skates, you're slow?"

"I'm just average," Mario replied, "and average is not good enough to catch passes in the NFL."

Take that, Coach Cope.

Part Three

Faith, Memories, and a Few Opinions

Chapter Fifteen

Mildred,
the Bad-Luck Girl

"Hey, Mom, how y' doin'?"

Why am I asking when I know you're going to say, "Fine"—and say it with a smile. That was the response I got practically every night I returned home from work, right through the years you were tortured by pain. You did not fool me, Mom. I knew you had made up your mind that you were not going to visit your suffering upon me and the kids if you could help it.

In case you're not keeping track, it's been almost eight years since you left us. We're doing okay. I don't know what the rules are up there or what the regimen is, or even if there *are* rules or regimen, so I have no way of knowing whether you've been able to keep track of us. That being the case, I'll mention that I took Danny and Elizabeth to the country club today for the Easter luncheon buffet, which of course you always enjoyed. An attractive blond woman walked through the dining room wearing a broad-brimmed straw hat with a decorated band—the kind of hat we used to see all around us on Easter Sunday but I suppose is now worn mostly at beaches. Elizabeth said, "Look at that hat, Dad!" I told her, "I think it looks terrific." I pass this along, Mom, because it was you who caused me to realize that small talk is good for the soul. Whenever I came home from the station, sometimes with a knot in my stomach if the talk show had gone badly, your telling me the latest from the neighborhood or from Elizabeth's day at school helped me reenter the real world. There's much to be said for small talk.

Anyhow, rain began to fall right after lunch and is still coming down steadily, and if you're aware of all this, I know what you're saying as I sit down to write. You're saying, "Are you putting me into that book? Stop right this minute." No, I have not forgotten you always preferred to remain in the background and that when interviewers occasionally asked to visit you for a family-type feature, you cooperated pleasantly but wished they'd left you out. You liked the old rule you were taught as a child. "A woman," you sometimes said, "should have her name in the papers only three times—when she's born, when she marries, and when she dies." Say that today, Mom, and a feminist is apt to spring from the woodwork and bawl you out.

I respected your privacy and rarely mentioned you in my broadcasts, but you may be thinking, "What about that Thursday-night football game?" Oh, yes, the Steelers were playing the Oilers in Houston when suddenly I remembered that Thursday nights I hauled our trash up the driveway so it would be there when the garbage truck came by very early Friday morning. "I almost forgot—it's Thursday night!" I hollered on impulse into my microphone. "Mildred, if you're listening, take out the garbage!" Jack Fleming, my partner in the booth, almost fell from his chair laughing. The next year, the Steelers again played a Thursday-night game, this one in Miami. "Mildred!" Jack bellowed in the midst of our broadcast. "Take out the garbage!"

Now I suppose you're saying, "Why can't you leave me out of that book?" Tell you what—I'll make a deal. I'll try to keep this chapter short, okay?

Meantime, remember when I stumbled into broadcasting part-time, more or less by accident? I'll bet you were as surprised as I to find I instantly became a ham when a microphone or camera was placed in front of me. Filming a commercial or posing for still photographs, I'd ask, "You want some mugging?" I mugged six different ways, and when you saw the result you must have said, "Is this the man I married?" I'm not sure whether you smiled with me or at me when I sang and danced for videos that actually jacked up the station's ratings.

Anyhow, as you well know, Mom, our society has long been a culture that exalts celebrities beyond reason. Of course, even for this big fish in a small pond, advantages came with celebrity. Remember all those total strangers who would send a round of drinks to our table? But you also surely remember the trouble you had getting me to go to shopping malls and how, when I did, I walked with my head down, because I hated being recognized.

Anyhow—and you'll scoff at this—now that I'm a creaking geezer, strangers constantly approach me and say, "You're an icon! You're a Pittsburgh legend!" I don't know it for a fact, but I suspect that at WDVE-Radio—the Steelers' flagship station now—the guys who have me on their show on mornings that follow Steeler games are on standing orders to introduce me as "the Pittsburgh legend." Quit laughing.

Seriously, Mom, I have told Elizabeth so many times that she's probably sick of hearing it, "There is no such thing as a celebrity. There are only people who *think* they're celebrities." I shake my head when I see them preen.

All right, how did I get started with all this blabber? Simply because I can't recall having ever mentioned to you that if at any time I stood in danger of getting a swelled head, you would have to put a stop to it swiftly. How can I forget the night we went to DeBlasio's Restaurant for a charity party, the night Donnie DeBlasio had hired a jazz band and cleared away tables to make room for a small dance floor? That good-looking six-foot brunette came to our table and said, "Myron, let's you and I jitterbug." I went out there on the floor—you've got to admit this, Mom—and showed that big gal a move or two, and the room applauded. You offered no comment. You were nothing if not good company driving home, but when we retired that night, you reached to turn off the lamp on your night stand and gave me a terse review of my performance on the dance floor.

"Myron, you're such a showoff."

So saying, you turned off the lamp.

What about the time I came within a hair's breadth of dying? Did you believe it or ever give it a second thought? You'll remember, now that I'm bringing it up, that one morning I drove to Dr. Laughlin's office because I had laryngitis, which I feared might develop into bronchitis, and asked for a shot of penicillin. Dr. Laughlin accommodated me, as he had in the past, only because he knew I made my living talking. I bent over his table, and practically the instant his needle penetrated my backside, my knees buckled. "Doc, I'm having a reaction!" I piped.

Not only was I dropping but my hearing, even as I collapsed and heard Dr. Laughlin call for his nurse, had turned weird.

He caught me, barely, and managed to lift me onto the table. It seemed as though all of me was breaking down—everything but my brain, for I still could think clearly. Dr. Laughlin's voice seemed off in a distance. My tongue thickened, impeding my speech. My spine hurt like holy hell. I was paralyzed, and I could feel my heart thumping a mile a minute. Dr. Laughlin, with help from his nurse, began shooting an antidote, adrenaline, into my arm.

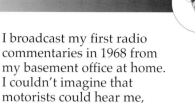

I broadcast my first radio commentaries in 1968 from my basement office at home. I couldn't imagine that motorists could hear me, so I started shouting and never stopped.

Evidence that an irate Penn State fan was not entirely wrong when he wrote to me. He said to look at myself in the mirror and I would find a man with squinty eyes, a big nose, a crooked smile and tobacco-stained teeth.

With play-by-play man Jack Fleming, my partner in the Steeler broadcasting booth for 24 years. Jack was the consummate pro who suffered (not entirely) in silence when the rank amateur joined him.

My son Danny (left), Mildred and me, and daughter Elizabeth (right).

Hall of Fame linebacker Jack "Splat" Lambert saw that I was properly moist for the shooting of a 1985 television commercial advertising a water ride at Pittsburgh's Kennywood Park.
(*Chapter 23*)

During take after chilly take, Splat and I headed for the waterfalls. To make certain we appeared soaked, a man sat in the front of the boat and hurled buckets of water at us.

As a writer, I had not suspected I had an ounce of ham in me. As a broadcaster, I found that if the photographer said, "Mug," I mugged six different ways.

With my current Steeler broadcast partners, former Pro Bowl Steeler tackle Tunch Ilkin and play-by-play man Bill Hillgrove.

I believe citizens in the position to open the right doors should open them. Here I am posing with one of my young friends. I try to do what I can to raise a few bucks for children in need.

At a retirement party for Steelers executive Joe Gordon. As publicity director, Joe encouraged Terry Bradshaw to think before he spoke.

Shortly after the beginning of the war in Afghanistan, U.S. soldiers at an undisclosed location in the Middle East display their secret weapon.
(More on the Terrible Towel in Chapter 16.)

On the babble-for-pay circuit, I worked cheap and never knew what fate awaited me. Here I am with Hall of Famer Franco Harris (left).

At the 25th anniversary reunion of the Steelers' first Super Bowl Championship team, with defensive tackle Ernie "Fats" Holmes (left) and linebacker Andy Russell. Fats, by this time, had mellowed considerably. (Chapter 12)

Many have good-naturedly called me "Coach Cope," and I did get a chance to coach the Pitt intrasquad game in 1974. My scheme to stop Tony Dorsett remains the plan of the decade, at least in my own mind. *(Chapter 14)*

I moderated a panel discussion in which (left to right) Pete Rose, Joe Frazier and Bob Knight proved to be a surprisingly good combination. Their hilarious anecdotes brought down the house. *(Chapter 17)*

In a milk ad with Steeler star Jerome Bettis, who has mistakenly credited me with nicknaming him "The Bus." *(Chapter 20)*

Carlton Haselrig sent me this photo after I lobbied the Steelers to select him as their final pick in the 1990 draft. A wrestler, he had not played any college football but later made the Pro Bowl. *(Chapter 24)*

Nobody had to draw a blueprint for me. I knew I was at death's door, do you yet believe it, Mom? Often I've read or heard of people who found themselves on the brink of doom and afterward related that their entire lives had flashed before them. Mine chose not to. I simply thought, "I'm going to die with my pants down." Then I had a second thought. "I'm scheduled to give a speech in Derry, Pennsylvania tonight, and the toastmaster's gonna have to get up and say, 'Our main speaker cannot be with us tonight, owing to the fact that he's dead.' "

I'm not sure how long Dr. Laughlin kept me on the table, but when he at last helped me down he sat me in his waiting room for at least half an hour. Then he beckoned me into his office and held his thumb and index finger so close together they almost touched. "Do you know," he asked, "that you were this close to cashing 'em in?"

I said, "Damn right, I knew all along."

I drove home—it was about noontime—and as you may remember, Mom, I found you napping on the sofa in the family room. I tugged at your shoulder to awaken you and said, "Mildred, do you know that I just almost died in Dr. Laughlin's office?"

"Tell me about it later," you said, and rolled over to get on with your nap.

Later, as you'll recall, a test would confirm that all the shots of penicillin I had absorbed over the years sensitized me to the drug, making me susceptible to an acute reaction. Again remembering people who have survived close brushes with death, I know that lives have been turned around by the experience—men and women have dedicated themselves to constructive works, to their faith, to family, to all that they had neglected. Mom, *you* know it never occurred to me to change my worthless ways. All I did was sometimes tell the story of my close call to friends we were having dinner with, just for laughs, your nap serving as the punch line.

I'm guessing you still suspect I was exaggerating. Hey, if you thought it important, you could have called Dr. Laughlin to check out my story. Admit it, you thought, "He's dramatizing himself again." The point is, Mom, that no, a swelled head was not a possibility living with you.

Well, night is falling on another Easter, so I'll knock it off for today. Am I holding to my promise to keep it short? I'll do my best to end this expeditiously when I get back to the typewriter. Quit frowning.

I suppose you could say we really pulled off an upset, didn't we, Mom? We had a great marriage despite being an odd match. There I was, the writer. And there you were, formerly the head lab technician at a major hospital. What did I know of chemistry or most any other branch of science? And what did you care about syntax? You read voraciously— novels, nonfiction, magazines, newspapers—but you either liked what you read or did not. You did not issue critiques. Whenever I showed you my latest story, fresh off a magazine stand, you read it and gave either of two verdicts: "That's good, Myron," or "That's very good, Myron." You never said, "That's bad," but I knew that all of my work could not possibly have held your rapt interest. After all, you were not crazy about sports to begin with.

Intermarriage remained relatively rare at the time we married, you 33, I 35, both making the plunge for the first time. Jewish women hearing of a marriage such as ours would lower their voices and say, "He married a *shiksa*"—a gentile. I was tense, I tell you, Mom, when I took you to my parents' house to meet them. They were of the "conservative" division of the faith—the middle ground, not orthodox—but they kept a kosher house with separate sets of dishes for meals that included meat and those that included dairy ingredients, the two forbidden to be eaten at the same meal or even from the same dishes. I expected Ellis and Elizabeth to be shocked when I broke the news, and I suppose they were, but if so, they hid their shock well. They liked you at once, as did every member of my family—my sister Violet loved you as she would a sister and mourned your passing hard. Hey, Mom, there you were, this woman with a West Virginia drawl certainly not common to Pittsburgh, but without a trace of affectation and as easy to pass the time with as anyone's best friend.

You were the church-going Catholic, later to switch to United Presbyterian and hear me kid that you switched only because the Presbyterian church was a shorter drive. That you made the switch did not surprise me, because your family, the Lindbergs, was all over the religious map. Your mother, Margaret, as you told me, had spent time in a convent till she decided a nun's life was not for her; your dad, Gus (Lefty Lindberg when he pitched in the minors), taught Methodist Sunday school; and your sister, Leola, was a Presbyterian. Seriously, I say you made the switch because Westminster Presbyterian Church on Sunday mornings had a child-care room in which the woman in charge was terrific with handicapped children, among whom was our retarded son, Danny.

Correct me if I'm wrong, Mom, but we were not a couple to examine our psyches and our souls in depth in intense conversations between the two of us. I always have thought that one reason we had a great marriage was that we allowed one another room for private thoughts. Anyhow, we had a good thing going, and I'm sure it helped that I was an agnostic. I wasn't confident that God existed, so I could not make religion an issue and suggest you convert to Judaism. I took pride in my heritage—pride in the fact that our tribe had survived down through history in the face of all manner of no-good crap artists frustrated by their own inadequacies. They've searched for scapegoats, usually us, to blame for their plight, bent upon rallying legions of similar knuckleheads. Not only have we Jews survived but we've done it with a smile, producing a rich line of professional comedians. In my talk show, I myself invoked Yiddish humor. "*Mazeltov!*" I told bewildered athletes—*mazeltov* meaning congratulations on their latest achievements. I cannot remember if I told you this one, Mom, but in 1982 the Steelers selected as their first-round draft pick a running back from Baylor University named Walter Abercrombie. They flew him from Texas to Pittsburgh for a news conference that evening, sending a man to pick him up at the airport. The driver played our ongoing draft broadcast on the radio as he drove Abercrombie to Steeler headquarters, and upon arriving, introduced Walter to me. "Tell me," Walter said. "What does *mazeltov* mean?"

In your last years, Mom, you dropped the smile—oh, maybe only two or three times—and said, "I'm just a bad-luck girl." You made that observation—and I knew you could have said the same thing through many other trials you'd endured over many years—when a specialist ordered up tests for scleroderma, a rare but frightening shrinkage and stiffening of tissue that posed a variety of dangers. The specialist assured you the chance of your tests being positive was minuscule. Bad luck, the tests were positive. You already were battling cancer—visiting scleroderma upon you was piling on.

But here it came, and so your hands turned blue and painful. On our final drive to the hospital, where you would spend your last 16 days, you told me you feared the effects of scleroderma (which in its advanced stages might turn one's face grotesque) worse than you feared dying of your cancer. And you asked, how can there really be a merciful God?

He forgave you your doubt, I'm sure.

You left us, to be exact, on September 20, 1994. No more than several days later, I glanced out the window of my study, which looked out onto the front lawn. You had told me early on, about 20 years before, "You're the gardener." I was a lazy gardener, so our three rose bushes dwindled to two, and those two became scraggly. Only in spring and early summer would they pop up a few yellow roses. Yellow was your favorite color, so I yelled for you whenever I saw a rose coming into bloom. Now, I noticed through my office window in late September that a single rose had begun to bloom on the tallest branch of an otherwise bare bush. That rose fairly burst into fullness, huge and glorious. I beckoned Elizabeth, Mom, and you surely must know that as close as the two of you had been, she had reacted to your death horrendously, unbelieving. "Look," I said. "Do you suppose Mom is speaking to us through that rose? Do you think she's telling us to hang tough?"

Through the rest of September and into October—a brisk, sometimes downright cold, October—our yellow rose stood robust atop that branch. On the final day of October, the rose wilted and died.

So ended my agnosticism. As you know, Mom, if you've been able to look in on us after our rose died, I have not felt called upon to alter my life any more than I had after I nearly died in Dr. Laughlin's office. But I know you're there.

Chapter Sixteen

The Terrible Towel

For more than two decades now, the question most frequently asked of me is, "How did you come up with the Terrible Towel?" This says, I suppose, that I have led a trivial life—a piece of terrycloth will be the monument to my career.

The Terrible Towel is, of course, the Pittsburgh Steelers' well-known good-luck charm. More than that, it became the flag of the Steeler nation, whose citizenry, regardless of where across America or around the globe their employment takes them, remain intensely loyal to the Steelers. NFL teams that have trouble filling their stadiums know that when the Steelers come to town, thousands of displaced Steeler fans can be counted upon to gobble up tickets and show up flying their Terrible Towels. Oh, how the Towel has traveled. It has been flown by mountain-climbers from a peak in Nova Scotia, hung by tourists from the Great Wall of China, decorated barrooms from Maryland to Manila, and been planted at the South Pole by a University of Pittsburgh scientist on an expedition. He hammered the flagstaff into ice-covered ground the day before the Steelers played in —and won—a Super Bowl.

One never knows where the Towel will pop up. Many years ago *TV Guide* asked me to write an article about controversies that had surrounded previous Super Bowls. My piece resulted in a football player suing the magazine for libel. In my opinion, the lawsuit was strictly a nuisance action by which the athlete and his lawyer hoped to extract a small settlement, but I had to travel overnight to a town in eastern Pennsylvania to give a deposition in the rather shabby office of the player's lawyer. Later, as the lawyer walked me and *TV Guide*'s lawyer to the door, he said, "Wait a minute." He then went to his office and returned carrying a Terrible Towel.

He asked, "Myron, will you autograph my Terrible Towel?"

"Counselor," I replied, "you can stick that up your ass."

Meantime, the Towel's fame spread worldwide. In 1996 the Steelers played the San Diego Chargers in a preseason game in Tokyo. A Japanese reporter with notebook and pen clambered aboard one of the buses that would take players and media to practice. He found me and said, "You man who made Tellble Tile?" In 2000, the Steelers played the Indianapolis Colts in a preseason game in Mexico City. Mexican fans clearly chose the Steelers to root for; they flew Terrible Towels throughout the 100,000-seat Azteca Stadium. Several years earlier, I had assigned the Steelers exclusive rights to market the Towel. They would pay all royalties to Allegheny Valley School, which cares for severely retarded and otherwise badly disabled persons. Following the game in Mexico City, I said to the Steelers' director of marketing, Tony Quatrini, "Boy, Allegheny Valley School will get a nice chunk of money from this game."

"No," Tony replied. "All those Towels you saw were knockoffs." The NFL religiously cracks down on pirates who try to peddle club merchandise. Would anything be done about these Mexican knockoff artists, I asked Tony. He shrugged and said nothing. Clearly the NFL wanted no international fuss.

All right, how *did* I come up with the Terrible Towel?

In the 1975 NFL season, the Steelers in the next-to-last week of play clinched both a berth in the playoffs and home-field advantage. The season before, they'd beaten a strong Minnesota team to win their first Super Bowl championship, so their fans were ecstatic at the prospect of their team making it two in a row. Now, in '75, their first playoff game lay two weeks away, against the Baltimore Colts at Three Rivers Stadium. On a fateful December afternoon, Pat Bertalanits, the secretary to the vice president and general manager of WTAE-Radio, Ted J. Atkins, phoned me at my desk.

"Can you step over to Ted's office?" she said.

Crossing the hall, I found the tall, burly GM huddled with the vice president for sales, Larry Garrett. Atkins got quickly to the point. "As the Steelers' flagship radio station, we think we should come up with some sort of gimmick for the playoffs—something that will involve the people."

Atkins paused, then barked at me: "Come up with a gimmick!"

"I am not a gimmick guy," I replied. "Never *have* been a gimmick guy."

Garrett, the sales exec, spoke up. "You don't understand," he said. He explained that were I to successfully promote some kind of object the fans could wave or wear at the playoffs, advertisers would be so impressed by my hold on the public that they would clamor to sponsor my daily commentaries and talk show. "Besides," said Garrett, "your contract with us expires in three months."

No, he was not threatening that I might be let go. He was suggesting that a Steeler gimmick, if successful, would give me leverage for a nice raise. "I'm a gimmick guy," I conceded.

Atkins hurriedly summoned advertising sales persons to his office, turning it into a think tank in which all of us could train our brains on the vital search for the unknown gimmick. Brainstorms erupted. "I've got it!" cried a salesman. "Chuck Noll's motto is 'Whatever it takes,' right?" The salesman proposed that we dress every fan entering the stadium in black costume masks upon which Noll's motto would be printed in gold lettering. At the time, Three Rivers Stadium held 50,000 spectators (later, 60,000), so Atkins reached for his phone and called a novelty supplier for a price on 50,000 such masks. "Fifty cents apiece," said the supplier. Twenty-five thousand dollars. Atkins and Garrett immediately concluded that masks were not the crowd-pleaser we were looking for.

My eye on their gimmick budget, I said, "What we need here is something that's lightweight and portable and already owned by just about every fan."

"How about towels?" Garrett suggested.

"A towel?" I said. It had possibilities. I ruminated. "Yes, we could call it the Terrible Towel. And I can go on radio and television proclaiming, 'The Terrible Towel is poised to strike!' "

The room stirred. A voice piped, "Gold and black towels, the colors of the Steelers."

"No," I said. "Black won't provide color. We'll tell 'em to bring gold or yellow towels."

"Yellow and gold will fly!" cried a sales voice. "Tell 'em, if they don't have one, buy one, and if they don't want to buy one, dye one!"

"I'll tell 'em they can use the towel to wipe their seats clean," I said. "They can use it as a muffler against the cold. They can drape it over their heads if it rains."

Atkins sent out for champagne.

While we toasted our brilliance, Atkins suddenly said, "Myron, we've got to go upstairs and get approval from Mr. Snyder." Franklin C. Snyder headed both our radio and television stations and was general manager of the entire Hearst Broadcasting System as well. A rugged man, he listened as we presented our plan, then banged his desk and said, "No!"

No?

"We must have black towels, too," he said gravely. "If we exclude black we'll be asking for trouble from the Human Relations Commission and the FCC."

All right, black towels, too.

A few days later, on the heavily watched Sunday-night 11 o'clock television news, I introduced Pittsburgh to the Terrible Towel, making a damned fool of myself by hurling towels at the anchorman, the weatherman, and the floor director. Throughout the week leading up to the playoff opener, I would implore my radio and television listeners who held game tickets to bring towels. Early that week, however, Atkins experienced misgivings.

"Suppose the Steelers lose," he said to me. "Suppose the players say you jinxed them with your Terrible Towel. Those goofy Steeler fans are liable to come out here to the station and burn the place down. What I want you to do," he continued, "is go to the Steelers' locker room and poll the players—do they want the Terrible Towel or not?"

Okay, upon arriving there, I entered the trainer's room where linebacker Jack Ham and defensive tackle Fats Holmes sat on tables, having their ankles taped for practice. I carried a clipboard on which to record votes. Ham responded first. "I think your idea stinks." Holmes, never a man to trifle with, narrowed his eyes and slowly said, "Marn, I don't want you to do this."

Hey, I'd already campaigned on the air for the Terrible Towel. "What's needed in this locker room," I told myself, "is a banana-republic vote." I found Terry Bradshaw seated on a stool at his locker, reading the farm reports. "How do you feel about the Terrible Towel?" I asked him.

He looked up and said, "Huh?"

I check him off as a yes.

I made my way across the lockers, using similarly conscientious polling technique, until I had a clear majority on my clipboard. But co-captain Andy Russell stopped me as I crossed the locker room. "What's this crap about a towel?" he growled. "We're not a gimmick team. We've never been a gimmick team."

His words had the ring of familiarity. Hadn't I said something like that to my bosses? Still, turning back was not an option. "Russell," I said, "you're sick." I reported back to Ted Atkins that the Steelers overwhelmingly approved of the Towel.

Mind you, I did not see the Terrible Towel as witchcraft to hex the enemy. It would be a positive force, driving the Steelers to superhuman performance, but if it experienced a yen for mischief and created fatal mistakes by opponents, I would tolerate that. Not entirely sane by now, I daily intoned on the air, "The Terrible Towel is poised to strike!"

At last, game day arrived. As soon as the stadium gates opened I sat down in our broadcast booth and trained my binoculars on the fans as they took their seats. No towels in sight! Even as the Steelers and Colts went through warmup drills, barely a dozen towels could be seen. Had the public scoffed at my call for towels? That very morning, the *Pittsburgh Post-Gazette* had protested that I was trying to turn Three Rivers Stadium into a tenement district, such neighborhoods being characterized in that era by wash hung out to dry. Now, at least one newspaperman strolled into our booth to snidely ask, "Where are all the towels, Cope?"

Nearing kickoff, the Steelers gathered in their tunnel for introductions, whereupon the crowd exploded—and suddenly, by my estimation, 30,000 Terrible Towels twirled from the fists of fans around the stadium! Where had those towels been? Well, the day was wet and nasty, so I supposed all those fans either had been sitting on their Towels or had stuffed them into their coats. Whatever, my reputation was saved and my next raise assured.

Yes, the Terrible Towel was born that day, Dec. 27, 1975, bursting into the world like a bawling infant. Frank Lewis, a swift Steeler receiver, raced across the middle in the rain and made a scarcely believable one-handed catch of a Terry Bradshaw bullet. A young woman named Lisa Benz would soon mail me the following verse:

> Now how could you, Frank
> Try what you tried
> In weather so wet and so foul?
> "There's one thing to thank,
> I had my hand dried
> On a piece of the Terrible Towel!"

Late in the second quarter, Bradshaw went down with a leg injury. When the Steelers at halftime emerged from their locker room to begin the third quarter, the crowd groaned—Bradshaw had not returned. Seconds before kickoff, however, he trotted onto the field. Benz cheered his recovery, to wit:

The crowd was amazed,
They all wondered how
Could his leg heal in such a short time.
"We wrapped it," he praised
"With the Terrible Towel
And it healed up this poor leg of mine."

But the Towel saved its best work for Andy Russell, the linebacker who had wanted no part of it. He scooped up a Baltimore fumble at his own seven-yard line. Lacking natural speed and playing on a gimpy leg, Russell nonetheless lumbered 93 yards to a touchdown while a cordon of ten blockers jogged alongside him. Benz outdid herself.

He ran ninety-three
Like a bat out of hell,
And no one could see
How he rambled so well.
"It was easy," said Andy
And he flashed a crooked smile,
"I was snapped on the fanny
By the Terrible Towel!"

The Steelers pasted the Baltimore Colts, 28-10, then beat the hated Oakland Raiders and the Dallas Cowboys to gain their second straight championship. The following season I received a phone call from Gimbel's, a major department store chain wanting to market the Terrible Towel. Now it would go first class—its name and logo stamped onto thick, rich terrycloth. Three years before Ted Atkins had convened that think tank in his office, the Miami Dolphins, charging through the 1972 season undefeated, had encouraged their fans to cheer big plays and touchdowns by waving white handkerchiefs. Tens of thousands of fluttering hankies made for a nice show of enthusiasm but came across too dainty for the game of football. Miami's hankies soon disappeared. The Terrible Towel, by contrast, was robust and ready for the long haul. It continues to this day to reign as the champion talisman of American sports.

On days or nights when the Steelers play, the Towel is draped by fans over television sets and radios, even fastened around dogs, cats, and babies. In years that the Steelers reach the playoffs, it hangs from windows, lampposts, and roofs. Across professional and college sports, puny copycat towels have been distributed to spectators, but these towels are usually white, undersized, cheaply made, and bearing the name of a bank, radio station, or some such sponsor who's footing the bill. The spectator who bothers to take one home has gained a dust rag.

Somewhat more than three years after the Terrible Towel first appeared, Steeler president Dan Rooney handed me a copy of a publication called *Sports Business—the Management Newsletter for Sports Money Makers*. Rooney pointed to an item he knew would interest me. Under the advisory "Watch for Fans," *Sports Business* confided to the club owners who subscribed to the newsletter:

"Special, almost unclassifiable gimmicks like the Steelers' 'Terrible Towel' are a fan turn-on. The keys to the most successful of these devices seem to be 1) Color and 2) Motion. Crowds dressed in the same color clothing can make an impact, but it is passive. Color plus motion in the stands creates a kind of framework for the contest itself, making the entire experience more memorable for the spectator. We suggest a look at the Japanese and British sports crowds for examples of dynamic display of color and motion."

I, as the Towel's creator, could not decide which impressed me more —*Sports Business*'s expertise in determining that color plus motion had made the Towel a success, or the audacity I had showed by creating the Towel while ignorant of the fact that I was mixing a precise formula that would produce a "special, almost unclassifiable gimmick."

"Your idea," Rooney said, "was pure genius. But you were too stupid to know what you were doing."

On Dec. 27, 2001, the Terrible Towel celebrated his 26th birthday. (I usually have employed the masculine gender when speaking of the Towel and sometimes have complained to my audiences that he was eating me out of house and home. To refer to him as "it" is much too impersonal.) I would not have been surprised had he withered and expired in the latter 1980s when the Steelers went four straight years without making the playoffs. Among fans, his heights of popularity were reached whenever the Steelers entered the playoffs. But he survived lean years nicely, and when the Steelers—in the 2001 season—won the AFC Central Division title and then, in the playoffs, battered the mouthy Baltimore Ravens (the defending Super Bowl champions) Terrible Towels filled the air in numbers I had never seen.

You were right, Rooney. I was too stupid to know what I was doing.

Chapter Seventeen

Talk Shows and Shock Shows

In late summer of 1973, WTAE-TV-Radio lured a successful Los Angeles radio executive, Ted Atkins, to Pittsburgh to be vice president and general manager of radio. Upon signing Atkins, Frank Snyder, the boss of both our television and radio stations, instructed him that for his first day on the job he should closet himself in a hotel room and spend the day listening to our station. Keep a legal pad handy, Snyder told him, and list your thoughts.

The first words Atkins wrote on his pad were: "Fire Myron Cope."

He had listened to my morning sports commentary and reacted much as do strangers motoring through the Pittsburgh area, their car radio tuned to our station. Hearing my voice assault their eardrums for the first time, they exclaim, "What *is* that!" I suppose Atkins's management colleagues persuaded him that he might change his mind about firing me if he remained patient and heard more of my stuff. Years later, Atkins revealed to me that he'd been poised to fire me, and he guffawed. Somehow, I had difficulty smiling.

Back there in '73, WTAE-Radio's format consisted primarily of music but included newscasts and an evening one-hour sports talk show conducted by a veteran sportscaster named Tom Bender. Atkins, soon after his arrival in Pittsburgh, altered his opinion of my value and called me to his office to inform me that he was removing Bender from the talk show and wanted me to take his place.

"I can't do that," I said. "For one thing, Tom and I have been friends for years."

"It's not a matter of your taking his job," Atkins replied. "His show just isn't working. If you won't give it a try, I'll simply drop the show and replace it with music." Atkins had made his reputation in L.A. with a sense for music format.

Meantime, Tom Bender's problem was twofold—he was a good-natured man, plus he had come up in an era when sportscasters rarely (and then, only lightly) criticized local teams. Talk shows were still in their infancy when Tom had been given his; he had been conditioned to avoid controversy and disliked taking calls from fans bent upon belittling club owners, coaches, or athletes. At the time, as best I remember, there existed only one other talk show in town—not a sports show but a general show—whose host had opted for the tough-guy shtick, regularly hanging up on callers in mid-sentence. Now, Atkins appealed to my company loyalty. "I'm trying to turn this station around, and you can help me," he argued.

I knew that accepting the talk show would bring my writing career virtually to an end, because the combination of broadcasting the show and the preparation that I knew to be mandatory would be piled upon my radio and television commentaries and Steelers broadcasts. When would there be time to write? But I told Atkins:

"All right, I'll try this show, but I have great misgivings. I'll be sitting there punching up phone calls and not knowing what kind of idiots will come crawling out of the woodwork. At the same time, don't expect me to use the hang-up-on-'em technique. My parents bred me right. I'm not going to be rude. Also, you say you want me to take over the show at the start of September? Okay, but let's agree that when the end of the year comes around, I can drop the show if I'm not enjoying it and *you* can drop it if you don't think it's working."

On that reluctant note, I entered a new landscape, one that would do wonders for my broadcast career. To that point, many listeners had found my commentaries and football broadcasts informative and entertaining, I liked to think, but they had little idea who Myron Cope was. A call-in show, for reasons of sheer length and one-on-one conversation with callers, in time can explain its host to its listeners and develop a bond between them. My sing-song delivery of prepared commentary scripts had inspired no warmth from the audience, but I do believe the talk show rectified that. At the outset, I told myself that the show should more or less replicate the many evenings I had spent as a teenager idling with pals on a street corner in front of Sol's Pharmacy, across the street from Ross's Poolroom. We debated the sports issues of the day past nightfall, or until a familiar red-faced cop arrived in a patrol car and ordered us to disperse.

"There's your talk show, Cope," I thought. "Go back to the street corner. Nothing pompous. Make it fun, because that's what sports is supposed to be."

I would conduct my talk show for almost 22 years and would see it expand from one hour to two, which I believed to be the maximum span inasmuch as I was convinced that a successful show should leave its listeners wanting more. Of course, there were evenings at the mike I could have done without. For example, an elderly listener phoned to relate a humorous anecdote about a baseball umpire. "That's good," I said, "but I'll top it."

I mentioned the name of a pro football talent scout, Fido Murphy, an acquaintance of mine. An unabashed braggart, Fido claimed to have been a superb athlete in baseball, football, and basketball. He maintained that in the days when baseball games frequently were umpired by a single man, he once laid down a trickling bunt, and while the umpire hovered over the ball to see whether it would remain fair, he, Fido, sprinted directly across the pitcher's mound and came to rest on second base. The bunt stayed fair. Fido's opponents furiously protested his shortcut to second, but as Fido told the story, the ump replied, "Aw, dry up. You guys just wish you had Murphy's speed and could take two bases on a bunt."

About halfway through my telling Fido Murphy's tale, I heard the sounds of loud snoring on the telephone line. I said, "Obviously, caller, you don't find my story arresting." I discontinued it and went on to the next caller. Soon after, I learned that the sounds I had taken for snoring actually were the labors of a man gripped by a heart attack. Alas, his family returned home that night to find him slumped at the telephone, dead.

Many were the evenings I signed off disgusted with myself for having had a flat show or having failed to offer a suitable answer to a caller's question, but I have no problem whatever in pinpointing the most difficult, probably the worst, talk show I ever conducted. The date, in fact, was January 16, 1991. I had invited Brian Colleary, the athletic director of Duquesne University, to come to my studio and be a guest for an hour. Duquesne basketball was not a particularly lively topic, but at times I felt an obligation to give struggling organizations exposure. As luck would have it, shortly before Colleary and I went on the air, CNN began the first live telecast in history of an American war—the Persian Gulf War. Yes, President Bush had ordered a devastating bombing of Iraq. While Operation Desert Storm lit up the sky over Baghdad and CNN televised the bombing from the scene, Colleary and I discussed Duquesne basketball.

"Nobody," I told Colleary, "is listening." Not one person phoned. We struggled through an hour of talking to one another. During commercial breaks I apologized to the athletic director for a televised war having upstaged his opportunity to tout his basketball team. He said he understood.

Merrier shows, to be sure, often occurred. Heading toward my first talk show on September 3, 1973, I conjured up an award I would bestow upon callers who made particularly brilliant contributions. I called it the Cope-a-nut Award. I asked one of our radio engineers to put together a sound effect of a coconut falling from a tree. My audience would hear a rustling sound simulating the tree being vigorously shaken . . . then a long, whistling sound as the coconut descended . . . and then, bong! It had struck the caller smack on his noggin. Before triggering the sound effect, I said, "Caller, you have made a contribution so brilliant that I'm tempted to make you a Cope-a-nut."

"Oh, my God," such callers took to pleading. "Please, please. Do it, Myron, do it!"

"Where are you, in the kitchen?" I would ask. If so, I would say, "Bow your head, and get a firm grip on the kitchen counter. This will hurt."

Bong! Silence. Then the caller might say, "I'm on my knees, but my head is clearing. I'm delirious with joy."

"You do know, don't you," I would say, "that once made a Cope-a-nut, callers immediately experience an upturn in their fortunes—a job promotion, for example."

From the beginning of my broadcast career in 1968, I had signed off all of my commentaries and, later, talk shows by saying, "This is Myron Cope, on sports!" Urchins followed me in the streets crowing, "This is Myron Cope, on sports!" My daughter Elizabeth's elementary school classmates tormented her—she hated it—by calling out those words. At any rate, in the final talk show I would conduct, in April of 1995, a show expanded on this occasion to three hours, I found myself with but a couple of minutes remaining, whereupon a woman piped up with the last call of my long run.

"My two-year-old spoke his first words on an evening when we watched you giving your television commentary. You said, 'This is Myron Cope . . . ' and he joined in, 'on sports!' Those were his first words."

I had long been told that my voice, however grating to adults, fascinated two-year-olds and dogs. Dogs barked at the television set. Still, this kid was special. I made his mom a Cope-a-nut and promised her a promotion at her place of work. About three months later, I attended the

Pittsburgh Vintage Grand Prix, an auto-racing event that I had cofounded and seen become the foremost vintage-car attraction in America, raising important money for charity. On a grassy hilltop in Schenley Park, my final caller approached me and introduced herself.

"Three days after you made me a Cope-a-nut," she said, "I got a promotion."

One evening in the early 1970s, I found myself standing at the bar in the press lounge at Three Rivers Stadium, awaiting the start of a Pirates game. A slightly built man in his 30s, perhaps only two inches taller than I, pranced into the room—he seemed to walk on only the balls of his feet —and lightly patted my cheek. "Hi, My!" Sam Nover said. Thus did he greet me from time to time. He had come from Detroit to be sports anchor for television station WIIC. For whatever reason—was it the pat on the cheek or the fact nobody else called me My?—Sam's greeting always caused me to wince. (In recent years, my fellow Steelers radio analyst Tunch Ilkin has taken to calling me My, but I have not minded, so I suppose that in Sam's case, it *was* the pat on the cheek.) At any rate, Sam possessed both a rich voice that he seemed to bring up from the pit of his stomach and a highly favorable opinion of himself. Also, he carried in his pocket a small mirror with which to make certain that every hair on his head was perfectly combed.

One day an automobile dealer for whom I was performing commercials said to me, "I got a phone call from Sam Nover. (They played golf at the same club.) Sam said to me, 'How about me doing your commercials?' I told him, 'Myron Cope does our commercials.' And he said, 'I know. But you can use me instead.' "

The auto dealer declined. "Well," I thought, "it's a free country, but wouldn't you think that within the media circle a man would respect another's turf?"

Nover also gauged that my evening talk show was vulnerable to incursion by a serious and versatile talent, meaning himself. But first, the background. My show had been in existence at WTAE more than seven years, occupying the 7 to 8 p.m. hour all that time. Our sales department charged high advertising rates in so-called "drive time," which ended at 7 o'clock, but because my show was a hit, the sales staff found itself able to continue commanding drive-time rates clear to 8 o'clock. Naturally, other radio stations began to see the potential in sports talk. One rival, KQV, put sportscaster Stan Savran on the air from 6 to 7:30, KQV's strategy being that when the clock struck seven, Savran might hold his listeners and leave me with fewer as I opened my show. In style, we were opposites. Stan possessed an impressive memory for factoids and loved to delve into sports trivia. Whenever my callers expressed an urge to talk trivia, I said, "Sorry, you're in the wrong store. I consider trivia to be facts not worth knowing." My memory leaned to anecdotes, preferably humorous.

Eventually, our company hired Stan away from KQV to be a television sportscaster, and when he insisted in his negotiations that he be given a talk show on our radio station as well, management as a courtesy asked me if I minded Savran following my evening show with an hour-long show of his own. "Fine with me," I said. Stan was developing a following and could add strength to our broadcast format.

When Stan left KQV, that station offered his show to the television anchor Nover, who eagerly accepted the additional work. Soon after, *Pittsburgh Magazine* brought together the three of us—me, Savran, and Nover—to sit down to a taped exchange of thoughts about sports talk shows. The interviewer began:

"A casual observer would say that the three of you are doing battle for the same group of listeners. How much competition is there among you?"

"I was a little startled," I replied, "to read Sam being quoted in the newspaper as saying, 'Myron Cope will not see the light of day from 7 to 7:30.' " Translated, Nover's prediction meant he would rapidly build a huge audience for his show and so fascinate his listeners they would not so much as think about switching at 7 o'clock to my show. "Although I've survived some competition in the past," I continued, "I suppose I ought to pack my bags. I told my wife maybe we better move to a smaller house."

Nover then responded, "I wouldn't want you to do that. We would all be in the wrong business if it wasn't competitive, and there probably are very few people who feel as confident about their innate skills and their ability to be successful in this market as me. . . . My bark has always been bigger than my bite. That statement was just a reflection of my own personality. It was a cute phrase, and it worked."

"It worked?" I said. "You mean the dust is settling on me already?"

"Anyone who thinks he's going to walk in and kick mud in your face is foolish. But it's fun to talk that kind of game."

"I just wish," I persisted, "you'd give me a timetable so I know when I have to start looking for a job."

Turning to the interviewer, Nover said:

"All kidding aside, this is a very difficult situation to get into, inasmuch as Myron has been so dominant for so many years. Then Stan got into it and raised a great deal of interest by virtue of a uniquely different style. Myron is entertaining and knowledgeable. Stan has the best recall of anybody in this industry in Pittsburgh. When Stan showed that he could cut into Myron's rating numbers a little bit, 'TAE decided the important thing was to try to buy up the market in it. . . . " In other words, have *both* of the city's sports talk hosts under one roof.

I bristled. "You said that Stan was cutting into my numbers," I piped. "Stan was building his own numbers but not at the expense of mine. It was like comparing the numbers"—the populations—"of China and Luxembourg. And I wasn't Luxembourg."

Well, girls will be girls. Savran at last got a word in edgewise, saying to me with good sportsmanship, "Obviously, your numbers were as strong or stronger than they'd ever been before."

By the way, Sam Nover's show died a quick death.

Almost 20 years later, by which time I had gone into semiretirement, a television current affairs talk host named John McIntyre working at the same station as Sam invited me to appear on his evening show. At the very outset of the show, McIntyre asked, "You haven't always been Myron Cope, have you? Didn't your name used to be Myron Kopelman?"

"Yes, it was," I said and then related, as I have in this book, that in 1951 a newspaper editor had changed my byline as a condition of employment. Now, however, I was furious. At the first break for commercials, I growled, "Where'd you get that question?"

"Well, I spoke to someone in the newsroom."

"You got that from Sam Nover, right?"

McIntyre nodded.

Why had I minded the question? Having grown up in Pittsburgh and written for the campus newspaper at Pitt, and having employed Yiddish words and phrases in my talk shows, I certainly never hid my Jewishness. Yet I was sure that Nover, though Jewish himself, had planted the question with McIntyre in the hope of embarrassing me, as though by taking the name Cope I had been trying to pass for Gentile and would now be exposed. Don't invite Sam Nover and me to the same party.

Thankfully, for the majority of the years I worked my talk show and delivered commentaries, the Federal Communications Commission governed broadcasting rigorously, seeing to it that broadcasters observed civility. The age of shock radio and shock television had not yet come to pass. No performer dared utter vulgarities on the air.

Radio and television licenses were precious, especially TV licenses; cable had not yet come into existence to fill TV screens with competition, so the few televisions companies that held licenses in effect possessed a permit to print money. Thus broadcast companies, be they television or radio, lived in fear that others aspiring to a license might report them to the FCC for lapses and challenge their right to continue to hold one. At the least, the broadcast stations would have to pay large fees to attorneys to defend themselves.

What a pristine world we broadcasters lived in then! Imagine not being allowed to speak foul language into a microphone! Yet I had no desire to, nor did it even occur to me that the restrictions placed upon me might constitute infringement of my freedom of speech. For more than a decade now, the FCC, so far as I know, has paid no attention to the ruination of manners; it is preoccupied examining multimillion and billion-dollar mergers of broadcast behemoths. "Shock talk" flourishes. Were the FCC to attempt to crack down, I'm fairly sure the American Civil Liberties Union would rise to the defense of talk-show hosts who, for example, tell callers, "Kiss my ass," or invite them to come to the station and perform oral sex upon them. I regard the ACLU as an indispensable defender of constitutional freedoms, but at least in my town, the ACLU chapter leaps to the defense of high school students who defy teachers and would not surprise me by springing to defend the rights of bedbugs to inhabit beds. Alas, when it comes to manners, I'm surely a generation gap behind. Maybe two.

It's not that I'm a prig. I enjoy a "dirty" story, told at the right time and place. I cuss as much as the average man but normally reserve my cussing for team locker rooms, the men's grille at the golf club, or selected bars. On the golf course, I employ coarse language to lament a poor shot, of which I make many. At the club where I hold membership, I once played a round with a fellow member who at about the sixth hole told me he wished I would choose my language more carefully, informing me that he was a lay theologian. I immediately complied. I played in a celebrity charity tournament—the type of tournament in which sports figures are teamed up with paying foursomes—and was assigned to play with four strangers. I know that in these tournaments, my teams expect me to regale them from time to time with stories from my experiences or with stories of any kind, some of them apt to be somewhat off-color. In this instance, sitting down afterward to dinner with my team, I said, "I hope I didn't offend any of you out there today. For all I know, one of you might be a clergyman."

"As a matter of fact," replied one of the golfers, "I am a clergyman." He laughed and said, "Don't worry about it. All of us had a good time."

As readers of this book by now may have noticed, I've occasionally employed obscenities that, it so happens, I find objectionable in newspapers and magazines. I am of the persuasion that such language is permissible in books if serving the purpose of flavor or accuracy, because people who read books are usually sufficiently intelligent to understand the nature of book-writing, a print entity unto itself. Children who rise beyond children's books likewise may be presumed to realize that authors have license, to be employed within reason.

To illustrate—and I caution the reader that the illustration requires a somewhat involved anecdote—in January of 1970, when I was still dabbling in broadcast commentaries as a sideline to my writing career, I read that the Associated Press had conducted an international survey to choose the Athlete of the Decade and that the great golfer Arnold Palmer had won the award. Yes, he was chosen the greatest athlete in the world through the 1960s. I knew Palmer personally, for I had written about him in a magazine or two, but I went on the radio and said, "The choice is ridiculous. Golfers are not athletes."

Do golfers deserve to be called athletes, or do they fall into the category of marksmen? It's a tired, ongoing argument, so I shall not lay out my reasons for carping about the AP's conferring so singular an award upon Palmer. All that aside, several months later, with springtime arriving, I found myself standing on the first tee at Laurel Valley Golf Club, an ultraexclusive national club nestled in the Laurel Mountains of Western Pennsylvania, not far from Palmer's home in Latrobe. Members—high-powered corporate CEO's—felt proud to point out that Palmer was Laurel Valley's titular club professional, and it happened that he had dropped by the club that morning and spied me from the grille above the first tee. He lit out for the tee practically jogging.

"Now we're going to see what an athlete looks like," he said as I addressed my drive.

Swell. To be specific about my game, I have never in my lifetime broken 100. The night I conducted my final talk show, Jim Carter, then general manager of our radio station, appeared in my studio with a going-away gift—a book of tickets entitling me to ten lessons from John Rech, the pro at Rolling Hills Country Club where I regularly commit atrocities from tee to green. Five tickets still remain in my desk. I hadn't the stomach to ask Rech to continue a hopeless project.

Meantime, if you're a hacker who's never teed off under the watchful eyes of a world-famous champion, I refer you to Ira Miller, an old sportswriter friend. Decades ago, Palmer's administrative assistant and righthand man, Doc Giffin, invited Ira and me to play golf with him at Latrobe Country Club, which Palmer owned, and Arnold graciously walked us to the first tee to see us off. Miller at the time was golf editor of United Press International, yet he now visibly shook and proceeded to hit a pop-up drive that carried no more than 15 yards.

"Mulligan!" chirped Palmer. Ira teed up again and duplicated his first drive. After three such attempts, he said, "The hell with it," and played his ball.

I could have done without Arnold Palmer demanding, as I stood over my ball at Laurel Valley, that I demonstrate my athleticism. "Look at him," said Palmer. "His golf shirt's faded. His slacks don't fit."

I waggled my club, but he wasn't through.

"He's got a grip like a kangaroo wearing boxing gloves trying to . . . " No, the kangaroo was not trying to grip a driver. Masturbate, I guess, is the proper synonym.

"Dear God," I prayed as I entered my backswing. "Please let me make contact."

I whacked a gorgeous line drive that traveled right down the middle of the fairway and settled about 200 yards away—for me, a prodigious drive. I held my follow-through as I watched the ball in flight and did not so much as glance back at Palmer. Being the last in our foursome to hit, I merely crowed, "Stick *that* up your ass, Palmer!" and headed directly off the tee toward the fairway.

I ask you, could I have related the anecdote as effectively had I scrubbed it totally clean? I think not. At yet another charity tournament recently, I related the story with exactitude to the four golfers I had been assigned to play with and polled their opinions of whether I should spare no vulgarity when telling the story in my book. They voted unanimously —tell it just as you've told it to us. I nonetheless have compromised.

Yet as inconsistent as it may seem, I rather would forfeit a week's pay than intentionally utter vulgarisms on radio or television. *Silly* as it may seem, there were times when I let slip the word hell—and immediately recalled it by saying, "I mean heck." I firmly believe in the power of the microphone to influence society for better or worse. Every day, hundreds of millions of Americans, children among them, are tuned in. For many, profanity issued over the airwaves becomes acceptable public idiom. In other words, if that stuff makes it across the airwaves, it's our language, right?

Okay, I'm being preachy. Yet it is my conviction that when broadcasters abandon manners, they help create societal meanness that in turn produces hardened and irresponsible citizens. As I'm writing this book, I read that the downtown branch of the Minneapolis Public Library found it necessary to ban, temporarily, the playing of chess in its building. Why? Well, spectators—kibitzers, I gather—to the chess matches had taken to employing "boisterous" language and turning foul mouths on security guards who tried to shush them. The library suspended chess until signs could be posted stating rules of conduct. But, then, I supposed the American Civil Liberties Union would have something to say about *that*.

Shortly after I turned 60, when I cut back on my radio talk show from five evenings a week to two, I noticed that so-called shock radio had extended from Howard Stern's syndicated servings to sports, for had not Stern shown smut to be hugely profitable? A young man named Rocco Pendola, about 25, came to our station from somewhere in Florida to host a late-night sports talk show. He did not stay long, moving on to Dallas, but his shows gave me a grounding in the elements of shock radio when applied to sports.

"Darn!" I told myself. "If I'd latched onto that shock shtick years ago, I could have cut my work day in half."

No more 70-hour weeks. No more racing to a hockey or basketball or baseball game when my evening show ended, so that I could keep in touch with the scene and visit the locker rooms to hear what the athletes, coaches, and managers were saying. Such attentiveness to being informed would be impossible, because given the fact that successful shock shtick combined vulgarity with hard-hitting, merciless evaluations of sports figures, a visit to a locker room might have brought me, at the least, an embarrassing dressing-down from one of my targets, or at the worst, a punch in the mouth. I might have had to miss a long stretch of shows while having my broken jaw repaired. No, I could have just read the sports pages and selected my targets. Sports columnist Bob Smizik of the *Pittsburgh Post-Gazette* once wrote that I was the hardest-working member of Pittsburgh's sports media. I took that as a compliment. Had I realized the minimal time and effort required of a practitioner of the shock shtick, I easily could have escaped Smizik's compliment.

Never have I been sued for slander, and it may be that one reason was that I followed a dopey rule by which I never called an athlete a name or uttered a criticism of him that I would not be willing to repeat to his face, if asked. Was it not stupid to follow the policy that if you roughed up, say, a hitter in a slump, you nonetheless presented yourself in the clubhouse lest you be thought of as a coward? To think of the hours I wasted mingling with athletes when I could have sat at the neighborhood bar drinking beer!

Worse, I knew slander and libel law and therefore knew how easily I could have pilloried people and gotten away with it. Our law provides public figures—meaning politicians, sports figures, film stars, and just about anyone whose name is even vaguely known to the public and therefore can be classified by lawyers as "limited public figures"—with only a small window through which they may sue. They must show in court that the defendant has pursued the plaintiff with "malice" and/or has acted with "reckless disregard" for the truth. It's a difficult lawsuit to win, so public figures normally resign themselves to being punching bags rather than invest the time and legal costs necessary to wage courtroom battles. With shock shtick, I could have been a terror. Listeners could not have been expected to know the law and therefore would assume that every word I spoke about my targets was true, else my targets would sue.

Editorial writers and pundits, when writing about matters in which they have a personal, or vested, interest, sometimes alert their readers by employing the word "disclosure." All right, disclosure: As I express my view of shock shows, I am under unremitting fire from a Pittsburgh sports shock host named Mark Madden. In his radio show in the spring of 2000, he began peppering me with assertions that I was washed up. By fall, he stepped up the tempo by describing me as a "short little drunk" and accused me of drinking while on the air. The last part was true. During my early broadcast days, a veteran radio engineer gave me a tip. "You shouldn't drink soft drinks while you broadcast," Cecil Stuchell said. "They contain sugar that makes you salivate and gulp. Drink coffee or beer." In a football broadcast booth (open in front), coffee quickly grows cold, so when beer is available I drink it.

Thirst-quenchers aside, a letter written by my lawyer to Madden's company brought an immediate halt to his "short little drunk" stuff and reduced him to dismissing me as, for example, "a walking corpse." But on the night of May 17, 2001, I went to a charity party attended by a number of former Steelers and fell into enjoyable conversation with two of them, Frenchy Fuqua and Frank Lewis. I wound up violating the restriction I'd put on myself in old age: Leave parties early. I banged up my car en route to my home and was charged with driving under the influence.

"We're off the hook!" Madden proclaimed on the air, directing those words to company lawyers. He hammers me, I gather, on an almost daily basis. He concocts outright lies and is surely guilty of "reckless disregard for the truth." He promises to hound me "forever"—malice, wouldn't you think? Should I sue? At this stage of my life, do I have the stamina for a lawsuit that in the end would be in the hands of an unpredictable jury? Nobody appreciates being labeled, more or less, the town drunk. I had hoped to live out my senior years in relative quiet, but it was not in the cards.

The reader, meanwhile, may wonder, what was it that triggered Madden's filibuster in the first place? He and I never had exchanged cross words. In fact, he had spoken of me as his "idol." I am left only with a theory. I had entered the twilight of my career in good standing with the public. I had entertained audiences and found time to play a part in worthy causes. The combination made me perfect grist for Madden's shock-radio mill. I was material, simple as that.

I've spoken of the advantages that accrue to sports shock hosts and now offer one more. By failing, years ago, to sense the trend toward people-bashing, I missed the opportunity to achieve almost-perfect objectivity. As I have said, the shock-radio host stays miles away from his targets; not knowing them, he runs no risk of finding he likes them. Thus he has no compunction about ripping them on the air. Not long ago, I was out for a Sunday drive with my daughter and mentioned that I had been hired to perform an interesting job the next morning. The National Board of Boiler and Pressure Vessels Inspectors—yes, I swear to the name—was opening a weeklong convention in Pittsburgh and bringing together basketball coach Bob Knight, former baseball player and manager Pete Rose, and ex-heavyweight boxing champion Joe Frazier to entertain and motivate the conventioneers. I had been engaged to join the three of them on a small stage and pose questions to them for 90 minutes.

"Knight," I said to Elizabeth, "is known for grabbing his players by the throat, stuffing people into trash cans, and throwing a plant against a wall to make a point with a secretary who displeased him. In short, he's a madman. Pete Rose," I went on, "is banned from baseball because he bet on baseball games while managing the Cincinnati Reds, and he served a little time for income tax evasion."

Elizabeth laughed and queried, "Are you going to put questions to them about all that stuff?"

"No," I explained. "This will be an interview but not an exercise in journalism. I'm not being paid to go into that hotel ballroom and start a ruckus."

The next morning I reported to a salon off the ballroom where I and my three interviewees were to pose for photographs with one another and with convention officials. I had known Pete since he was a rookie, had seen him off and on, and knew he would remember me, for he possessed a photographic memory, not only for baseball statistics but for names and faces. I knew Frazier not at all. I had met Knight just once—when he played basketball for Ohio State in the 1960s—and had no expectation he would remember me.

Joining the others for photos, I intended to introduce myself to the burly demon of college hoops, but he flung out his hand and said, "Good to meet you, Myron. I've heard a lot of great things about you."

Well, now. Was I going to like this guy whom I had pegged from afar to be a tyrannical horse's ass? I would see.

Onstage, he pondered my questions (not all of them routine) and served up thoughtful, insightful answers, all the while dishing out hilarious comments and anecdotes that brought the house down. At one point both Knight and Rose—with no prodding by me—fetched up the circumstance in which for years now we have seen athletes, often born-again Christians, invoking their religion to explain their victories. "Somehow," said Knight, "I cannot see God hanging around a ballpark to pull a pitcher through a game. If He's hanging around, my guess is He's at a children's hospital or a food kitchen for the homeless."

Right on! One of my pet peeves is football players who, when I interview them in my postgame Steelers locker room show, put off my first question until they have said, "First, I want to thank the Almighty and praise Jesus Christ for making my successes possible." I thought as I listened to Knight, watch it, Cope, you're starting to really like this maniac.

Lest he appear too grave, Knight said, "I once had a player who crossed himself every time he stepped to the foul line. One night, a priest seated in the first row tapped me on the shoulder and said, 'Coach, get him to stop doing that. He's one for eight at the line and starting to give the church a bad name.'"

Pete Rose put in his two cents. "In Cincinnati, we had a player who crossed himself every time—I mean *every* time—he stepped up to the plate. One day, the pitcher facing him watched him cross himself and stepped off the mound and made a show of crossing *him*self. We had a tie."

From the first time I had met Pete, I had been fond of him, but in my broadcasts I had agreed with baseball's not only having banned him from the game but from the Hall of Fame as well. Yet whenever I said so, it hurt. If only I had adopted the shock shtick, I could have ripped him and called him a dirtbag without wincing, knowing that in the unlikely event I ever met up with him, he probably would not have heard my show.

Meantime, back at the convention of the National Board of Boiler and Pressure Vessels Inspectors, Joe Frazier felt impelled by the others to address the role of God in sports. Attired in a black pinstriped suit and a wide-brimmed black felt hat, Joe recalled his first fight against Muhammad Ali, a grueling 15-rounder at Madison Square Garden where he successfully defended his championship.

"The bell rang for round one," said Joe, "and we met in the middle of the ring. Ali screamed at me. He said, 'You're in the ring with God! Don't you know I'm God?' I said to him, 'God, you're in the wrong place.'"

Our program ran ten minutes beyond our allotted 90 minutes because I could not stop Pete from regaling the packed hall with yet another anecdote. Finally, I said, "No more, Pete. These people have to go to lunch." As I was about to step down from the stage, Knight threw an arm around me. "Myron," he said, "I've got to tell you, you did a great job with the program. I mean it. A really great job."

Idle flattery? Maybe. But of course, I thought not. I had spent hours preparing my questions, and I chose to think that the lunatic coach, from his experience in coaching, recognized detailed preparation. I left the hotel thinking, "Now what would I do about this guy's reported antics if I still were conducting a talk show and delivering commentaries?"

My objectivity had been dented. But hey, this was sports, not the White House beat. Were I running a shock-radio show, I simply could have said, "Thank you, Coach, I appreciate it"—and gone to the studio and verbally bludgeoned him that evening, knowing he had caught a plane out of town. Let's see. I could have begun by saying, "Bob Knight, the all-time bully of college coaching—I caught his act at a convention this morning. He wowed his audience. You cannot believe how phony this man can be when he's making a buck. . . "

I allowed more than enough time to drive to the South Side, taking into account afternoon rush-hour traffic and the consideration that it would be unwise to arrive late for my first ARD class. ARD stands for Accelerated Rehabilitative Disposition. When charged with a DUI in Pennsylvania, one must attend a series of classes lasting up to four hours apiece, during which time those in attendance are lectured on the risks posed by consuming alcohol and other stuff. My first class was to start at 5:30 p.m., but to my surprise, traffic moved smoothly and I arrived in plenty of time to cruise by my destination—a faded, yellow-brick rowhouse converted by the county into classrooms and offices. I found a parking space about a block and a half away, then glanced at my watch and saw that I was forty minutes early. How to kill the time?

Walking toward the rowhouse, I passed a bar called Ruggers Pub. This was early December, but the day was so warm even as dusk settled that Ruggers Pub had kept its front door wide open. A customer called out, "Hey, Myron! Come on in. We'll buy you a drink."

Through the establishment's front window, I saw three middle-aged men and a woman seated at the bar. "Why not?" I thought. I took a stool immediately to their left and ordered a vodka martini on the rocks. I quickly sized up my new acquaintances as being what we old-timers in Pittsburgh call "Pittsburgh guys"—as in, "Oh, he's a Pittsburgh guy," meaning he or she is down to earth and without airs. But I knew a question was coming.

"What are you doing in this neck of the woods?" the man to my far right asked.

I had ready a rhetorical answer: Don't you know the Steelers practice on the South Side? Indeed, for almost two football seasons now, they had practiced at the sprawling, state-of-the-art University of Pittsburgh Medical Center's (UPMC) Sports Performance Center. But again, I liked my newfound friends, so I gave them a direct answer.

"I'm on my way to drunk class."

They guffawed. They knew the rowhouse, for its clientele frequently gather outside around the doorstoop during class breaks. In Ruggers Pub we turned to regaling one another with tales about the Steelers. "Ouch!" I finally said. "It's 5:25, I gotta run." The bartender reached for a camera and asked me to pose for a picture outside the bar, but I said, "Sorry, I can't be late for my first class."

I found a brunette, probably in her 30s, seated alone on the stoop, smoking a cigarette. "Hi, Myron," she said. "They told me they're not starting in there just yet—there's time for a smoke." I lit up, whereupon she forlornly gave me an account of her DUI arrest in every detail. We then entered an upstairs classroom, which held about 25, and spotted vacant seats in the front row. Glancing around the room, I saw that I was the only senior citizen. I felt lousy. Instantly recognized, as well.

Our instructor, a pleasant blonde, introduced herself to the class as Cindy Holmes-Dawkin and announced she would call the roll and then administer to each of us a breathalyzer test. *What?* Did I hear Cindy correctly? Had I not just enjoyed a martini at Ruggers Pub? Small, sealed packets containing plastic tubes—to be inserted into an instrument held by Cindy—were passed around the room. "We'll take you by rows," said Cindy. "Let's start with the first row."

My God!

Only two days earlier, I had telephoned the Alternatives/DUI Regional Chemical Abuse Program to enroll in class. To the woman who answered the phone, I said, "I know it's short notice, but you have a class Wednesday on the South Side. I don't go to court till next month but I'd like to get some of my classes out of the way."

"No problem. In the holiday season, we get quite a few who put off their classes. We'll have room."

The lady asked my name, then let out a chirp and showered me with enthusiasm for the Steelers. "Who'm I speaking to?" I eventually asked.

"My name's Janey," she said.

Janey, Janey! Why didn't you tell me about the breathalyzer test?

"I can't take this test," I piped to Cindy. "I just had a drink down at the corner saloon."

Just about everyone in the class roared.

What was it I wrote in the first chapter of this book? "Humor sometimes takes the form of the unexpected . . . humor often comes unannounced from left field." I had not come to drunk class to play for laughs.

"What'd you have?" a voice called out from the rear of the room.

"A martini."

"A margarita?"

"No. I hate margaritas. I had a martini."

The room practically shook with laughter. Why?

To Cindy I said, "Can I just leave and come back another time?"

"Take the test," she replied. "Then we'll test you again at the end of class. If you had only one drink, it'll be gone." Yes, it went. After Cindy's instrument failed to light up with numbers she said, "Myron, I could tell all the people here really liked you." At halftime, I'd gone outside to the stoop and answered questions about the Steelers while, like others, having a smoke.

"Well, that's nice to hear, Cindy," I said, "but those people departed here with their No. 1 gossip item for immediate use wherever it is they're going: Myron Cope was at DUI class—not only that, he flunked the breathalyzer test." By morning, probably five times the number of persons at the class would know. I would not fault my classmates. Gossip is human nature. Actually, my heart had hung heavy with sympathy for them, all much younger than I. Some may have been addicted. Almost none, I suspected, could afford the fines, court costs, restitution, and other charges. A man about 40 had said in class, "I lost a $50,000-a-year job because my driver's license is suspended."

"What do you do?" asked Cindy. "Are you a truck driver?"

"No, I'm a plumber. I can't work if I can't drive."

Late the next morning, my license not yet having been suspended, I drove to Chartiers Country Club, a venerable club where the Fraternal Societies of Greater Pittsburgh had reserved the ballroom (merrily festooned with poinsettias) for its annual Christmas luncheon. Pittsburgh is a city of many ethnicities—Polish, Serbian, Italian, Slovak, you name it. My hosts were a confederation of ethnic organizations involved in good works. So it was that they presented to me a contribution of $1,000 to one of my favorite charities and a pledge of $3,000 more and gave me a plaque designating me the recipient of their 2001 Humanitarian Award. Big shot? Uh-uh. By evening, Mark Madden trumpeted on his talk show that Mr. Double Yoi, as he referred to me, had attended his first "alcohol rehab class." He said he'd learned so from a phone tip. He promised his listeners to provide reports on each successive class I attended.

Neither film stars nor superstar athletes have been accorded media coverage of their DUI classes. Well, not many folks are given special recognition twice in one day. I was on a hot streak.

Chapter Eighteen

Nearly Fired, Thanks to Sinatra's Telegram

In 1972 Franco Harris, a rookie fullback the Steelers had drafted from Penn State, became an immediate NFL sensation. As his fame spread across the country, so did that of a fan club he'd acquired—Franco's Italian Army. The Army consisted of perhaps a score of Steeler fans of Italian heritage, its name inspired by the fact that although Franco's father was black, his mother was Italian. She'd married an American soldier after they had met in Italy during World War II.

Tony Stagno, a burly man who owned a baking company, commanded the Army as its five-star general; next in command stood four-star general Al Vento, who operated a pizzeria. The Army showed up for Steeler games wearing battle helmets and carrying a full-sized flag of Italy as well as baskets of Italian foods and wines. From time to time, the high command squired Franco, with no attendant publicity, to such places as hospitals or schools for handicapped children. A big-hearted guy, he went willingly.

Franco's Italian Army was nothing if not enterprising. One evening, as I was in the midst of delivering my commentary on the six o'clock television news, the Army burst into the studio in full battle dress—well, helmets—and kidnapped me right off the set, carrying me bodily as they plunged out the door. I was stunned. But from the corner of my eye, I caught sight of John G. Conomikes, the general manager of our television station, standing in the corridor laughing. Good. Franco's Italian Army had observed protocol by asking permission.

The next morning, when it came time for me to deliver my radio commentary, I spoke *sotto voce*. "They blindfolded me when they brought me here," I whispered, "so I cannot tell you, dear listeners, where I am held. However, I did hear them discussing ransom. I think I heard one of them say he figured WTAE might pay $20 to get me back…" As a reward for my good sportsmanship, and notwithstanding the fact that I possessed no Italian blood, the Army inducted me with the rank of one-star general. Much later that year—in fact, when the Steelers were about to play the Miami Dolphins in an AFC Championship game at Three Rivers—Franco's Italian Army hired an airplane to execute a propaganda bombing of the Hilton Hotel, where the Dolphins were staying. The plane showered the Hilton with leaflets that cried, "Surrender!"

Alas, the Dolphins did not. They beat the Steelers, 21-17.

En route to the playoffs, the Steelers had faced a critical game in San Diego. It would be the final game of the regular season, and if the Steelers won they would gain the first divisional title in the 40-year history of their franchise. Chuck Noll, taking into account that his team would be playing a mid-December game in a warm climate, issued orders for his squad to spend the week practicing and acclimating in Palm Springs, and as I departed for that California resort aboard the team charter, I had my own orders from the Italian Army.

"Frank Sinatra," General Stagno had told me, "lives in Palm Springs, as you may know." I also knew that Sinatra had been in retirement for about two years. He later would emerge from retirement and again pack concert halls, but in the meantime, he lived in virtual seclusion, having refused even to be photographed in all that time. "We're giving you a mission," General Stagno went on. "You're to find Sinatra, bring him to practice, and induct him into the Italian Army. Make him a one-star general."

In Palm Springs, various Italian-Americans claiming to be among Sinatra's *buoni amici* promised me they would establish a line of communication to the Great One, but none of them came through. A stroke of luck, however, would save my mission. On Wednesday evening, I sat at a long table in a posh restaurant called Lord Fletcher's, in nearby Rancho Mirage. Our party consisted of about ten—reporters and Steeler front-office personnel. The club's traveling secretary and contract negotiator, Buff Boston, sat across from me. "How goes your mission?" Boston asked.

"Nuts to the mission," I replied. "I'm in Palm Springs to have a good time. I'm not wasting any more time searching for a connection to Sinatra."

Boston sat facing the entrance to the restaurant. Minutes later, he said, "Don't look now, Cope, but here comes your man through the front door."

Indeed, here came Sinatra in the company of the controversial baseball manager Leo Durocher, the professional golf star Ken Venturi, and a tall, comely brunette. I reached for a cocktail napkin and wrote:

> *Dear Mr. Sinatra:*
> *I apologize for the intrusion. We are a bunch of media bums and front-office types traveling with the Steelers. You no doubt have heard of Franco's Italian Army, of which I am a one-star general. I would like to invite you to Steeler practice tomorrow to be inducted into the Army as a one-star general.*
> *Myron Cope*
> *P. S. Franco's from Hoboken.*

The last was a lie. Franco had not come from Sinatra's hometown but from Mt. Holly, NJ. What the hell.

I beckoned the proprietor, whom I assumed to be Lord Fletcher, and handed him the note. "If you think this is an intrusion, forget it," I said.

"He'll get a kick out of it," Lord Fletcher replied.

As the restaurateur strode to Sinatra's table on the far side of the room to my left, heads swiveled the length of our table.

"He's getting the note!" piped one of our party.

"He's reading the note!" chimed in another.

"Quit staring," I said. "You'll embarrass me."

"He's getting up! He's coming over."

So here came Sinatra, trailed by his two flunkies, Durocher and Venturi. Almost at once, I learned of one reason he'd responded with alacrity. Since the start of the week, a shadow had hung over the Steelers' prospects for defeating San Diego. Terry Bradshaw in the previous week's game had suffered a dislocated pinkie on his throwing hand. Steeler fans fretted. Would Bradshaw be able to throw effectively? Gamblers wondered which team to back, and as it happened, rumor had it that Sinatra bet heavily on football—as much as $10,000 a game. Happily, earlier that day at the Steelers' hotel I had said to Noll, "All you've said about Bradshaw's finger is that it's fine. *Is* it fine?"

"It's fine," Noll reiterated. Then he added, "Look, for the first time in his career, he's throwing the ball with touch. Instead of drilling it every time, he's having to put a little touch on the ball."

Sinatra yanked a chair from a vacant table that stood beside us and sat down at my side. The first words out of his mouth were, "How's the quarterback's finger?"

"Yep," I said to myself. "It's true. The man bets football." I then told him, "Mr. Sinatra, the quarterback's finger is fine, I assure you."

He smiled and agreed to attend Steeler practice the next day and be inducted. After he returned to his table, Lord Fletcher brought bottles of wine to ours. "It's the finest in our cellar," he said. "Courtesy Mr. Sinatra."

"Cope," Buff Boston said. "You've got to phone Stagno and Vento and tell them Sinatra's coming to practice. Maybe they can grab an overnight flight and be here for the induction." An induction, mind you, was a ritual—participants drank Italian red wine and ate cheeses and prosciutto, and the Army's high command planted wet kisses on both cheeks of the inductee.

It was 10 p.m. in Palm Springs but 1 a.m. in Pittsburgh. Nonetheless, I found a phone and awoke Tony Stagno and his wife in their bed. Groggy, she handed him the phone. Instead of rejoicing at my news, the bakery owner said, "Myron, I can't fly out there. Christmas is little more than a week off, and I'm behind on my Christmas cookies."

Later I would learn that when he hung up the phone and explained the call to his wife, she shrieked, "My God! You've got a chance to meet Frank Sinatra, and you're not going?" The truth, as I later was told, was that Stagno had a deathly fear of flying.

About eleven the next morning, I left our hotel to board one of the team buses for practice but was stopped by Noll. Word had gotten around. "What's this I hear about your planning a distraction at my practice?" he snapped.

"Listen," I replied. "In the first place, I celebrated the Sinatra thing hard last night. I've got a killer of a hangover, and I don't need aggravation. In the second place, you're almost my age, which means you grew up on Sinatra. Don't badger me."

With that, I boarded the bus.

When I arrived at the practice site—a minor league baseball park where the California Angels took their spring training—I found dozens of photographers ranging the sideline, having gotten wind of Sinatra's impending appearance and hoping to get the first photos of him to hit the newsstands in two years. However, when practice got underway, nobody sighted Sinatra. Presently, one Pittsburgh reporter and another sauntered over to me and said, "Cope, you're a loser again." An hour into practice, Buff Boston picked up a pay phone fastened to the outside wall of the baseball clubhouse and phoned the team's media relations director, Joe

Gordon, who had gone to San Diego to visit that city's media and publicize the upcoming game.

"Did Sinatra show?" Gordon asked Boston.

"Sinatra's a no-show. Cope's a loser again."

No sooner had Boston issued those words than he felt a finger tapping him on the shoulder. He turned to find a fellow wearing an orange sweater and, characteristically, a white porkpie golf hat. "When Sinatra says he'll show," said Sinatra, "he shows."

"He's here, Joe, he's here!" cried Boston as he watched Sinatra turn and walk toward the sideline. It turned out that for an hour he had sat alone in the bleachers watching practice.

Photographers muscled one another for position. And as I stepped forward to greet Sinatra, I saw two figures wearing battle helmets jogging toward us, carrying baskets of wines and foods. Yes, Stagno and Vento, taking advantage of a three-hour gain flying west, had arrived. Breathing heavily, they presented themselves to officiate at Sinatra's induction, but I said, "Hold everything! We've got to have Franco in this."

Not thinking twice, I strode briskly into the middle of Noll's practice.

"Franco!" I shouted. "Get over there. The man's here." Then I thought, "Jesus! Noll will kill me."

A humble rookie who wanted no special privileges from his stardom, Franco replied, "I can't do that, Myron. I'm practicing."

I turned to Noll. He pointed a thumb at the sideline and, revealing himself to be a Sinatra worshiper, barked, "Get over there, Franco!"

Sinatra's induction commenced. Franco, sporting the abundant Afro and huge sideburns fashionable in that day, towered over the group. Stagno and Vento had flown west fully equipped. Not only did they unfurl a flag of Italy attached to a four-foot stick but placed upon Sinatra's head a one-star battle helmet on the right side of which had been pasted Italy's national colors. Sinatra thoroughly enjoyed every hug and kiss and held his wine glass high for a toast. The induction done, I drove Stagno and Vento to our hotel so they might freshen up in my room before heading to the airport—Stagno, after all, had Christmas cookies to turn out. Once in my room, he phoned his wife.

"It was like kissing God," he told her.

On the coming Sunday, the Steelers thrashed San Diego to gain the playoffs and the next week, in Pittsburgh, defeated the Oakland Raiders on a play forever remembered as Franco's Immaculate Reception, the wondrous shoestring touchdown catch of a ball that deflected off the shoulder pad of Raiders safety Jack Tatum. Approximately an hour after that game had ended, Franco, the only player remaining in the locker room, sat on a stool in front of his locker, still accommodating a semicircle of reporters. Joe Gordon approached and handed Franco a telegram, which said:

GO, STEELERS, GO
COLONEL FRANCIS SINATRA

Standing on the rim of the reporters, I moved forward to look over Franco's shoulder. Sinatra had forgotten his rank of general, but I said to myself, "Hey, he bet the Steelers, all right. That telegram's worth putting on the air." I glanced at my watch and saw that it read two minutes to five o'clock. Knowing my station had a five-minute newscast scheduled to start at five, I hurried to a wall telephone in the team's equipment room and said to the newsroom, "I got something cute here at the stadium. Put me into the newscast, live."

"Okay, hold."

I held, and kept holding. The newscaster was new to the station, a retired army major who had worked for *Stars and Stripes* and thus was able to "double-dip" by taking retirement pay and a fresh job in communications. Trouble was, he did not know which button to punch to enable me to hear his newscast or hear him say, "Now we go to Myron Cope at Three Rivers Stadium." My wristwatch told me just one minute remained of his newscast. Furious, I said aloud, "What the fuck!"

I was on the air.

The game had been played on a Saturday afternoon. Monday morning, Dick Ross, the general manager of WTAE-Radio, telephoned me at home. "Myron," he said, "I know what you said on the air was an accident, but when you get in here this afternoon, drop into my office. We've got to have a meeting."

I met with Ross and his director of programming, Bernie Armstrong. This was 1972, mind you, when the Federal Communications Commission governed broadcast language strictly, as I noted in the previous chapter.

"We're required to have this meeting," Ross began. "We're required to inform you of the possible penalties for what you've done. And by the way, Mr. Snyder"—the big boss, two floors above us—"is going up the wall."

Frank Snyder was a regular guy, but like myself, a total prude in his governance of material put into the airwaves. "Well, what are the possible penalties?" I asked.

"Up to two years in jail," Ross replied, "and a fine up to a maximum of $10,000."

"Who does the two years, me or Mr. Snyder?"

"Mr. Snyder."

"Good," I said. "I'll send him a fruitcake."

As matters turned out, the FCC received only one complaint and disregarded it. I myself received only one letter, written by a man on the letterhead of an insurance company. He wrote, "Until now, I couldn't stand you. Now, I'm a fan."

About 25 years later, Bill Hillgrove, by then our play-by-play broadcaster of Steelers games, told me a story I'd never heard. Snyder, he said, had departed that playoff game at the wheel of his station wagon, his wife seated beside him. In the back of the wagon sat program director Armstrong and his wife. Snyder of course had his radio tuned to our station. He glanced backward at Bernie and said, "On Monday, you *will* fire that man?" Apparently, he was persuaded to think it over. In fact, now that I think of it, I would bet that it was Snyder himself who a half-year later persuaded Ted Atkins, the new radio GM he hired from Los Angeles, the man who upon hearing my voice made a note to fire me, to think it over.

Chapter Nineteen

Was the Most Publicized Play in American Sports Kosher?

In the autumn of 1997, the *New York Times*, prompted to telephone me by the fact that the 25th anniversary of Steeler Franco Harris's Immaculate Reception would occur in late December, asked me to write a piece about that astonishing play for the *Times's* Sunday sports section. The Immaculate Reception, after all, had created lasting controversy. Was it a legal catch? If not, a referee's call in the waning seconds of a 1972 NFL playoff game had outrageously deprived the Oakland Raiders of near-certain victory and made them 13-7 losers.

When the *Times* phoned, I hesitated—I had not written for either a newspaper or magazine for many years and feared I would be rusty. But I agreed to attempt the piece because I'd proclaimed myself through the years to be the world's leading authority on Franco's play. In importance, of course, this self-conferred distinction ranks well below being, say, the leading authority on the African tsetse fly. Be that as it may, the following is my story that ran in the Sunday *Times* on Dec. 21, 1997.

What became of Amelia Earhart?

Where is Jimmy Hoffa buried, if not in Giants Stadium?

Have creatures from outer space really sampled New Mexico's tourism?

And then, yet another of the great unanswered questions of the 20th century: Was Franco's Immaculate Reception kosher? Was it legal?

The Immaculate Reception doubtless will not be remembered as far into the future as the Catholic doctrine from which its name derived. Yet thanks to the energies of NFL Films, which profitably and constantly feeds the appetites of television networks and syndicators, Pittsburgh Steeler rookie Franco Harris's catch revisits our screens to this day, heading toward its 25th anniversary Tuesday, as the single best-publicized play to have been executed in an American sports competition, ever. Mary would be amazed, if not irked. TV is not giving us Bartolome Estaban Murillo's timeless 16th century painting "The Immaculate Conception", is it? TV is showing the Reception.

Ah, but Mary and Franco share. Some doubt the Virgin Birth (which, by the way, non-Catholics confuse with the Immaculate Conception). John Madden, then the coach of the victimized Oakland Raiders, doubts the Immaculate Reception. Again, was it legal?

It was. I know so. I know where the proof lies this very day.

After the game, I dined with my wife, then drove to Pittsburgh's WTAE-TV studios to deliver a commentary on the game for the 11 o'clock news. Meanwhile, a Steeler fan in his late 20s, Michael Ord, was celebrating Franco's catch at a downtown bar fittingly named The Interlude. Boisterous fans toasted the victory. Ord climbed upon a chair and with a spoon tapped his glass for attention.

"This day," he proclaimed, "will forever be known as the Feast of the Immaculate Reception!"

Then, to a friend, Sharon Levosky, he suggested, "Call Myron Cope."

When my phone rang in the newsroom, I listened to Sharon's suggestion and said, "That's fantastic. Let me give it some thought." The Immaculate Reception? Tasteless? I pondered the matter for 15 seconds and cried out, "Whoopee!" Having conferred upon Franco's touchdown its name for 11 o'clock news viewers to embrace, I accept neither credit nor, should you hold the moniker to be impious, blame. Whichever, I can lead you by the hand to the repository wherein lies the proof that Franco made a legal catch of Terry Bradshaw's pass.

But first, a memory refresher.

On a Saturday afternoon, two days before Christmas of 1972, the Steelers and Raiders engage one another at Pittsburgh's Three Rivers Stadium in a first-round playoff game, the winner to advance to the American Football Conference championship game. With but 22 seconds remaining, the Raiders lead, 7-6. The Steelers' offense faces fourth down at its 40-yard line, needing 10 for a first down.

One of NFL Films's marketed videos is especially arresting. Bradshaw breaks the huddle, jogging to the line behind No. 56, center Ray (the Old Ranger) Mansfield. Whoops, was not Jim Clack centering for that play? True, but NFL Films had no particularly dramatic from-the-rear film of the Steelers breaking that huddle, so an earlier play had to do. The Old Ranger, who died of an apparent heart attack in 1996 hiking down a mountainside in the Grand Canyon, is preserved for posterity. That's OK. The revisionist Oliver Stone might have plugged in JFK snapping the ball from a Hyannis Port touch-football game.

Anyhow, Bradshaw drops into the pocket but is soon chased backward and to his right by the Raiders' right defensive end, Horace Jones. Bradshaw slips Jones, who grazes a hand across Bradshaw's midsection, and desperately rockets a pass that travels 37 yards from his fingertips to the Raiders' 34. He has spied John (Frenchy) Fuqua, an undersized but talented halfback, hooking into the middle of the field, racing free. Raiders safety Jack Tatum, however, also has spotted Frenchy. He abandons the tight end he was covering and advances upon Fuqua. At the instant the ball arrives, a fierce collision occurs.

Tatum will say afterward, "I thought I might have a chance for the ball, until he got in front of me. But when he did that, I just went for the man," meaning Fuqua. Tatum, whose autobiography published years later was titled *Call Me Assassin*, delivers a Tatum special—a wicked right forearm that appears to strike Fuqua's head, flush.

At that moment, the ball emerges from the collision, flying back toward midfield. And here comes Franco.

Says Dick Hoak, the Steelers backfield coach then and still today:

"Franco's assignment was to stay in the backfield and block the outside linebacker. If the guy didn't come, Franco was to try to chip someone, then get out for a pass."

Franco finds nobody to block or even chip. He glances over his right shoulder and, seeing Bradshaw in trouble, gallops downfield. Little does he suspect he is about to collect a priceless reward for good practice habits.

"From the day he came into the league that year," Hoak remembers, "he ran them out. In practice, no tackling, he'd run clear to the end zone from 40 yards out. In games, he was always around the ball, whether he'd run a pass pattern or was blocking. If he ran a pass route to one side of the field and Bradshaw threw to the other side, Franco would run there. Maybe the pass would be batted into the air, or maybe there'd be a fumble.

I tell our young guys in practice, 'Run to the end zone. Get to know it. Franco Harris did it every time and got to the Hall of Fame.' "

Franco's simple explanation following the Steelers' victory? "I started running to block if Frenchy caught the ball."

But here comes the ball, and Franco cups it in his upraised palms, possibly as neat a shoestring catch as the many Roberto Clemente made in this same stadium. Scarcely breaking stride, Franco points himself at the left corner of the end zone. Raiders defensive back Jimmy Warren angles in pursuit from the middle of the field. Inside the 15-yard line, Franco reaches back with a stiff arm, fighting him off. At the 11, Warren lays hands on Franco's back. But he slides off, landing on his belly. As Franco crosses the goal line, a reported hundreds—but actually, maybe not even a hundred, the estimate being significant, as we shall see—pour onto the field.

But was this a touchdown? The referee does not signal touchdown.

The rule book at that time specified, as it no longer does, that for a pass to be legally caught, two players of the same team could not touch the ball consecutively. The NFL frowned upon receivers playing volleyball. Thus, if Bradshaw's pass had touched Fuqua en route to Franco, it was *traife*—not kosher. But if it had caromed off Tatum to Franco, fine.

Referee Fred Swearingen confers with his crew, particularly with umpire Pat Harder and back judge Brian Burk, the two officials presumed to have had the best view of the Tatum-Fuqua collision. Remarkably, Swearingen then disappears into a Pirates baseball dugout, escorted to a telephone by a Steeler official, Jim Boston. Swearingen phones the press box, asks to speak to NFL Supervisor of Officials Art McNally, then emerges to throw up his arms. Touchdown! Did Babe Ruth, having had a lemon hurled at him as he knelt in the on-deck circle and being jockeyed mercilessly by the Chicago Cubs dugout, predict his 1932 World Series line-drive home run by pointing to Wrigley Field's center field wall? Or was he merely gesturing, or not even doing that? History is a mess. Did Franco make a legal catch? How shall we ever know the answer?

We will. Here.

And now, a word about the principals.

The Corpulent Coach—John Madden, head coach of the Raiders, described as more stunned than angry in the Raiders' locker room, declared, "If the officials really knew what happened, they'd have called it right away." The Corpulent Coach had a point.

The next day, Madden spent a miserable Christmas Eve back in Oakland reviewing game film. He subsequently asserted that Bradshaw's pass could not have ricocheted off Tatum because Tatum had positioned himself behind Fuqua. Perforce, the ball had struck Fuqua.

But Madden was rationalizing. The Raiders' game film had cleared up nothing. (Nor had the Steelers' film.)

Nonetheless, the Corpulent Coach plunged forward, charging that Ref Swearingen had phoned the press box for Supervisor McNally to review instant replay. NBC-TV was televising the game but not to Pittsburgh. Though the game was a sellout, Congress had not yet gotten around to pressuring the NFL into televising home-game sellouts. Television carried the game into Three Rivers on at least one monitor, but the telecast played to the public only beyond a 75-mile radius of Pittsburgh. Steeler fans, if still sober, held their foul breath in Youngstown, Ohio, motel rooms.

Instant replay remained 14 years from being approved as an officiating tool, so it could not be invoked by Swearingen or McNally. Yet Madden, furious, charged that McNally had stolen a peek at a replay. Several days later, a United Press International article datelined Oakland reported:

"Oakland writers said Steelers Public Relations Director Joe Gordon told reporters in the press box that the NFL officials had made the decision from the replay."

"That's total fabrication," said Gordon, long regarded by pro-football writers across the country as the nonpareil of NFL publicists. He had answered the phone call from Swearingen, called McNally to the phone, and stood by, hearing McNally's end of the conversation. Gordon says McNally never viewed a replay. He says Swearingen simply was checking with McNally to determine that his interpretation of the applicable rule was correct. If so, Swearingen had no business making the phone call. A high school official would have understood the rule.

Madden pressed on, taking an additional tack. "There was no way they were going to call it any other way with all those people on the field. Somebody would have been killed."

Hey, the stands had by no means emptied. Was this a Bogota soccer game?

The Assassin—"I didn't hit the ball," Tatum said.

He is, of course, remembered as the man who delivered the blow to New England receiver Darryl Stingley that put Stingley in a wheelchair for life. Stingley reviles him for afterward showing only minimum interest in his—Stingley's—fate. If you depended upon this man's testimony, would you put him on the witness stand?

The Frenchman—One of my all-time Steeler favorites. A black man from Detroit, John Fuqua called himself Count Frenchy, claiming to have descended from a French count. To teammates and beat writers, he was simply "the Frenchman." He confided that at weigh-ins at the start of training camp, he carried a five-pound weight in his athletic supporter so as to make 180 pounds and avoid being cut.

Down through the years, he has insisted he knows whether it was he or Tatum who touched the football but that he will reveal the truth in his own good time. About a dozen years ago, in a Detroit hotel bar, the Frenchman urged me to write his autobiography. Short of time, I declined with thanks. Was it a book that would reveal The Truth?

Forget it. The Frenchman has no idea whom Bradshaw's pass struck.

"Everything was dizzy," he at first told reporters crowding around his locker. Tatum's ferocious forearm had sent him sprawling.

The Frenchman seemed unaware of the rule that governed the Immaculate Reception. When reporters explained it to him, his mischievous mind cranked into action. "No comment. I'll tell you after the Super Bowl"—a game the Steelers did not reach, having gone on to lose to Miami in the AFC Championship game. "I'm not chopping down any cherry trees"—perish the thought Count Frenchy would fib—"but no comment."

Twenty years later, Steeler free safety Mike Wagner opined:

"He doesn't know. How could he? He was getting drilled from behind."

Divine Intervention (possibly?)—Father John Duggan, sojourning from Ireland to study in Boston for a doctorate in psychology, had made the acquaintance of several sons of Steeler owner Art Rooney, Sr. A good-luck charm, they decided. "Get him to the games," Rooney ordered. Relatively young for a priest, his face cherubic, Father Duggan in this fateful season had attended 12 games, preseason included. The Steelers had won 11 of them. Saturday nights he conducted Mass for Steeler Catholics and candidly admitted he prayed for Steeler victories.

Friday, the day before the playoff game, he looked on as the Raiders took the field at Three Rivers to practice. Notwithstanding Father Duggan's collar, the Raiders suspected a spy and ordered him off the field. Said the priest in his rich Irish brogue, "I consulted their manager, a Mr. Madden, of all names, and told him I would speak to my superiors about this."

You asked for it, Madden, and you got the Immaculate Reception. Franco, for his part, allowed in the dusk of that Dec. 23, "I'd believed all along, but after today I believe in Santa Claus, too."

Not far east of Pittsburgh, in a woodland favored by deer hunters, stands WTAE's 1,000-foot-tall television tower and, about 150 feet distant, a squat, concrete-block, one-story, fenced-in structure. In the basement are stored film and videotapes of times past. There lies my proof that the Immaculate Reception was legal.

On Christmas Day of '72, two days after the Immaculate Reception, I obtained from our television newsroom the film of Franco's catch that one of our cameramen had shot. Neither it nor the excerpt from NBC's telecast had made it the least bit clear to audiences whether Tatum or Fuqua had touched that football. I then ran the film through a device called a viewer, slowly cranking the handle that allowed me to watch the film frame by frame, again and again, at snail's pace.

No question about it—Bradshaw's pass struck Tatum squarely on his right shoulder. I mean, I saw it.

Bradshaw's powerful arm (he drilled that pass) combined with the inflexible polycarbonate plastic epaulet that topped the right side of Tatum's shoulder pads would account for the football rebounding a full eight yards into Franco's hands. At any rate, with great relish, I aired my findings. The film could not be televised frame by frame, so I simply related my findings in a commentary I scripted. That was that. In today's age of advanced technology, to say nothing of valued collectibles, that film, I suppose, would have been made airable in slow motion and then placed in a safe. For my part, I had magazine and broadcast deadlines to meet and an AFC championship game for which to prepare, so I simply returned the film to the newsroom shelf, from which it would in time be sent to WTAE's transmitter building for storage.

It lies there, proof of the legitimacy of the Immaculate Reception, but virtually unfindable.

"It would be like looking for a needle in a haystack," I am told by Steelers play-by-play radio broadcaster Bill Hillgrove, for many years the sports director of WTAE-TV.

All right, why?

"About 1977, our station went from film to videotape. In the film days, when Franco made his catch, TV people didn't think much about systematically filing stuff for the future. It was, 'Just get it on the air.' About two years after we went to tape, we became more conscious of future need, if for no other reason than legal purposes."

But would not the Immaculate Reception film have been stored chronologically, by date?

"It isn't. See, we played that film from time to time for a while— we'd get it from the transmitter, then send it back—but each time we sent it back, it was added to all the stuff that preceded it. Who can remember when we last used it, let alone know a date? To go in there and find it, well, you'd have as good a chance of hitting the lottery."

Absent the film, the Corpulent Coach might say I have concocted my story of viewing that film frame by frame. Would he be calling me a liar? If so, I would confront him and, to borrow a Madden trademark, pow! Then again, maybe not. I stand 5-feet-5, 140.

Back in early November, I had lunch with Franco, still a Pittsburgh resident and businessman. A huge, stately man, he wore a neatly cropped beard; if you put a turban on his head, you would have a Sikh warrior. Not long ago, he led a group that bought a venerable but failed sausage-making company in Baltimore—Parks Sausage. "God, it's hard work," he told me, "but we're getting near to turning the corner." The coming weekend, though, he would be in Philadelphia to watch the Princeton-Penn football game. His alma mater, Penn State, would be playing Michigan at Happy Valley, where he wanted to be, but his son Dok—not a football player—had enrolled at Princeton.

"I've never attended an Ivy League game," Franco said, wincing. Then, hesitantly—but what father could resist mentioning it?—he said, "Dok made 1,600 on his SATs."

I told Franco about the film I had put through the viewer. "Wow!" he exclaimed. "Can I see it?"

Sorry, Franco. Laying your hands on it is as unlikely as a second Immaculate Reception.

ADDENDUM

Recently I read that Terry Bradshaw had explained Referee Swearingen's call on the Immaculate Reception by saying, "He went to the dugout phone and told his boss in the press box, 'If I call it no catch, we don't get out of here alive. If I call it a catch, we get out alive.' So the guy upstairs said, 'Call it a catch.'"

That's Bradshaw, as I indicated in an earlier chapter—say it if it pops into your head. In It's Only A Game, *a book he and a collaborator published in 2001, Bradshaw states that the referee, whose name the collaborator misspelled, examined replays on a TV monitor suddenly brought to the sideline for that purpose. I phoned Joe Gordon and said, "I don't remember a TV monitor on the sideline." Gordon replied, "That's because there was none." Terry's imagination is, you might say, a figment tree. Moreover, his assertion that Swearingen ruled in favor of the Immaculate Reception in order to save himself from mob violence was actually a canard John Madden had spouted and clung to for years. Terry, it's a cute answer when you are asked if Franco's catch was legal, but it's an answer that does a disservice to your teammate. Think about it when you go for the laugh.*

Chapter Twenty

"How'd You Like Me to Call You Shorty?"

In the sixth round of the 1998 NFL player draft, the Steelers selected a 250-pound running back named Chris Fuamatu-Ma'afala from the University of Utah. Several colleagues and I were broadcasting the draft on radio from a small office at Steeler headquarters. Whenever the team made a selection, Mike Fabus—normally the team photographer but on draft day a "runner"—would scribble the name, position, and college affiliation onto a slip of paper and walk down a lengthy corridor from the so-called War Room (where coaches and scouts huddled) to the media room to inform reporters. En route, Fabus would pause briefly at our broadcast site so that we could have a quick look at his slip of paper, jot down the information, and immediately put it on the air for the benefit of draftnik listeners waiting breathlessly. Alas, Fabus's handwriting sometimes was legible only to himself.

Chris Fuamatu-Ma'afala? I blurted into my microphone, "The Steelers have just made their sixth-round pick. He is running back Chris Fuamatu of Alfalfa State!"

Of course, no such college existed, but who knew? Taking time to better decipher Fabus's scribbling, I knew I had to act in self-defense, lest my tongue trip for however long Fuamatu-Ma'afala's pro football career might last. I thereupon announced a reasonable facsimile of his name and told our audience, "From here in, that guy is Fu." I always have had a fondness for nicknames. Anyhow, soon after Fu reported to training camp, he put on a one-man show in a practice scrimmage against the Redskins. Pounding for yardage, he took the Steelers on a long drive. I stood at the end of the Steelers' bench and shouted, "Way to run, Fu!" Lee Flowers, the safetyman, said, "Fu?" He then turned to his teammates and yelled, "Myron says he's Fu!" They chorused, "Way to go, Fu!" That season, whenever Fu ran for sizable gains, Steeler fans crooned, "Fuuuuuu." For several decades now, spectators at American sporting events have been issuing similar sounds of approval to cheer athletes whose names prominently include a vowel that rhymes with, well, boo. Born in Honolulu of Samoan blood, Fu as a Steeler rookie expressed surprise at the nickname I had given him. When I first met him in training camp, I said, "I guess I wasn't being original when I named you Fu. Surely they called you Fu when you played for Utah."

"As a matter of fact, no," he replied.

Will someone please check Utah football fans for a pulse?

Way back in my boyhood, probably half the professional athletes in America carried nicknames—Pudge, Joltin' Joe, Smokey, *ad infinitum.* I am not sure what caused nicknames to run out of fashion, but I'll guess they began to vanish in the 1960s when American blacks, fighting for their civil liberties, began demanding respect. Black athletes not only took up Muslim names but insisted they be addressed by their given names— a Robert no longer cared to be called Bob; a Richard was Richard, not Dick or Dicky or Rich or Rick. Sportswriters soon eschewed assigning nicknames to players, let alone picking up on one that was in the process of being popularized by a broadcaster. Long after the wave of formality among black athletes waned, most sportswriters, and sportscasters as well, clung to it. In 1999, Lethon Flowers, approaching his fifth season with the Steelers and by then a starter, took me aside in training camp and said:

"Myron, would you do me a favor? Tell your friends in the media that I'm asking they please stop calling me Lethon. My family and friends have been calling me Lee all my life."

In the summer of 2001, oddly enough, I found myself rejecting a player's nickname. In the second round of the draft that year, the Steelers had selected Kendrell Bell, a linebacker from the University of Georgia. Early into preseason training camp, Kendrell's performances on the field made it appear likely that the Steelers had drafted a second-round steal. So I said to him:

"Do people back home call you Kendrell, or do you have a nickname?"

"They call me Ken or Kenny," he replied. "My mother's always called me Kenny."

Hmmm. Unknown to Bell, he had created for me a dilemma. I told myself, "If this young man is to achieve national recognition as a star, he'll get there faster as Kendrell Bell than Ken Bell." Sure. Kendrell Bell rhymed. If he played as well as I thought he could, the name that rhymed would stick in the minds of fans and media. Never mind Ken or Kenny, Cope. At the end of the season, Kendrell Bell was elected the NFL's Defensive Rookie of the Year. The decision I made in his behalf made it possible. Don't argue.

But normally I'm a nickname guy and pleased that lately I think I have detected a ray of sunshine melting the virtual moratorium on nicknames. When the Texas Rangers in 2001 gave the most lucrative contract in baseball to shortstop Alex Rodriguez, sportscasters across the nation called him A-Rod. His new Texas teammate, catcher Ivan Rodriguez, already was known as Pudge, thereby reviving a long succession of Pudges that seemed to have no visible heirs. Perhaps the Rodriguezes of sport were anointed by a higher power to blaze a trail back to the friendly humor that baseball nicknames almost always implied. In any case, I am rooting for the trend. In golf, happily, we have the cognominal giant, Tiger Woods. A trivia question: What's his first name? At this instant, I cannot recall. In basketball we have Shaq. In football, we've had Deion (Prime Time) Sanders, but Prime Time was not a nickname—it was a billboard.

As I mentioned in Chapter One, I hung nicknames on athletes, teams, even cities, but in one instance I had to back off. In 1971 the Pirates fetched up from their farm system a tall, skinny, 21-year-old pitcher named Bruce Kison. He showed no tolerance for hitters who leaned over home plate. No matter their credentials or fame, Kison, expressionless, fired fastballs under their whiskers. Personally, I loved his messages to the hitters, for I believed in the pitcher's right to claim his space. In my commentaries I dubbed the rookie "Killer" Kison. One night soon after, I strolled to his locker with other reporters after he had rung up a victory.

"What's this Killer stuff?" he asked me from his stool.

"You don't like it?" I said.

Kison rose to his full height, 6-feet-4, and stared down at me, a foot below. "How'd you like me to call you Shorty?"

He spent 15 years in the big leagues, as Bruce. Oddly, nobody in my lifetime has called me Shorty. Come to think of it, Shorty Cope would have made a great byline.

Meantime, nicknaming away through the years, I allowed myself a smile when I heard my nicknames become part of the Pittsburgh vernacular, employed by news announcers and fans alike. Not as if there's a crying demand, I herewith offer a brief glossary of some of the monikers I have served up.

The Cinci Bungles—Glen Sheeley, a Pittsburgh sportswriter who covered the Steelers in the 1970s, in an article one day referred to the Bengals as "the Bungles." I immediately embraced this handle, giving Sheeley due credit on the air, and have perpetuated it every season the Bengals have bungled away; such seasons, of course, have been many.

The Cleve Brownies—In my own mind, if in no one else's, this has been a means by which to dismiss the Steelers' hated rivals as if they are little more than a pack of mildly bothersome toddlers. Now and then, until club owner Art Modell moved his team to Baltimore and renamed it the Ravens, I also called the Brownies Modell's Meatballs.

The Denver Yonkos—In some neighborhood bars around Pittsburgh, any customer who bored the drinker seated on the next stool with inane, endless conversation came to be labeled a yonko. Astute drinkers chose a stool beside a known yonko only when it was the only one unoccupied. At any rate, in 1977 when the Steelers were to meet the Denver Broncos on the day before Christmas, it crossed my mind to write a lyric, to be sung by me on radio to the tune of the carol *"Deck the Halls."* I could carry a tune, all right, but of course my voice was another matter. Moreover, the only instrumental recording of *"Deck the Halls"* to be found in WTAE's music library was played at such a rapid tempo that it forced me to spit out the words in a fashion that bordered on gargling mouthwash. Nevertheless, the idea was to bash the Broncos, so I came out singing.

> Deck those Broncos,
> They're just yonkos,
> *Fa-la-la-la-la, la-la, la-la...*

Listeners surely thought I had gone insane, yet they wanted more; thus my Steeler Christmas carol became an annual musical event at Christmastime. The third year, as I recall, our television station asked me to videotape my carol for the 6 o'clock news. I put on a Santa Claus hat and a white costume beard and sang away while a stagehand, unseen by viewers, stood atop a ladder, dumping fake paper snow on me, some of it entering my mouth as I sang. Some time later, a writer for the magazine *Inside Sports* invited me to dinner at a Pittsburgh hotel so that she might interview me. Naturally, I hoped for a favorable writeup and out of the blue received an encomium from a fan that surely impressed the writer. A woman approached our table. After pardoning herself for interrupting our dinner, she said, "When you sang, I swear to God my whole family was pissing in their pants."

Nonetheless, a year after, Fred Young, our director of television news said to me, "We won't be needing your carol this year."

"Okay," I replied, "but do you mind telling me why not?"

"Well, for one thing, my kid says it stinks."

"How old's your kid?" I asked.

"He's ten," said Young, if I remember the correct age. I responded, "That's a real first-class survey you have there."

"Another thing," Young pointed out. "When you sing that thing, spittle forms on your lips. For the viewers, it's disgusting."

Young, normally an astute executive, had spoken, so I sang my carol for radio only. Television viewers lit up our switchboard. "Where's Cope's Christmas carol?" they howled. The following year, Young said to me, "Why don't you resume your carol for television? We'll put up with the spittle."

I wrote and sang a fresh lyric every Christmastime until I retired from virtually all my radio and TV duties save my Steeler football broadcasts. One of my favorite carols began:

> Deck the halls
> With Modell's meatballs
> *Fa-la-la-la-la, la-la, la-la...*

Now where was I? Oh, yes—my glossary.

Diego Chargers, Diego Padres—I just liked San Diego's name sans the San.

Jack Splat—Adapted from a popular nursery rhyme ("Jack Sprat would eat no fat...") to describe the sound of the great Steeler middle linebacker Jack Lambert sacking a quarterback. Splat!

The Bus—On draft day, 1996, the St. Louis Rams traded 5'11", 250-pound running back Jerome Bettis to the Steelers. That season he battered his way to 1,431 yards, leaving would-be tacklers prone as if hit by a bus. Along the way, I seemed to recall that back in his Notre Dame years, Bettis sometimes indeed had been called the Bus, so I jumped on the nickname. Meantime, wanting to give credit where credit was due, I phoned Notre Dame's sports information office.

"Who was the first to call Jerome the Bus?" I asked.

"Some sportswriter for the college paper, I think," came the answer.

"What was his name?"

"I have no idea, and I'm not even sure he was the guy."

I asked Jerome. He had no idea.

Okay, I tried.

Not to give my glossary of nicknames the thickness of *Webster's*, I'll just gloss over the Chi Bears, the Chi Cubbies, the K.C. Chiefs, the Minny Vikes, and the Dallas Cryboys (who blamed their loss to the Steelers in Super Bowl X on lenient officiating). I do hope that an old friend, Dick LeBeau, now head coach of the Cinci Bungles, does not succeed in turning around that miserable outfit. Nothing personal, LeBeau. I simply would hate to lose Bungles from my lexicon.

Chapter Twenty-One

On Smoking

I cannot recall where it was that I saw the term "health Nazis" used to describe Americans who are on a crusade to save our populace from poor habits, but afterward I muttered those two words just about every time I was forced to leave a building to smoke a cigarette, or because of unavoidable circumstances found myself in the self-righteous and screwed-up state of California, where I always opted for hotel room service because restaurants are forbidden by law to allow my kind to indulge.

I took up smoking in my teens, for the usual reasons. Were not my friends—excuse me, peers—smoking? Nobody at that time heard warnings that cancer might be the result. Jocularly, we were told, "Those cigarettes will stunt your growth." If a serious study of that possibility is ever attempted, I suppose I'm a likely case history. At any rate, knowing what we long ago learned about the health hazards that go with smoking, I'm pleased that neither of my children smoke, but I learned to *enjoy* cigarettes—in my 20s and 30s, horrors, I smoked cigars and chewed tobacco as well—and I take responsibility for my own welfare. Barring a scientific discovery that makes me young again, I don't care to reach my 90s, nor have I formed a plan to sue a tobacco company if the smokes get me.

Meantime, I'm practically certain that the obituaries of me in our local newspapers will include this sentence: "He was a heavy smoker." If the writers of the obituaries happen to be health Nazis, they may even put down those words with a measure of glee, as if to say, "See, Cope, you got yours. How about the others you poisoned with secondhand smoke?"

In 1964 U.S. Surgeon General Luther Terry issued the first "Surgeon General's Report on Smoking and Health," but smoking did not become a supposed scourge in America until 1982 when a self-promoting surgeon general named C. Everett Koop issued a call for a "Smoke-Free Society." Affecting a beard of the kind that over years had been assigned to Hollywood versions of scientists, Koop obtained all the statistical and anecdotal material he wanted from the study industry, portions of which are happy to make a living providing answers that are wanted. However, I remember that as I was shaving one morning, an announcer giving the news on my radio reported that Yale University had conducted an independent study that found the effects of secondhand smoke to be virtually nil. Koop's speeches and tapes became ubiquitous, doing no harm to his bank account, I assume, and there emerged a technology company that bore his name. I found it satisfying when I read in *Newsweek* that Dr. Koop.com had "swooned in the market."

I saw signs, as early as 1989, that the health Nazis were closing in. Aboard the Steelers' chartered plane headed for a preseason game, I lit up. Smoking was still permitted aboard airplanes, but three rows in front of me, a rookie receiver from a military college turned his head and piped, "Sir, would you please put out that cigarette?"

"Why?" I asked. "Am I imperiling your health?"

"Yes, you are."

"Well, then, I guess you're just going to die, because there is no rule that says I can't smoke on the plane."

Bubby Brister, the irrepressible quarterback, sat in the row directly behind me. "Hey, rook," he called out. "You don't seem to know it, but this guy is one of the Steeler owners."

I heard no further protest from the rookie, and on the Monday morning that followed the preseason game, Chuck Noll cut him. Noll found him too slow, but I wondered if the rookie, as he packed his bags, figured I had had a hand in his release.

In 1992, the new Greater Pittsburgh International Airport opened, a magnificent structure. Following the Steelers' first road trip that year, the team returned home at about 3 a.m. The airport was deserted. I made my way to the trains that carry travelers to the airport exits. There I encountered Ralph Berlin, the trainer. It had been one of his pleasures in life to light a cigar when he left a plane. "I picked up a tail," Ralph told me. "A security guy came up behind me and said, 'This is a nonsmoking airport.'"

I said, "You should have told him you don't give a damn whether the airport smokes or not."

I certainly did not smoke in the company of people afflicted by asthma or whatever ailment they might call to my attention. But it puzzles me that among nonsmokers who have no such condition, many object to so-called secondhand smoke while others express no complaint whatever. I suppose nostrils differ. Meantime, the health Nazis—the really vehement crowd to which politicians pay attention as they tax smokers, most of them said to be poor, to their teeth—began to pound on a variety of doors in the middle of the night, so to speak. Not satisfied to crush smokers under their collective heel, they fanned out in other directions, attacking people for being fat and airlines for serving peanuts. H. L. Mencken, held by some to be the greatest American essayist of the first half of the 20th century, wrote that "it has been my firm belief ... that all persons who devote themselves to forcing virtue on their fellow men deserve nothing better than a kick in the pants."

That said, Mencken offered an equation that he called Mencken's Law: "Whenever *A* annoys or injures *B* on the pretense of saving or improving *X*, *A* is a scoundrel."

A also creates confusion. For example, some conservationists and health-care busybodies embarked on a movement to segregate wearers of perfume and stamp out secondhand fragrance. In California—where else would the policy start?—Marin County required restaurants to provide perfumed and nonperfumed seating. I wondered, what emotional toll did this take on reformers who strove for Cigarette Prohibition but coveted their perfumes and colognes? Aftershave lotion was under siege, I learned in a column written by John Balzar in the *Los Angeles Times.* Noting also that pollen allergies were even more widespread than perfume allergies, Balzar asked, "Should we be required to collectively dig up our lawns and flower beds?" With obesity rampant, he reported movements afoot to place a sin tax on greasy fast-food meals. How would *that* go over with non-smoking, nonperfumed health Nazis who love cheeseburgers and have only a half-hour for lunch?

As the year 2001 neared an end, our latest surgeon general, David Satcher, indeed declared war on obesity. He vowed, I read in my morning newspaper, he "will launch a campaign equivalent to the one the surgeon general's office launched in 1964 against smoking." It was not clear to me what weapons Satcher would employ, but I made it 100 to one that taxpayers, fat or skinny, would pay millions—if not billions—for Satcher's war. Mencken was right. *A* is a scoundrel.

And Harry Truman was right. "There are lies, damn lies, and statistics," he said. A couple of years ago I told a doctor friend, "For about three years now I keep reading that we smokers cost the country $400 million a year in health-care costs. *Your* outfit, the American Medical Association, is one of the organizations that put out that figure. Tell me, how do they arrive at a very round figure like $400 million, and how come the statistic hasn't changed? Also," I asked, "if we're killing ourselves by smoking, how are we costing the country money? A lot of us won't make it to the nursing homes to hang around for years with Alzheimer's or you-name-it. We're *saving* the country money."

The doc had no answer. I have not seen that $400 million statistic for a while, but I read just a few weeks ago that smokers, according to the Robert Wood Johnson Foundation, now cost the nation $138 *billion* a year. My God, in practically the wink of an eye, we became almost as expensive as a missile defense system.

Art Rooney, the legendary founder of the Steelers, beloved as "the Chief" by the populace, was rarely seen without a cigar—he either smoked one or bit one into pieces and chewed it or carried one, lit or unlit, between his index and middle fingers. After his death, a statue of him was placed outside Three Rivers Stadium (and later transferred to Heinz Field, the Steelers' new stadium). Fittingly, the statue held a cigar in its fingers. One morning after the Chief died, a sign went up in the Steelers' press room: No Smoking. As best as I could learn by probing, a quarterback in a meeting room 30 or more feet down the hall had complained that he could smell cigarette smoke through an overhead ventilation system. I went to Dan Rooney's office and appealed the ban, but he gave me no satisfaction. "Times change," he said.

"Are you going to send somebody out there to the Chief's statue," I asked, "to chop off the cigar?"

The health Nazis came to be everywhere. In the hours before a Steelers game against the Arizona Cardinals in Tempe, I stood in the rear of our radio booth, listening to colleagues conduct a pregame show and smoking a cigarette. A security man wearing sergeant's stripes on the sleeve of his brown uniform—was that not the color the Nazis wore early on?—entered the booth and said, "Sir, there's no smoking here."

I thought fast and replied, "Sergeant, with all due respect, you don't seem to be aware of NFL rules. Visiting broadcasters' booths are treated as embassies. They are inviolate to home-team interference."

The sergeant pointed to a private box adjacent to our booth and separated from us by only a pane of glass. "Sir," he said, "the club owner's daughter sits there with her party. If you smoke, she's going to phone for me, and I'll have to come back here and make you quit smoking."

As matters turned out, owner Billy Bidwill's daughter failed to show up. Her box remained vacant. To our radio audience I related my conversation with the security man and extracted revenge by saying, "Bidwill's team is so awful his daughter doesn't show up for the games. But what else would you expect of a team that has nothing better to do than concern itself with protecting the owner's daughter from smokers?"

I recall visiting my sister Violet and her husband, Hal Grodsky, who were having family to dinner at their apartment. As Violet brought an ashtray to where I sat in their living room, their son Larry, just back from a trip to Spain, said, "Uncle Myron, you ought to move to Spain. Everyone there smokes."

"I know," I said. "I've been there."

Those ill-informed Spaniards need to be told the statistics so they will quit enjoying themselves as they please. Meantime, turning again to H. L. Mencken and this time paraphrasing him, reformers are people who are haunted by the fear that somebody, somewhere, is having a good time.

I sleep lightly, listening for the clatter of the health Nazis' boots.

Chapter Twenty-Two

A Closer Look at Me

(Which Rhymes With "Just a Closer Walk with Thee,"
Which Louis (Satchmo) Armstrong Put to a Wonderful
Dixieland Beat!)

It may surprise those who listened to the radio talk show I conducted for almost 22 years that I left a lot unsaid. I have been a fairly private person. On the air I did not often mention personal matters or relate adventures in my household. Many talk show hosts do. I don't fault them, but I always wanted to keep a piece of myself for myself. Also, I was there to talk sports. I believe it was Larry Merchant, at the time a richly talented sports columnist for the *Philadelphia Daily News*, who first termed sports "the toy department." That's how I've always treated it. Let's just get on the air and have fun.

At 73 now, I look back on my life and know that it included more misfortunes than, dare I say, the average American's life, yet fewer or less severe misfortunes than have been suffered by Lord knows how many.

For starters, at 15 I began to lose my hearing. A doctor identified the condition as otosclerosis, surely inherited because my older sister Violet likewise had lost a portion of her hearing. From which branch of the family tree we received the gene, I have no idea. But losing hearing was no help to a kid who by then was developing a passion to be a reporter. Many years later, when Chuck Noll held his weekly news conferences from the head of a long table, I made certain to grab a seat at his elbow. I am sure some reporters said, "Who does he think he is, Helen Thomas?" But those who knew of my deafness helped me out when afterward I asked them for quotes I had missed. I came to be totally deaf in my left ear and as a result hated to have strangers call out to me in public. Walking up the aisle at an arena, I could hear them only through my right ear, so I would say to myself, "Which side did that come from?" I had to guess. When I turned the wrong way to acknowledge their greetings, they surely said, "That guy acts goofy."

At times, however, my deafness was good for a laugh. In 1978 the PGA championship tournament came to Laurel Valley, the lush golf course that lay about an hour east of Pittsburgh. I set down my typewriter and work papers on a table well to the rear of the huge media tent and went to work. Soon a tournament official entered the tent and spoke into a microphone up front. "Gentlemen, may I have your attention?" he said. He had a bulletin to announce. "I regret to inform you that Pope Paul has died."

"Boog Powell!" I cried out, speaking the name of the longtime Baltimore Orioles slugger whose baseball career had ended only a year earlier. "He's too young to die!"

Never has a Pope's death resulted in such laughter as rolled through the media tent.

Eleven years earlier, our first child, Martha Anne, had been born prematurely and lived but five days—easily long enough to love her and clearly remember the face I saw through a hospital nursery window when I visit her grave, marked by a small, flat, heart-shaped stone. Our second child, Danny, was born brain-damaged, apparently having received insufficient oxygen at birth. He is 34 as I write but has never been able to speak a word—he makes only sounds—or comprehend abstract concepts. I remember that when he was four, with beautiful features and yellow hair that caused an ad-man friend to tell me he wished I would let Danny pose for commercial photography, Danny stood one summer evening in our driveway and watched neighbor kids tossing a ball in the driveway across the street. I saw a tear or two roll down his face, for he knew he could not take part.

Well, 'tis a "world of toil and snares," as Velma Middleton, Satchmo's robust vocalist, sang when she belted out the hymn.

The fact is that in taking stock, I consider myself a *lucky* man, for three principal reasons (other than Mildred and our daughter Elizabeth). One is that I never had to fight a war and risk being maimed or killed in my prime. I was drafted for the Korean War but of course was rejected because of my deafness. I shall not for a minute suggest I departed the draft board's headquarters disappointed, but I wondered, "Why don't they take me and put me to work banging a typewriter at a military post and thereby free up another to fight the war?" I suppose they had good reasons. At any rate, I was spared the horror of war. All three of my brothers-in-law had served in Europe in World War II—Marie's husband, Kenny Joseph; Shirley's husband, George Meyers; and Violet's husband, Hal Grodsky. Not once since, at least in my presence, did any of them speak a word about the war. To those who have fought my wars, I offer my thanks, with embarrassment.

Another reason I call myself a lucky man is that not for a single day have I found myself out of work. Once in my newspapering days and another time as a broadcaster, I sweated out 11th-hour management-union negotiations that averted strikes, but I never missed a paycheck. The late Jim Murray, a Pulitzer Prize-winning sports columnist, published his autobiography in 1993, and as I read his first words on Page 1, I scribbled in the margin, "Describes me!" Murray wrote:

"I was a Depression child. With all that connotes.

"That means you never trust the system again. You know what can happen to it. That means you go through life never able to fully enjoy it. That means you have a never-ending sense of foreboding. I don't know how it affected other people but I have never been off a payroll in my life. I'm sure I would get the shingles if I didn't know I was getting a paycheck. I never quit a job in a huff. I swallowed guff.

"I don't recommend it," Murray continued. "It's just the way I was. A legacy of hard times, constant fear of the future. I was disgusting. Good Soldier Schweik. That's because the most terrible thing in life to me was to be out of work. I had seen what it did to people. To families. To marriages."

I, too, had been a Depression child and lived out Murray's fears almost identically. Oh, it's true, as I related in an earlier chapter, that I shucked a weekly newspaper paycheck to try my hand at freelancing for magazines, but again, I was single and confident that if I failed, I could find another newspaper job. Hadn't my sports editor bade me farewell by saying, "Kid, you'll be back in six months"?

Still, the Depression haunted me, as it did Jim Murray. When economists and Wall Street analysts debated whether a recession was under way, I thought, "Are you kidding? It's here. And a depression may be around the corner, and if it comes, it'll be far worse than the last one because in *these* times the vast majority of jobless, hungry men already will have acquired guns."

Not to dissolve into total despondence, I'm prompted to recall that Jim Murray and I once played a round of golf in Lewistown, Maine, the unlikely site of Muhammad Ali's first title defense against Sonny Liston. Later, in at least two of his syndicated columns, Murray wrote, "Myron Cope is the worst golfer I have ever played with."

The third principal reason that I feel as lucky as a shipwreck survivor fished from the ocean is major medical insurance. I have no doubt whatever that after I moved from writing to full-time broadcasting, many colleagues in the media and even readers who followed my work concluded, "He did it for the money." Writers, of course, were expected to be underpaid. It was taken for granted that broadcasters who topped the ratings cashed in big-time. But no, I did it for major medical.

Danny was born in January 1968. The surprise phone call I received from a radio station asking me to take on a morning sports commentary as a sideline came little more than a month later. By the time Danny reached his second birthday, we knew something was wrong. He had been slow to crawl, and when we placed him in a bassinet in the backyard and a neighbor's dog barked, Danny screamed so fearfully that we took him back into the house. Our pediatrician said, "He's just developing slowly." As time passed, Danny's unpredictable behavior caused Mildred to become a virtual prisoner in our house. Whenever she took him along to the supermarket, there was no telling when he would unloose piercing screams—or if, in the checkout line, without warning, turn and deal a swift kick in the shins to the woman behind him. Baby-sitters usually disappeared after one try.

It was not until Danny reached six that we heard of a local psychologist versed in a little-known affliction called autism. Danny was indeed autistic, the psychologist told us, and advised us that his only hope of improvement—for modifications of his behavior—lay in placing him in a facility with knowledge of autism. None existed in Pittsburgh. In one instance, I told a friend my son was autistic. He replied, "It must be nice to have a kid who can draw."

We traveled the east and on up into New England, inspecting one place and another, sometimes finding housing that appeared close to squalor. Our clear choice, our only choice, was a large old house in Chester County, near Philadelphia, operated by the Devereaux Foundation well off its main campus and supervised by a Canadian expert in autism, Dr. Austin DesLauriers. The bills began coming in—approximately $6,000 per month, if I remember correctly.

Major medical at that time in the 1970s was a new wrinkle in health insurance, rarely accessible. But the American Federation of Television and Radio Artists to which I belonged provided it to members, so I put in a claim for benefits. Not so fast, I was told. The union's insurance carrier rejected my claims, contending that autism was a mental illness, a category not covered. Autism is no such thing. It is a physical disorder caused, as simply as I can put it, by wires in the brain being crossed incorrectly at birth. Its victims, though they vary widely in symptoms and capability, often live in fear of normal environments. They raise their hands before their faces and wiggle their fingers, as if defending themselves. Small changes around them prompt them to scream and even butt their heads against the nearest wall, as Danny did. It's mental illness, said the insurance carrier.

I had a lawyer send a letter, threatening a lawsuit. Soon after, I received a call from the head of the union in New York. "Good news," he said. "I went to the insurance company and spoke to them in the language I learned growing up on the south side of Chicago. They're going to cover your claims." Later, I would learn that actually, officers of my Pittsburgh local—principally, a television performer named Bill Cardille —had rescued me by putting fierce pressure on New York union headquarters. I was going broke paying Devereaux's bills, my savings disappearing. That new-fangled insurance, major medical, dictated that I make a career of broadcasting, not writing.

The day we first deposited Danny at his new home and hugged him goodbye at the door and then got into our car for the drive back to Pittsburgh, Mildred wept for a long while. I felt helpless. Once a month, we fetched Danny home for a weekend. Thursday nights I would leave the radio-TV building after my talk show at about 8:15, check into a Chester County Holiday Inn at about 1:00 a.m., pick up Danny around 9 a.m., and head back to work at WTAE, where Mildred awaited to drive Danny to our house. Sundays, she took over the chauffeuring, departing late in the afternoon and returning Monday. Air travel was no option. Who could predict Danny's behavior on a plane? We could not take him off a plane over, say, Scranton. At any rate, Danny stayed at Devereaux eight years, or until we heard that the Home for Crippled Children in Pittsburgh had begun to receive autistic children. There he lived for two years—the maximum allowed for patients. Through these years—and I have no idea why—Danny's autistic symptoms gradually waned. No more finger-wiggling, no more butting his head against a wall or having to wear a helmet. He still emits short screams when feeling threatened by whatever, but no more long, piercing screams that used to force us to leave restaurants in the middle of dinner while those at other tables stared at us. Now, I simply classify Danny, when asked to, as brain-damaged.

From the Home for Crippled Children, we moved Danny at 15 to Allegheny Valley School, an outstanding nonprofit Pittsburgh organization that has grown to operate campuses and group homes that serve more than 800 retarded and otherwise afflicted persons clear across Pennsylvania. There, as far as I can tell, Danny will live out his life. I once invited a group of hardened cops to tour Allegheny Valley School's Patricia Hillman Miller campus, which specializes in retarded kids so crippled and deformed as to be pathetic. When the cops left, I spotted nary a dry eye.

Yet such is the callousness of our society and, in particular, of our politicians toward the need for sufficient funds for havens for the mentally disabled that good-hearted workers in these places exist on wages barely above the legal minimum—or at least they do in Pennsylvania, where I am knowledgeable. For the same reason, political indifference, a model organization such as Allegheny Valley School is forced to tell parents (some of them of an advanced age and not knowing what will become of their child when they die): "Sorry, there's only the waiting list.

In the 1970s, not long after we enrolled Danny at his first home-away-from-home, Devereaux, there occurred a development in the book-publishing industry that gave me pause. Publishers began dishing up sizable advances, some in six figures, to writers of sports books, which historically had been targeted at the children's market and made little money. In 1960, however, Jim Brosnan, a Cincinnati Reds relief pitcher, had published *The Long Season*, an engaging diary that for its quality of writing and imagination produced adult sales. Publishers took notice. Three years later, my agent telephoned.

Doubleday & Company had signed the great Cleveland running back Jim Brown for an autobiography, she told me, and had offered him his choice of three collaborators, myself included. He chose me, for when I had profiled him for *Sport Magazine*, he found my story to be a sensitive portrayal that went beyond his feats on the field. At the time, Brown easily ranked as the greatest running back in football, and to this day I regard him as the best ball carrier I have seen—a 230-pound bruiser possessed of a 32-inch waist and huge thighs, a runner who, when necessary, would shift into a higher gear that made him nearly impossible to catch.

Doubleday paid Brown $8,000 as an advance against royalties. I got $4,000. Brown would receive two-thirds of the royalties, and I, the remaining third. For a sports book, these were good numbers. I told myself, "With Brown's name working for us, who knows? Maybe even the bestseller list?"

In the ensuing months, we met frequently in the living room of his small house on the east side of Cleveland, and while we talked, his toddler twins sometimes played on the floor or climbed upon his lap. "Myron," he lectured me, "you really ought to get married. It's a good life." I married Mildred late the next year; Brown, embarking on a film career in Hollywood at about the same time, split with his wife. Meantime, our book, *Off My Chest*, had received many reviews, all favorable, and been serialized in newspapers, for Brown had straightforwardly unburdened himself of stories he had previously secreted. For one thing, he described obstacles that race prejudice had placed in his path. If read today, the book would seem tame, but in 1964 black athletes kept their mouths shut.

In any case, my agent (or was it Doubleday?) told me, "We've got a problem. Brown's made just one appearance for the book. He appeared at a Dallas department store and sold out the inventory—1,000 books. But he refuses to make any more appearances."

I found it difficult to believe that the store had stocked as many as 1,000 copies, but I phoned Brown to see if it were true that he'd refused to make further appearances.

"Yes," he said. "I couldn't even find the book at my neighborhood bookstore. If Doubleday can't distribute it properly, why should I spend my time promoting it?"

Because, Jim, if for no other reason, I had a chance to make a big score.

My guess was that Brown had by then become preoccupied with dreams of Hollywood. Though still a devastating football player, he retired after the next season, 1965, a Hollywood contract in hand. He debuted in a major role in *The Dirty Dozen* but his film career petered away. While it did, newspapers splashed his name in print for, in one instance, being accused of throwing a woman off the balcony of his apartment— and in another, for allegedly becoming involved in a heated argument with a motorist, who thereupon sat on the hood of Brown's car, only to have Brown forcibly remove him.

"Hmmm," I said. "Are there sequels to *Off My Chest*? *Off My Balcony*? *Off My Auto Hood*?"

Close to 30 years later, I ran into Jim Brown in Pittsburgh. Both of us were to speak at a huge televised dinner that former Steelers cornerback Mel Blount has organized annually for the benefit of his Mel Blount Youth Home. Those who were to occupy the dais were lined up backstage for a grand entrance—in alphabetical order. "B" as in Brown immediately preceded "C" as in Cope. He turned his head and said, "Hello, Myron."

I said, "Hello, Jim."

End of conversation.

Meanwhile, back in the mid-1970s, as I noted earlier, sports books hit their stride. Big-time advances were being paid to major sports figures *and* their collaborators, for television was building a vast and worshipful audience for sports. I knew I could have left broadcasting and cashed in. Jimmy Breslin, the well-known New York columnist and author, had said to me back in the days of my magazine career, "You're nuts for not moving to New York. Your byline's a name in the business. I guarantee you, you walk into the bar at Toots Shor's at the cocktail hour, you'll get offers to write books and screenplays."

I remembered Breslin's words. I knew I easily could top the money I was earning from Pittsburgh broadcasting without even having to leave my hometown. But no. Going out on my own again would mean losing major medical. Jim Murray would have understood.

Eddie DeBartolo, Jr., whose family once owned the Pittsburgh Penguins hockey team and later the San Francisco 49ers football franchise, appeared on my talk show less than an hour after his father had announced the hiring of a new general manager, Tony Esposito, who had ingratiated himself to the DeBartolos at the expense of General Manager Eddie Johnston. During a commercial break, DeBartolo said to me, "How come you're not with the networks?"

A nice compliment. Maybe lack of ambition was the answer. ABC, NBC and CBS dominated television, for cable had not yet bitten off huge chunks of audience. The networks certainly knew about me. Whenever I asked their publicity departments to provide a big-name guest for my show, they at once came through. (The gambler-turned-TV-star Jimmy the Greek—with CBS, if I recall correctly—proved to be the surliest guest I ever interviewed; ordered to report to my show during Super Bowl Week, he had been delayed from attending parties, I assumed.) I once heard that a network executive had said, "Cope's big in Pittsburgh, but will his act fly in Detroit or Cedar Rapids?" I thought it would, but never in my career did I submit a tape of my stuff to a network or anyone else. I knew that all I had to do to join a network was to send them a history of my ratings—year after year at the top, except in the category of 12 years old and under, and doing it with a weak 5,000-watt radio station whose signal disappeared at dusk from a vast area to Pittsburgh's north. The networks could not ignore such data. Casting about, they kept paying big money and providing chauffeured limousines to a number of stiffs who came and went.

One network, not among the Big Three, did phone. As I was dressing in the morning, Mildred said, "You had a call while you were in the shower. A man called from Atlanta, and he wasn't very nice. I told him you were in the shower, and he said, 'Get him out of the shower.' "

"Sounds like a television executive," I said.

Yes, it was Bill MacPhail, who had been head of CBS Sports and now was charged by Ted Turner with organizing a cable television network, Turner Sports Network. "I'm forming a three-man studio sports team," he explained when I returned his call. "I've hired Steve Zabriskie to be my anchor man and a woman who's pretty good." Zabriskie and I had worked together in Pittsburgh before he went off to ABC to broadcast college football. "What I need to complete the team," MacPhail continued, "is an off-the-wall guy." This was the first time I'd heard the expression, which I supposed meant creative, unpredictable, and somewhat weird. "Zabriskie tells me you're he best off-the-wall guy in the country."

"Well, thanks," I said, "but it happens I'm in the middle of a contract."

I told others who phoned the same. In my talk shows and commentaries, I never hesitated to blister sports figures who capitalized on a big season by demanding their contracts be renegotiated. My conscience was clean. I never told management of job offers to exert leverage for a new contract before the old one expired. I was business-stupid, sure. But I believed a signature on a contract, or even a handshake, was sacred, and I slept well.

Headhunters phoned. One asked if I would be interested in a Cleveland job that would include broadcasting Browns games. I knew that Art Modell, the club owner, had admired my magazine writing and followed my broadcasting career. He backed a film starring Walter Matthau, who in one scene relaxed on a Caribbean island listening to a Steelers radio broadcast delivered by me and my partner Jack Fleming. I later said to Modell, "You've never paid me a cent for appearing in your film." He replied, "I'll pay you the same amount you pay me when I appear on your talk show."

Anyhow, I told the headhunter, "I'm in the middle of a contract."

Another headhunter phoned. Would I be interested in a New York broadcast job that included the Jets' games? Hoo-boy, New York! "I'm in the middle of a contract," I said.

San Francisco. This one was cute. I would become sports director and sports anchorman for a television station and broadcast the 49ers' games. Eddie DeBartolo, Jr. by then operated the 49ers, so I guessed he had okayed the phone call. But I also sensed a strategy at work. In Pittsburgh, our chief rival in radio and television was KDKA. That station had hired a television sportscaster from North Carolina named Bill Currie, billed as the Mouth of the South, who appeared in gaudy sports jackets with a flower in his lapel. He cared little about sports, I always suspected, but he had a talent for humor and was able to script commentaries that made large inroads into others' ratings, gathering up women viewers who loved his stuff and never suspected when he had his facts wrong. He was good. The Westinghouse Broadcasting Company owned KDKA and also the San Francisco station that phoned me. If Westinghouse could lure me out of Pittsburgh, Currie would face less competition for the television audience and KDKA's radio arm no longer would have to contend with my talk show.

"I'm in the middle of a contract," I said.

Finally, I received an overture that did not come in the middle of a contract. Carolyn Wean, a nice woman who was general manager of KDKA-Television, phoned. "Your timing is good," I said. "It happens that my contract has only three months to run." We met in a hotel room —clandestinely, as was the practice when a station attempted to snatch a rival's employee—where she made me an offer that was a whopper compared to what I was earning. (No, I am not going into figures.)

"Okay, Carolyn, here's my answer," I said. "WTAE has been nice to me over a long time. I'll tell them your offer. If they match it, I stay there. Be sure this is your *best* offer, because if they do match it, I will not be coming back to you to try to get you to raise the ante. I won't play you and them against one another."

She said, "It's my best offer."

I brought into the negotiations with WTAE my lawyer, Les Zittrain, and a close friend, Sam Zacharias, an expert in insurance and pensions. Years before, at a time when I was haggling with television general manager John Conomikes, a friend since boyhood, I said, "John, it looks like I'm going to have to bring in my lawyer to do this stuff for me."

"Fine," John replied. "Instead of you talking with me, your lawyer will talk with our lawyers." A coward, I dropped the idea.

This time around, John welcomed Zittrain and Zacharias with a friendly handshake. WTAE matched KDKA's offer. I finally got paid what I was worth, but hey, no hard feelings about the long delay. Business was business. I simply had been a lousy businessman.

For example, a year or so after I married Mildred, we had bought our first house, a small split-level. Several years later, when we purchased a larger house, we put the split-level up for sale. I said to Mildred, "Why should we pay a fat commission to a real estate agent? This is a good little house. We may have to sweat it out for a while, but it'll sell." I chose a nice, round asking price—$40,000. We placed an ad in the newspaper and stuck a for-sale sign into the front lawn. The next morning, a woman visited—our first prospect. She said, "I'm very interested. I'll phone you this evening." A young couple was next to arrive. "Forty thousand?" the husband said. "We'll take it."

"Somehow," I told Mildred after the couple had put down a deposit and departed, "I have the feeling I underpriced this place."

Don't ask me about the stocks I bought that went down or the stocks I sold that went up.

To make a clean breast of it, my disinclination to express interest in broadcasting the games of the Browns, Jets, or 49ers stemmed not only from an obligation to honor my contracts but also from a fear of losing my enthusiasm for the role. Leave the Steelers broadcasts? Are you kidding?

In my teens I worked as a vendor at Forbes Field where the Pirates and Steelers played. It was rotten work. Vendors reported at about 8 a.m., hours before they knew whether they would get work. We would stand around in a large dungeon of a room in the bowels of the ballpark or if possible find space on a bench until the big boss called us into line for a shape-up. Sometimes you got work and received a blue uniform, other times you were sent home through an opening in the wall that put you onto the street, assuring you could not hang around to watch the game free. I worked Pirates games—it helped if you slipped a small bribe to one of the boss's lieutenants—but I meant to *see* Steelers games.

I cased the place. I observed that now and then one of the bosses would enter the dungeon through an iron gate that prevented us from slipping into the grandstands to enjoy a ballgame without working. If the boss intended to spend only a few minutes in the dungeon, he merely closed the gate behind him but failed to lock it. I waited for the moment. I darted through the gate and sprinted up the aisles of Forbes Field until I reached the very top of the right field stands. There I hid in a stall in the men's room where I memorized players' uniform numbers from the roster that appeared in the Sunday sports section. I waited for the ballpark's gates to open at 11 a.m. At eleven I sprang from the toilet to take a place in standing room behind the uppermost row of the ballpark, smack above the 50-yard line. Hundreds soon gathered there. They had no tickets but had slipped 50 cents to pals working the turnstiles. The Steelers usually played badly, and there were times when it seemed that standing up in right field, we almost outnumbered paying customers seated in the stands. No wonder Art Rooney considered it a victory whenever he met the payroll.

Bred a Steelers fan, I hated to imagine broadcasting another team's games. Yes, I had told the Steelers at the outset that I would thrill to their successes yet verbally beat on them when they stunk out the joint. How could I broadcast another team's games and have no emotional stake in the outcome? I might as well have signed on to broadcast Olympic bobsledding.

Chapter Twenty-Three

That Anal Voice

When I have been the subject of newspaper articles or mentions, "raspy" usually is the adjective employed to describe my voice. Going beyond that, Jerry Izenberg of the *Newark Star Ledger* once wrote in his nationally syndicated sports column that my voice "has all the shrill subtlety of an attack-dog whistle." On the other hand, *Inside Sports* found it to be "sort of mid-range sandpaper." Then there was Billy Davis, a Dallas receiver at the time the Steelers played the Cowboys in Super Bowl XXX. Billy had played for the University of Pittsburgh and thus heard my broadcasts. Chuck Finder, a Pittsburgh columnist, mentioned my name while interviewing him, whereupon Billy said, "He has that anal voice."

I believe he meant to say nasal, but then again, we hear of announcers and singers bringing up their voices from the pits of their stomachs — maybe Billy Davis was pinpointing the source of mine.

I suppose my voice falls upon the public's ears like china crashing from shelves in an earthquake. At Super Bowl XIII, the Steeler versus the Cowboys, the NFL put old George Halas—the longtime owner and coach of the Chicago Bears—into a handsome antique car and drove him to midfield to toss the coin. Meantime, broadcasting to Steeler country on radio, I forecast an interesting battle between the aging Steeler guard Sam Davis and the great defensive tackle Randy White. A technical glitch occurred. I have never heard of such a glitch before or since. Just as Halas flipped the coin, my voice took the place of those of the network television announcers. Across the nation, viewers heard me bellow, "Sam Davis will clean Randy White's clock!" Elderly ladies in Topeka probably dropped their knitting.

By the way, Davis cleaned White's clock.

Yes, it is true that listeners to my earliest radio commentaries bombarded the station with demands that I be removed from the airwaves, but in the years that followed I came to realize that my voice amounted to an asset. For one thing, it is identifiable. Few announcers have had a voice that was worse. Secondly, my voice practically demands the listeners' attention, just as motorists slow down to look when passing a wreck. Also, when I thought about it, I was reminded of Bob Prince, the longtime announcer of Pirates baseball games. Prince possessed a terrific broadcast voice, but more than that, it was a voice that cut through rooms, enabling listeners to continue hearing the ballgame when they went to the kitchen for a fresh beer. I think I, too, cut through rooms. In fact, at one time I was billed in a sales department brochure as "the voice that cuts through concrete."

Advertisers came calling with invitations to perform radio and television commercials. Hey, talk about easy money! A half-hour's work, a day's work, and they send you a check. Jack (Splat) Lambert and I were cast to do a television commercial for Kennywood Park, a popular Pittsburgh amusement park. Kennywood was installing a new ride—a water ride in which patrons rode a boat that carried them beneath waterfalls that soaked them. Because Kennywood as yet had not completed construction of this attraction for masochists, we were dispatched before the amusement park season opened to film at a place in Richmond, Va., that had installed the water ride the previous season. An ad agency crew of about 20, whose duties I could not entirely identify, likewise converged on Richmond.

The day dawned cold and damp. Time after time, "take" after "take", the ad men had Lambert and me step off a small pier into the boat and head for the falls. To make certain we appeared soaked, a man sat in the front of the boat out of camera range, hurling buckets of water at us. After about the 15th take, Lambert climbed back onto the pier and stared down at me. His false teeth chattered.

"This," he said, "is a lot of shit."

"Listen, Splat," I replied. "This is like robbing a bank."

He reflected for a few moments, then said, "Cope, you're right."

For whatever reasons, advertisers saw Lambert and me as a team, perhaps because the image of the tall, lean, furious linebacker contrasted comically with that of a loud-mouthed runt. We heard from a ruddy-faced, volatile businessman named Frank Fuhrer, who had dabbled in Pittsburgh sports ownership and now had purchased a Budweiser distributorship that covered the whole of Western Pennsylvania. A sport, Fuhrer signed both Lambert and me to generous contracts to perform Budweiser commercials. Believe it or not, we even did singing commercials. Anheuser-Busch flew an expert team of music producers from Nashville, the Music City, to Pittsburgh to direct our recording session, the equivalent of having Leonard Bernstein conduct a heavy-metal band. At the end of our first year under contract, Fuhrer phoned us.

He told me, "St. Louis"—Anheuser-Busch headquarters—"wants to take over your contract and Lambert's. It makes no difference to me, but if you don't like it, the hell with them."

"It's okay by me," I said. Lambert likewise agreed.

For the next three years, as I recall, we received a check from St. Louis every six months—and recorded no more than three radio commercials the entire time. Anheuser-Busch paid me, if I remember correctly, $60,000 for doing virtually nothing but going to the mailbox to extract the checks. Oh, I almost forgot—in one of the rare phone calls we received from St. Louis, Lambert and I were instructed to report to a parking lot at Three Rivers Stadium to pose for a Budweiser poster. A production company in Dallas sent a crew of about 30 to mastermind the photography. I said to the head of the production company, "St. Louis puzzles me. They keep sending me checks for doing next to nothing."

"That's not unusual," he said. "They're such a huge, labyrinthine outfit that things just get lost. We did a $35,000 job for them that never saw the light of day. The guy in charge got transferred, and he never told the guy who moved into his office about the project."

An ad agency executive once offered me friendly advice at lunch. "You don't charge enough," he said. I thought I was charging too much.

In any event, I have ample evidence that my voice, failing to mellow with age, sells products. Word reached me in my late 60s that Hardee's Restaurants, the national fast food chain, was airing a radio commercial in Chicago—a commercial spoken by an unidentified performer in a voice identical to mine. The next year, Hardee's moved the commercial to North Carolina, whereupon I asked a former colleague who worked at a station there to obtain a tape for me. Sure enough, except for a bare second when the performer lapsed into a New York City inflection, I heard my own voice. Either Hardee's had unearthed the only man in captivity who spoke as I did or had hired an impressionist.

"We can take 'em to court," my lawyer, Les Zittrain, told me. "But they've got an awful lot of money to fight the case, and there'll be no guarantee we'll win."

"Forget it," I said. But I would not be displeased if one of these days Hardee's was hit with a rash of lawsuits by customers claiming to have suffered ptomaine poisoning.

Perhaps one reason my *local* commercials succeeded was that, according to some, I speak to Pittsburghers in a dialect that is the quintessential Pittsburghese. Out-of-town speech professors and newspaper columnists whose occupations move them to Pittsburgh call our manner of speech just that—Pittsburghese. The professors conduct disapproving studies of it while the columnists poke fun at it. Yet I fail to recognize any peculiar nuances when I speak, nor when I hear other native sons speak. To my ear, we sound normal. However, way back in the 1960s the *Saturday Evening Post* sent me to Boston to put together a profile of Red Auerbach, the great Celtics basketball coach. Naturally, I sought out his star center, Bill Russell, for an interview, but Russell brushed me off my first day at practice and did so again the next day. Finally, I told him, "Look, at least tell me *why* you're not willing to talk with me."

Russell, who despised the Philadelphia 76ers and just about everything else in Philadelphia, replied, "You're from Philadelphia, aren't you?"

"No, I'm from Pittsburgh," I said. With that, we sat down to a lengthy interview.

Yet I'm accused of speaking Pittsburghese, which, for example, calls the Steelers the Stillers. Now, in my 70s, I am ready to concede. Roy McHugh, my friend and editor of this book, has spent most of his adult life in Pittsburgh but grew up in Iowa. Along with three or four other men, we had lunch not long ago with two gentlemen from Orlando who were planning a football museum for Heinz Field, the Steelers' new stadium. They wanted to elicit our memories of Pittsburgh football. Several times, one of the Orlando men, seated at McHugh's elbow, asked him to repeat my words. McHugh at last turned to me and said, "See, I have to translate you."

The clincher came while broadcasting the 2001 NFL draft. In the sixth round, the Steelers selected a receiver from Texas A&M, whereupon our producer hooked up our broadcast team—Bill Hillgrove, Tunch Ilkin, and me—for a telephone interview. I told the receiver, "Years ago, I spent a week in College Station"—Texas A&M's location—"and the president of your university took me to lunch at a sidewalk place that served the best barbecued beef I have ever tasted. That restaurant was very popular. Do you still have that restaurant down there?"

The receiver replied, "I don't know of any restaurant here named Donaire."

Tunch, raised in Chicago, guffawed. Case closed. Pittsburghese *is* a tongue, and I speak it. Combining that with my grating voice, I am to broadcasting what Vice President Dan Quayle might have been to a spelling bee. That said, another kind of bee comes to mind. A few years ago, WDVE, the Steelers Radio Network flagship station, arranged a dinner at which I was to be roasted. The onetime running back Rocky Bleier took a turn at the microphone; straight-faced and in his sonorous voice, he said:

"The bumblebee was not designed to fly. It was never meant to fly. Its body is too heavy for its wings. But the bumblebee does not know this, so it flies. Myron Cope was never meant to be a broadcaster."

Chapter Twenty-Four

Where Has the
Fun Gone?

Edmund Nelson, a stalwart defensive tackle for the Steelers in
the 1980s who went on to build a profitable insurance agency, said to me
at lunch not long ago, "Football's not as much fun as it used to be, is it?"

"To tell you the truth," I replied, "I can't honestly say. I've grown
too old to hang out with players in their 20s and 30s. I see 'em in the
locker room and watch them practice and play, but I can't *know* them like
I used to."

Now that I think about it, former athletes and a few active ones as
well have been suggesting for more than three decades now that the fun
has gone out of professional sports. The characters—the oddballs—have
disappeared, they say. Players carry briefcases. Money rules all. Free agency
makes it impossible to keep a team together long enough for the players
to bond. We shall see no more Steel Curtains, Purple People Eaters, or
Redskin Hogs.

Yes, I suppose it's true that much of the fun has been stripped from
sports, making uninhibited fun-lovers—like rhinos—an endangered species. They have been replaced by athletes often spoiled rotten by riches
and adulation and consumed with the possibilities lying ahead in their
next contract. Not by coincidence, I have known many sportswriters and
sportscasters who became jaded covering such athletes. Gene Collier, a

gifted columnist for the *Pittsburgh Post-Gazette,* gave up sportswriting at the age of 44. Two years later, after his employers had accommodated him with a general column, he wrote in the *Columbia Journalism Review*:

"It was in the Steelers' locker room, a Wednesday as I recall, and I was doing my famous milling act.

"Milling about, shuffling wordlessly along rows of lockers at the approximate pace of a drunk at a wedding, pulling my notepad out of my pocket, uncapping my pen, putting my notepad back in my pocket, capping my pen, waiting for some 20-something from the top one percent for gross motor skills to answer some questions for me.

"Some tragically measurable part of my life," Collier wrote on, "had been spent in exactly this pantomime, waiting for an athlete to get showered, get dressed, get treatment, get ice, get heat, get taped, get whirlpooled, get out of a meeting, or just get familiar with the common courtesy of making themselves available to someone who needed to talk to them."

Collier decided he had had it, as others before him had.

Yet I never gave a thought to leaving sports, for I knew that just around the next corner there would be a laugh, or at least a smile, that I could find only infrequently in any other sphere of reportage. As a writer and then broadcaster, the toy department suited me just fine.

I listened to Al Severance, a tall, red-faced, silver-haired basketball coach at Villanova University, address his players before they took the floor to play an important game against West Virginia. "All right, you guys," he said, "You wanna win a big one, huh? Well, let me tell you something. This is just another ballgame. To defeat West Virginia is not to ensure immortality. Victory on this seemingly critical occasion makes a superman of no man." Severance was obviously striving to keep his players loose by minimizing the game's importance. He rose to his tiptoes, wagging a finger at the acne-faced lads gathered before him, his voice now booming through the room.

"Cromwell! Cromwell!" he cried out. "I charge thee—fling away thy ambition! By that sin fell the angels!"

Severance surveyed the locker room. He found a 6-feet-8 youth named John Driscoll, known by teammates as Tweetie-Bird, slumped in a folding chair, his legs sprawled indolently in front of him. He was *too* loose, Severance decided, and thereupon turned on him. "Driscoll!" the coach thundered. "Tonight, Driscoll, you are Samson tearing down the pillars of the temple to destroy the Philistines! Do you hear me, Driscoll? Tonight you destroy the Philistines!"

Tweetie-Bird and his teammates lost to the Philistines, but I ask you, could I have heard such oratory covering city council?

I sat at a piano bar with Earl Weaver, the hugely successful manager of the Baltimore Orioles. Stubby and turning gray atop his outsized head (in the minor leagues players had called him Watermelon Head), Weaver eagerly awaited the pianist's arrival for the cocktail hour and meantime told me, "I got a good singing voice." I doubted that, for he spoke in gravelly sounds almost as grating as mine. This was 1975, but Weaver in fact not only knew the lyrics of hit songs dating clear back to the 1940s but could announce the years in which they were written. "I love 'My Hero' from *The Chocolate Soldier*," he said. "I still got a record by Nelson Eddy and Jeanette MacDonald"—a famous duet who sang operatic material in turgid, melodramatic love-story films—"that my wife almost broke over my head eight times." So saying, the manager whose record ranked him No. 1 in the big leagues shattered the polite buzz of the cocktail hour with a vocal.

"Come! Come! I love you on-ly, my heart is trooo . . . "

Had I later covered even the White House and been invited by Bill Clinton into the Oval Office to hear him play his saxophone, would I have had as much fun? No way.

I sat in Mamma Leone's Ristorante, much in fashion in Manhattan, with Dean Chance, a gangling young farmer from Ohio who just a few months earlier had won by a landslide the Cy Young Award designating him baseball's most valuable pitcher. To the waiter, Chance said, "Give me the baked lasagna and manicotti." The waiter stiffened. "Read-a the menu, pleeze," he said. He suggested Chance order just one main course, not two.

"Look," Chance replied, "I want baked lasagna and manicotti, and you can put some sausage on the side and gimme a Coke. Never mind what the menu says. You can charge me extra."

The waiter's face flushed with indignation. He had tended the tables of gourmets and perhaps princes, but now he had come to this. "Which a-one you want onna first course, and which a-one you want onna second course?" he bristled.

"Just gimme more o' the lasagna than the manicotti."

The waiter departed for the kitchen, his ears burning as the farm boy shouted across the crowded room, "Don't forget the sausage!" After dinner, we proceeded to the cloakroom to fetch our overcoats but found the attendant dawdling. "Hurry up," Chance barked at her, "or you don't get no tip."

I wished I had the temerity to speak those words.

I had hooked up with Dean Chance to write a magazine piece about the preeminent pitcher in baseball. He spoke of the day he left the family farm on a bus to report to his first minor league assignment—Bluefield, WV, in the Appalachian League. "That was the first day I'd ever left home alone," he said. Then he was moved to add, "If it'll help you any, you can write in the story that I was wearing overalls and work shoes. Hell, you gotta make a living, too."

As I have mentioned, I occasionally wrote music pieces for a break from sports; had I had dinner with Van Cliburn, the concert pianist who gained worldwide fame by winning the 1958 Tchaikovsky Competition in Moscow, would I have enjoyed myself as much as I did with the winner of the Cy Young Award? Impossible.

For me, watching games being played provided only a part of the pleasure—restaurants and bars, as the reader may be starting to suspect, provided as much enjoyment as witnessing a no-hitter. When in Baltimore the place to be was the Golden Arm, a restaurant operated by the superb Colts quarterback John Unitas. In the lounge one night, two Colts players fell into a disagreement. Alex Hawkins, a yellow-haired special teams player, claimed he knew how to ride horses, but defensive back Bobby Boyd scoffed. Hawkins then offered to bet $200 that he could ride a horse from the Golden Arm to his apartment, a distance of about four miles.

"I don't like the bet," Boyd replied.

"All right," said Hawkins. "I'll tell you what I'll do. I'll ride the horse buck naked. I'll pull a Lady Godiva."

"I still don't like the bet." Shrewdly, Boyd knew Hawkins was determined to prove his equine skills at any cost.

"Listen," said Hawkins, "I'll not only ride the horse buck naked to my apartment building, I'll ride him up the front steps and into the elevator. I'll ride him right into my apartment."

"You got a bet," said Boyd. Now all they needed was a horse. The bartender, a roly-poly man named Rocky Thornton, stepped into the street and shouted, "Hey, horse!" but no horse came. Phone calls to stables produced no rental horse, probably because the stables suspected Hawkins and Boyd were drinking. The bet off, Boyd explained to his teammate why he would have had no chance to win. Boyd's explanation bore out his reputation for thorough preparedness when studying football film of opponents' performances or pondering wagers for a sign of a sure thing. "I know your apartment building," he told Hawkins, "and I know your elevator. There's no way you can fit a horse into that elevator."

I drifted from writing into a broadcast career that saw my shows rapidly multiply to the point that long working hours (plus settling down and raising children) pared my opportunities to hang out in bars and nightclubs and let the good times happen. Still, I could make my own fun. Coming down the home stretch of the 1976 football season, the Steelers knew their hope of making the playoffs had been reduced to a prayer as they prepared for the next-to-last weekend of the regular season. The previous Sunday they had beaten Cincinnati and next would wallop Tampa Bay but still trail the Bengals by half a game in the race for the AFC Central Division title. The Bengals a day later—in a Monday-night game—would play the Oakland Raiders and seemed a sure bet to win and stretch their lead to a full game. The Raiders, you see, had already clinched a divisional title as well as home-field advantage for the playoffs; thus their owner, Al Davis, with no need of a victory and probably salivating at the opportunity to lift the Bengals to a title at the Steelers' expense, seemed certain to order his coaches to yank their starters off the field early in the game. Steeler players, meanwhile, publicly predicted the Raiders would tank the game, just go through the motions—a prediction issued in the desperate, and surely doomed, hope of motivating the Raiders. The Bengals, to my way of thinking, were a lock to win.

"If the Raiders beat the Bengals," I declared on radio and television, "I'll swim the Mon."

The broad Mon is the Monongahela, one of Pittsburgh's three rivers. When, to my amazement, the Raiders soundly defeated the Bengals, I knew, alas, the Mon awaited me. As matters had turned out, Al Davis wanted the victory more than he wanted to satisfy his hatred of the Steelers, who in the end went to the playoffs while the Bengals stayed home. At any rate, here I was, going on 48 and having sworn off exercise at 22, committed to swim that river.

Under darkness of a midweek night, with only television lights playing upon the water, I zipped up a wetsuit, strapped on goggles, and lowered myself into the cold river. I had not announced the date or time I would swim lest I create a traffic jam along the shore that would plunge the police department into a fit of rage, but Channel 4 would have the film in time for the 11 o'clock news. As a precaution, several men from the station would follow alongside me in a rowboat. Anyhow, to this day —more than two and a half decades later—people still ask me occasionally, "Did you *really* swim the Mon?"

"I *said* I swam it, didn't I?" I reply, feigning annoyance. "It was on television." I then turn the conversation to other matters, making it clear I do not enjoy having my integrity challenged.

But now, as they say in exposés, the whole truth can be told.

I swam the Mon, all right, but only half of it. I dropped into the water from the rowboat in the middle of the river. After all, I had promised only that if the Raiders beat the Bengals, I would swim the Mon—I had not specified shore to shore.

Swimming half the Mon is swimming the Mon, if I know the meaning of words. As it was, it was nasty work. During the 1970s Pittsburgh's steel industry collapsed, but the mills that lined the Mon had been polluting the river for decades. Unzipping my wetsuit ashore, I drove home and threw up for two hours. Even in a river, I could not keep my mouth shut.

To anyone who now accuses me of having fudged the truth, I'll answer, "I did no such thing, but if you look hard enough you might find a time or two when—call it show-biz license—I committed minor fakery." For example, during the second day of the NFL's 1989 player draft, I lobbied Steeler coaches and scouts to draft a stocky 270-pounder named Carlton Haselrig, who had won six national heavyweight wrestling championships while attending the University of Pittsburgh's Johnstown campus. I cornered an assistant coach who had taken a coffee break from the War Room.

"Do you guys know about Carlton Haselrig?" I asked.

"Yeh, the wrestler," the coach said. "But he hasn't played football since high school."

"What does that matter? Leverage is the key to playing in the offensive line, right? If a guy who's won six wrestling championships doesn't know a thing or two about leverage. . . " No, I did not promise to again swim the Mon, but I added, "He's certainly worth risking a late-round pick."

The coach patronized me with a chuckle and returned to the War Room.

The ninth round was coming on—the draft lasted 12 that year— when I began lobbying President Dan Rooney and every coach and scout who emerged from the War Room. "The ninth is the round. Take the wrestler." The ninth went by, and so did the tenth. No Cartlon Haselrig. With the 11th round starting, I poked my head into Rooney's office and hollered, "Will you please go down to the War Room and tell Chuck Noll and the rest of those stupid coaches and scouts to draft the wrestler?" Rooney grinned and remained seated behind his desk. (Later, I would learn that down in Miami, starting with the ninth round, Dolphin assistant coaches began pressuring head coach Don Shula to draft, yes, Haselrig. "I'm not drafting a wrestler who hasn't played football since high school," Shula snorted.)

At last, in the 12th and final round, the Steelers selected the wrestler. Was it to humor me? Or to shut me up?

In any case, I turned to a young production assistant and said, "Run up the street and get me a large cherry pie."

"A cherry pie?" he said.

"Don't ask questions. Here's money. Just get me a cherry pie and get back here as quickly as you can."

I had been broadcasting the draft on radio for two days, and now it was drawing to a close. I said to a Steeler publicist, "When this thing's over, fetch me Joe Greene"—by then the team's defensive line coach—"for an interview." Meantime, a cameraman from the station stood by, waiting to shoot a portion of my radio broadcast for the TV news. Greene, whom I had chosen for his sense of humor and massive presence, was delivered to me, and so was the cherry pie. During a commercial break, I quickly briefed Joe on my plan and gave him instructions. To the cameraman I said, "Be ready."

Coming off the commercial break, I lit into Joe. "All of you so-called football minds back there in the War Room wouldn't even have thought about drafting the wrestler if I hadn't badgered you through the last four rounds! How stupid can you guys be?" I carried on my tirade until Joe reached down to the floor. He came up with the cherry pie and splattered it in my face. Hey, on television, in contrast to radio, a visual usually helped. Besides, this was sports—keep laughing. Everyone enjoyed the gag except the janitors who had to clean the carpet of cherry pie that had run off my face onto the floor.

Haselrig, by the way, survived training camp to make the so-called practice squad (paid but ineligible to play in games). Noll dumbfounded me by assigning him to play defense, but later came to his senses and switched the Rig, as Haselrig came to be known, to offense as a guard, headed toward 290 pounds. The next year the Rig made the active roster and just two years later was selected for the Pro Bowl. Alas, alcohol addiction abruptly ended his career. But I still keep on a wall in my home a color photo the Rig sent me shortly after he was drafted. In the photo, he wears his wrestling togs and assumes a wrestler's crouch. The photo is inscribed:

"Thanks, Myron. You sure are one smart man."

It is my contention that every sportswriter and sportscaster should be beaten up—well, roughed up—by an athlete at least once in his career. Not severely, mind you. Just roughed up enough to leave the journalist victim with a story to tell friends for years to come. My beating occurred in Atlanta.

I had gone there to write a magazine piece about a football player and by coincidence found the Pirates staying at my hotel for a series against the Braves. Returning from interviews one night, I ordered a scotch high-ball at the hotel bar but then remembered a phone call I had neglected to make and went to a pay phone booth in the lobby. I was still dialing when suddenly two large hands reached into the booth, seized me by the throat, and started banging the back of my head against the rear wall of the booth. Don Leppert had come calling.

Leppert, 6-feet-2 and 220 pounds, had spent five years in the big leagues as a backup catcher and then been added to the Pirates' coaching staff to warm up relievers in the bullpen. Both as a player and coach, he was principally known as "the best man in baseball to have on your side in a ballfield brawl." In the bar I had noticed Leppert and several other Pirates coaches at a table. I knew Leppert. Our relationship was cordial. But as best as I have ever been able to guess, the coaches—as those in sports are prone to do over drinks—had sunk into an earnest discussion about rotten treatment from the loathsome media. Thus when Leppert strolled into the lobby and sighted me in the phone booth, he saw me only as a representative of the despised species, and went to work.

Well, it's difficult to fight a man in a phone booth, especially if you're the first one into the booth. Somehow, I managed to battle my way out. But Leppert locked his arms around my upper body, and as if I were a bowling ball, slung me the width of the lobby's marble floor. He strode toward me, ready to bowl again, when a great stroke of good fortune intervened. A three-man plainclothes detail of narcotics detectives, making their accustomed late-night rounds of hotels, entered the lobby. Clearly, they did not like my chances of winning the fight. They seized Leppert and pronounced him under arrest.

I told them, "Aw, he just had a few too many. Leave him be. I'll take him to an all-night diner for coffee."

At the diner, Leppert apologized profusely and thanked me for declining to press charges. Early the next morning the phone on my bedstand rang. I picked up the receiver but dropped it. I could not hold it, because as matters turned out, I had broken my right hand fighting my way out of the phone booth. The next time I saw Leppert at Three Rivers Stadium, I showed him a medical bill. "You know, I could sue you," I said, "or report you to the front office. Just pay me what I owe the doc, and it's water over the dam."

Leppert studied the bill and cried out, "Seventy-five dollars! Boy, you sure go to an expensive doctor."

So much for gratitude, but I knew that Leppert had attacked me not to settle any personal grudge but only to strike a blow against journalism. I chalked up the experience to occupational hazards. To elaborate, on assignment by the *Saturday Evening Post*, I spent about a week traveling the professional wrestling circuit with Cowboy Bill Watts, whom the wrestling hierarchy was promoting as the No.1 "bad guy"—the topmost villain—in the country. Following a bout one night, Cowboy Bill shot me a hard look and said, "You don't fool me. You don't think pro wrestling is legit."

"To be honest," I replied, "I don't."

Without warning, the Cowboy bent over and dealt me a sharp head-butt that dropped me to the floor. Not long after his career ended, he wrote me a letter from Japan to bring me up to date on his activities. He had gone into business and was enjoying success. He had gone from mauling and stomping opponents to selling perfume.

As a broadcaster I discovered a new source of enjoyment—my mail. I hated taking precious time to answer mail, but I had brought with me to broadcasting the author's tenet—if the letter is civilly written, you owe a personal response. Pat Bertalanits, who handled my secretarial work, told me the night I conducted my final talk show that she had calculated, conservatively, that I had answered a minimum of 30,000 letters. Still, I never knew when a gem might turn up. Early in the game, I received one from an anonymous listener who lit into my commentaries and sprinkled his letter with anti-Semitic language yet brought a smile to my face when he got to the point:

"Another thing there, Solly. Do you know what a parenthetical phrase is? If you managed to get through high school, you really ought to know a parenthetical phrase when you see one, and how's that, Cope? You say you do know what a parenthetical phrase is? Great! Then do us all a great big favor, will you, Cope? Connect the goddam subject with the predicate as soon as possible when you give us what is laughably supposed to be your 'sports news.' Do *not* separate the noun from the goddam verb by a series of unbearable parenthetical phrases.

"For example," my correspondent went on, "if you're trying to tell us Joe Blow broke his ass while sliding into second last night, do *not* inject a string of parenthetical phrases between 'Joe Blow' and 'broke his ass!!' ...Because when you talk like that—and that *is* the way you talk—the listener yells back at the radio: 'Cope, you sonofabitch, get to the goddam verb!'"

Of course, I have kept that letter from the bigot and treasure it.

My mail told me that I frequently disturbed fans of Joe Paterno, the lionized Penn State football coach. For one thing, I nicknamed him Darkglasses Joe—rarely in daylight did he not wear dark glasses. From a Penn State fan came a letter calling to my attention that Paterno was afflicted by a condition that made it advisable to wear tinted glasses to filter light. The fan upbraided me for, in his opinion, ridiculing the coach's appearance.

"Who do you think *you* are, a Greek god?" he asked. "Look at yourself—you're 5-feet-4, have a big nose, a bald spot on your head, a crooked mouth, and tobacco-stained teeth!" I gave the guy four out of five—my nose is normal-sized. Anyhow, he concluded his irate letter by writing, "Continued success in your field of endeavor."

I particularly irritated Penn Staters by accusing Joe from time to time of excessive piety. You see, for many years he seemed bent upon casting Penn State as an academic facsimile of Harvard and his football players as model citizens (when in fact some of them told me they received the benefits of rural isolation—no major newspaper there to snoop —and a friendly police force). Yet Joe never rebuked me for my sniping. Perhaps he remembered a summer afternoon at the Carlton House, a hotel in downtown Pittsburgh.

It was 1966, and he had just been promoted from assistant coach to head coach. He and Penn State publicist Jim Tarman were touring the state, inviting reporters to hotel suites; Penn State's athletic budget being limited, they carried with them a suitcase filled with booze so as to avoid hotel bottle prices when entertaining the media. (Considerately, they warned bellhops so as to avoid hernias.) I, a magazine writer at the time, had no working interest in Penn State, but I dropped in at the Carlton House anyhow. After all the others left Joe's suite, I sat on a sofa with him, just gabbing. He mentioned Terry Hanratty, a Pennsylvania kid who had been recruited to Notre Dame and was emerging as a soon-to-be All-American quarterback and *Time* cover boy. Hanratty, said Joe, could not have been enrolled at Penn State because of poor high school grades. After I departed the hotel, it occurred to me that although I was not in the habit of offering public relations advice to coaches, the rookie head coach could benefit from a word of caution. I reached him at his office the next day.

"You're lucky I was not at the Carlton House yesterday as a *working* reporter," I told him. "If I had been, Notre Dame would be in an uproar, and you might not have a chance to ever get them onto your schedule. You might want to be a little more careful of what you say."

Joe agreed and thanked me. His remarks about Hanratty, however, eventually made it into newsprint, infuriating Notre Dame, so I suppose Joe slipped up. Many years later, after he had attained near-deity status, a rumor circulated that he might quit his job to run for governor. He denied the rumor but at a party one evening urged me to leave the trivial world of sports journalism and consider entering politics as a press secretary. His?

Hanratty, in the meantime, had gone on to become a Steeler and then a successful broker on Wall Street.

When I look back upon the good times, I find myself sympathizing with today's athletes and wondering if it's possible for them to enjoy themselves as much as I enjoyed living on the fringes of sport. Athletes now possess wealth, all right, and I suppose that most have their favorite haunts where they share laughs with teammates and friends, but they would do well to be selective and on their guard. Strangers carry knives and guns and offer drugs. Also, for as long as I've been around, there has existed a particular species of barroom or nightclub bozo who wants to make a reputation by picking a fight with a known athlete. Times changed, and so did the bozos. Athletes had to start asking themselves, "Is this guy packing a weapon? Even if he isn't and I mop up the floor with him, will he sue?" The intelligent athlete turns his back on the agitator and leaves the premises, but when you are in the prime of life and physically gifted, that's difficult to do.

I would rather be young than be the septuagenarian I am, but then again, would it be as much fun loafing with this targeted generation of athletes?

Loafing—that's Pittsburghese but fast giving way, I notice, to "hanging out," the homogeneous American slang of the day. Long before "loafing" began its retreat, the local lexicon came to call Pittsburgh "the Burgh," an appellation that nettled me. In the 1970s, you see, sportswriters from across the nation poured into Pittsburgh to cover the Steelers in playoff games and jumped to the false assumption that our populace called their town the Burgh, which to my way of thinking conjured up a giant metropolitan hamburger. Some of those sportswriters went so far as to fabricate quotes in which locals referred to their town as the Burgh. Pittsburgh TV newscasters, often not of Pittsburgh origin, fell into line. So we became the Burgh. Just last night on the 11 o'clock news, I heard that a man from something called the Pennsylvania Resources Council had kicked off an anti-littering campaign by announcing, "We want to debug d' Burgh." I wanted to find him and slap him.

In the 1990s the Pittsburgh Brewing Company popularized an advertising slogan for its Iron City Beer—"It's a Burgh Thing!" The brewery invited me to perform a television commercial. Sure enough, that damned word appeared in the script. Well, I had lost the battle to repel the influence of outsiders upon Pittsburghese, so why not make an easy buck? I did the commercial, but I promise you—nobody again will hear me say "the Burgh," unless I am being paid to.

As a big fish in a small pond, I know my career is winding down. Long ago, when I turned 60, I started making it a practice to tell my bosses, "If you detect me losing a step or two in my Steeler broadcasts, just say so, and I'll walk out the door. No push required." I want no contract that runs more than one year. In the spring of 2001, I told Bob Roof, my boss at WDVE/WBGG, our FM and AM Steeler stations, "Last year, I found myself slipping a little—not 'seeing the field' as I used to. I had to give myself a talking-to and snap back."

"I never noticed it," Roof replied. "Our ratings went up again."

Meantime, being a prominent fish put me in a position to discover and rediscover the redeeming qualities of the human species, at least many of those members of it who inhabit my pond. Listeners mailed me contributions—unsolicited—to my favorite charities. I mean not to cloak myself in virtue by mentioning my involvement in charitable causes but only to express my belief that citizens in a position to open the right doors should open them. In 1982 a couple of vintage car buffs, Art McGovern and Mary Beth Gmiter, came to me with a plan. Nobody seemed to know, they explained, that Pittsburgh's Schenley Park, a vast expanse of public greenery in the heart of the city, possessed all the makings of the finest vintage racing course in the nation. Race drivers would love the park's winding roads and twisting corners; hillsides overlooking the roads offered a natural amphitheater for spectators.

I cannot identify a spark plug, let alone one vintage racing car from another, but I asked a woman named Louise Brown, the head of the city's Department of Parks and Recreation, to have lunch with us. We spread homemade maps of the park on the table and blew Louise Brown away. There existed only one problem. In 1889, a wealthy, civic-minded woman named Mary E. Schenley had gifted 300 wooded acres to the city and sold the city an additional 100 acres for a pittance, at a time when developers were thirsting to buy those 400 acres. But Mary Schenley stipulated in the deal that not only would the property be made into a public park but that no event ever staged there could charge the public admission. That's all right, we told Louise Brown—we'll sell a lot of hotdogs and T-shirts and dig up corporate sponsors. Twenty years later, the Pittsburgh Vintage Grand Prix ranks as the premier event of its kind on the continent, and possibly in the world. Race drivers have brought their cars to Pittsburgh from as far as France, Belgium, and Finland. But here was the key: The planning and staging of the Grand Prix requires some 1,200 volunteer workers, none ever paid a dime. Their payment has been the raising of well over a million dollars for charity—again, without charging admission! My luck was to witness the best of *Homo sapiens* from a ringside seat.

A year before the Grand Prix's inception, Foge Fazio, then the head football coach at Pitt, phoned me from his country club. "I've been sitting around here with some of the boys," he said, "and we've decided we ought to stage a celebrity golf tournament for charity. You name the charity." The first year, we raised fourteen hundred dollars and change. By now, the Myron Cope/Foge Fazio tournament has soared over a million bucks. Nobody involved has made a dime. I believe it important to shoulder a share of the workload it takes to stage a fundraiser, rather than to just have my name attached, but the others get none of the glory, only the satisfaction. Thanks, gents.

Am I claiming righteousness? Seeking a pat on the back? No—just saying I had an obligation.

Of course, braggarts meet their comeuppance, one way or another. For example, in the company of eight other sports reporters, I entered a noisy rathskeller one night and sat down at a long table where we ordered several pitchers of beer. A man wearing a tank top and staggering slightly from his liquor approached our table, pointing a finger at me.

"You're Myron Cope, aren't you?" he said.

"Yes, I'm guilty," I answered.

"Do you know I got your autograph 17 years ago?"

"Exactly 17 years ago?"

"Damn right, and if you'da died, it might be worth something."

"I'm sorry," I said, "that I could not accommodate you."

"Damn you!" the tank top said and returned to the bar.

Many so-called celebrities bathe in special attention and favors, but fate, I think, lies in ambush. I remember my radio station pressing me into service in 1983 to broadcast a season of Pitt football games, and I agreed to on one condition. I told my general manager:

"My favorite cousin is being married the same day Pitt plays a road game at College Park, MD. I'll miss the wedding, but I can make the reception if you charter a plane to get me out of College Park immediately after the game ends."

The pilot flew his single-engine craft through a cloudless September sky toward a fair-sized airport in Latrobe, PA, not far down the road from my cousin's wedding reception. He radioed in for a landing.

"Are you kidding?" the control tower shot back. "There's an air show going on here."

I had been aware of Latrobe's annual dazzling display of aeronautical gymnastics that drew thousands, but airport personnel had assured me the show would be concluded well before I landed late that Saturday afternoon. Poor advice.

To my pilot, a Maryland guy whose only knowledge of me was that I broadcast football games, I said, "Tell them your passenger is Myron Cope, and he's got to get to his favorite cousin's wedding reception."

I counted on the fact that Latrobe, where the Steelers pitched their training camp each summer, was ardent Steeler country. At any rate, the pilot shot me a quizzical look before he relayed the message. A lengthy silence ensued. Finally, a voice from the control tower spoke up. "Ask him if he can get four for the Cleveland game."

We landed. I wangled four tickets for the Cleveland game. The control tower had seen to it that my hat size remained seven and a quarter. Hey, in the course of my life I have neither performed liver transplants nor negotiated any global trade agreements. I've simply written and hollered in the toy department. A huge, garrulous, outgoing woman named Mary Blanda once summed me up. I spoke at a testimonial dinner for her son, the Hall of Fame quarterback George Blanda, at his hometown fire hall in Youngwood, PA. The man in charge of organizing the speakers to parade to the dais said, "Mr. Cope, get in line right behind Mrs. Blanda." She glanced down at me over her left shoulder and snorted, "Hmmp! *Another* bigmouth!"

An accurate description, yes, and concise. As an epitaph it would take up little space. I'll mull it over.

Acknowledgments

When, in my private thoughts, I take stock of those friends I hold dearest, I find that a handful of them encouraged and prodded me through the task of reaching back some 30 years to reacquire the skills (such as they were) by which I once made my living as a professional writer. More or less by accident, broadcasting had long since removed me from writing. When I returned to craft this book, I found those friends there to help me shake off the rust.

Roy McHugh, besides being a talented writer, was the most skillful editor I knew throughout my years as a newspaperman, magazine writer, and author. Through the first three chapters of this book, he made me rewrite and rewrite and rewrite until he finally said, "Now you've remembered how to write again."

Joe Gordon at one time held the title of director of media relations—"the publicity guy," as we called such men in those days—for the Pittsburgh Steelers. Most pro football writers across the country regarded Joe as the best in the business, nobody else in the same league. He rose to be director of marketing (all the while serving as invaluable troubleshooter for President Dan Rooney) and later retired, not suspecting he would become an editor. My chapters passed from Roy McHugh's hands to Joe's. My God, did I think I was writing a book for the ages? Two editors!

Make it three. At the outset, my next-door neighbors, Carol and Bob Pfaff, attempted in vain for three days to convert me from my 40-year-old Hermes 3000 manual typewriter to a computer. The fourth day, I returned the $1,300 worth of technology to the place where I'd bought it. So Carol took on the job of transferring my typewritten stuff to computerized pages while Bob, his curiosity aroused, read them. Wasn't I fortunate to have moved into a neighborhood where the lawyer living next door happened to be a former English teacher!

Speaking of lawyers, Les Zittrain has been mine for more than 30 years. One way and another, he made my book possible. Let's just say that I phoned him so frequently to draw upon his expertise and, indeed, brilliance, that I would be destitute had he run a clock on my calls.

Sam Zacharias, who for years counseled me in business matters, preventing me from losing my shirt, read my manuscript and phoned to exclaim generously, "It's a masterpiece!" Hemingway rolled over in his grave. Thanks for everything, Sam.

Index

Celebrate the Heroes of Pittsburgh Sports
in These Other Acclaimed Titles from Sports Publishing!

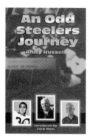

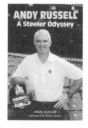

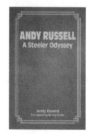